The Portuguese in Canada

From the Sea to the City

Edited by

CARLOS TEIXEIRA and
VICTOR M.P. DA ROSA

UNIVERSITY OF TORONTO PRESS
Toronto Buffalo London

© University of Toronto Press Incorporated 2000
Toronto Buffalo London
Printed in Canada

ISBN 0-8020-4754-8 (cloth)
ISBN 0-8020-8311-0 (paper)

Canadian Cataloguing in Publication Data

Main entry under title:

Portuguese in Canada

ISBN 0-8020-4754-8 (bound)   ISBN 0-8020-8311-0 (pbk.)

1. Portuguese – Canada – History.   2. Portuguese Canadians – History.*
I. Teixeira, Carlos.   II. Da Rosa, Victor M.P.

FC106.P8P67 2000   971'.004691   C99-932436-5
F1035.P65P68 1999

The University of Toronto Press acknowledges the financial assistance
to its publishing program of the Canada Council for the Arts and
the Ontario Arts Council.

Financial assistance for the publication of this book has been provided by
the Direcção-Geral das Comunidades Portuguesas – Secretaria de Estado
das Comunidades Portuguesas.

University of Toronto Press acknowledges the financial support
for its publishing activities of the Government of Canada through
the Book Publishing Industry Development Program (BPIDP).

Canadä

Contents

Figures and Tables

Figures

Tables

Foreword

It is entirely appropriate that the conference which elicited many of the papers in this book took place in St John's, Newfoundland, in 1997, the five hundredth anniversary of John Cabot's voyage from Europe. Portuguese navigators and fishermen have had a long association with the Atlantic coast of Canada, but, compared to the movement of many other European nationalities to Canada, the migration of large numbers of Portuguese is of remarkably recent origin. This book covers both long-ago and recent experiences of Portuguese in Canada – an intriguing juxtaposition. As someone from the Canadian prairies who is descended from Mennonite immigrant groups that left Russia in the 1870s and 1920s, I found that this collection opened a new world to me: that of the sea and of what life was like for immigrants in the great post-1945 European migration to Canada. Many significant facets of life play off one another as the reader goes from essay to essay.

The story of Portuguese immigration and of individual experiences in the new land is complex, and this book's comprehensiveness allows this complexity to emerge. Chapters 1 and 2 convey the broad picture of the Portuguese diaspora to various parts of the world, of which Canada is only one part; others reveal patterns of distributions and activities in Canada; and all this is brought to vivid life by essays about the personal experiences of people. I have rarely read a book where I felt so close to grasping what life is like for an immigrant group. The first wave of immigrants is alive and can tell us what it is like to arrive in a distant strange land where life is allegedly much better. In many cases this promise turns out to be inaccurate, at least for many years, until a considerable number of immigrants get established and a congenial, supportive community emerges.

Fortunately, devoted scholars and students of the Portuguese-Canadian community have documented, particularly in part I, the immigrant experiences at their earliest stages. Such recording was not done for many earlier migrations to what is now Canada, when peoples came from France, England, the United States, other European nations, and the Caribbean. This immediacy of the Portuguese immigrant experience, its sometimes heart-rending, sad realism, is an outstanding contribution of this book.

It is not only the essays on the immigrants that give rich intimate details of life, but also those in part II on the White Fleet. I recall with warmth the paper given by the congenial Jean-Pierre Andrieux in St John's, where he conveyed so clearly the pleasure he had experienced over his many years of dining with Portuguese sea captains of the White Fleet, listening and remembering their vivid yarns. These enabled him to record in chapter 4 shadowy aspects of the late years of the fishery, but he does this so innocently and subtly that one is hardly aware of the nautical tricks that took place. North Atlantic gales are vicious, and the high seas fishery has always been a demanding, dangerous life. Illnesses and smashed and broken limbs were inevitable in a stay away from home by 4,000 to 5,000 men for six or seven months. Hence the need for a hospital-supply ship that mended heads, while its chapel offered solace for mind and heart. We learn in chapter 3 of the sometimes-disturbing symbolism in the murals in the commander's quarters and in the chapel of the *Gil Eannes*. The fleet did come off the fishing banks to St John's for supplies and safety from hurricanes. Peter Collins's essay on memory, Newfoundland literature, soccer, and romance (chapter 5) is a gentle and lovely evocation of the cordial affections between Newfoundlanders and Portuguese fishermen. Above all, it reveals the mutual bonds and respect of folks who make their living on the sea and know as a daily fact of life its wild dangers and unceasing impressiveness.

In 1999 we still are very close to the great Portuguese migrations to Canada of the 1950s through the 1980s. In November 1998, I attended the ceremony opening the new Portuguese consulate on University Avenue in Toronto. A few words were spoken in English, but most of the speeches, presentations, and the blessing of the premises were in Portuguese, and the large assembly of guests listened closely and avidly. Clearly, a strong new Portuguese-Canadian community was well in place in Toronto, but its bonds with Portugal and Portuguese culture were close and highly valued. Most of the essays in this volume examine immigration themes and cultural changes in the new Portuguese communities in Canada.

The description in chapter 2 of the broader context of the movement of Portuguese to many other countries helpfully places Canada in world-wide perspective, especially in comparison with the migration from Portugal to the United States. A marvellous account of the migrations from the Azores in chapter 6 is based on a very touching story of the experiences of the first person to go from Pontas Negras on the island of Pico to 'a place called Canada.' The circumstance of the man's leaving his birthplace, including the reactions of his fellow villagers, and his first experiences and emotions in the new land are described. It is a story of the state of mind of all immigrants through time, who are inevitably caught for their lifetime with part of their being in two continents. The interviews with immigrant Portuguese women of the 1950s in chapter 7 reveals not only their own lives and responses to their new existence, but the working conditions in factories (some were sweatshops) in Canada and in the homes of Canadian domestic employers. The authors' reproducing the recorded interviews drives those experiences home. As always, the organization and continuation of family life fall mainly to women, and, along with that responsibility, the role of retaining much of the homeland's culture.

It is roughly half a century since the first large Portuguese migrations to Canada – time enough for significant changes in the lives of immigrants and their children, but a brief span for scholars studying themes such as language and ethnic identity (part III), the emergence of Portuguese communities in major urban areas (part IV), and literature and history (part V). Each author, investigating one or another of these themes in this volume, is very much aware that he or she is studying an extremely active social process, with the end result not clear. The scholars recognize their good fortune in exploring a society that is being created, and, since most are also part of that very community, they hold their breath, wondering just what will emerge.

In my very limited experience, occasionally teaching and talking to students of Portuguese background, I have become aware indirectly of the feeling of pride characteristic of parents everywhere that their children are acquiring a higher education in this new land. But they feel real apprehension as well – that this will change the children irrevocably. In thinking of this dilemma, I cannot help but reflect on other European immigrant groups that arrived on the Canadian prairies some generations ago, in the 1870s through the 1910s. That was mainly a migration to rural areas, to take up opportunities on the land to establish fairly isolated, contiguous communities. Groups such as the German-speaking Mennonites deliberately wanted to be, as they put it, *die Stillen im Lande*, 'The quiet (unobtrusive) in the land,' and the more conservative communities resisted English-language instruction in their local schools in order to fend off the outside culture. Neverthe-less, the potent external society increasingly affected even this rural group. Portuguese immigrants, in contrast, came to cities where they experienced the larger society immediately and directly, even though they created their own urban spaces. I am struck, in these essays, by how readily Portuguese immigrant families acknowledged that they were – and are – part of a new world. Yet phrases such as 'minority sta-tus' appear in the essays, and it is even suggested that Portuguese Canadians may comprise an *invisible minority*. That is self-perception, and one can anticipate that the term marks a rapidly passing phase and soon will not hold, just as *die Stillen im Lande* no longer applies.

These essays reveal the authors' concern about what kind of culture is emerging in the Portuguese-Canadian community, especially in the context of what the link with Portugal will be in the future. New fac-tors affects all recent immigrant groups in Canada: the ease of modern travel and communications and the ready movement of people and ideas. Bonds with Portugal will remain, officially through the consu-late and cultural organizations, and even more vitally through the con-tinuing interest of individuals about who they are and where their people have come from. An interest in former overseas homelands is characteristic of other ethnic communities in Canada, including groups whose ancestors arrived as early as the seventeenth century.

Perhaps part of the unease apparent in some of the essays about the nature of cultural change in the community stems from the fact that the authors themselves are part of that recent immigration stream: not only do they observe and analyse, but they experience personally the swift, sometimes bewildering change that is inevitable in this stage of the community's evolution. In other, long-established ethnic groups, many members maintain a strong, continuing interest in the former homelands. However, gradually the experiences of the community in Canada are woven into the general history of the country, or of one of its major regions.

Much debate continues in Canada about multiculturalism and rela-tions between cultural groups. In one form or another, using different terms, such discussions have been with us since population movements began in northern North America. Going beyond one's own culture is essential in life, and cultures different from, one's own should be appreciated in their own right. Ideally, mutual respect among cultural groups is implicit in multiculturalism. From the essays in this volume, it is evident how persistent cultures are. People grow up in a culture, and if they move to a new land they necessarily will experience cultures that are new to them. At the same time they find it impossible to discard all aspects of the life that they once lived, and that culture. Culture for immigrants and their descendants thus has many facets. Life is local, centred on family, community, and region, but it is lived as well in the wider framework and interplay of the new country, in the continuing perspective of a knowledge of one's forebears and the land of departure.

JOHN WARKENTIN

Acknowledgments

The editors wish to thank all of those who, directly or indirectly, helped make this book possible. Our thanks go in particular to Professors John Warkentin and R.A. Murdie of York University – the first, for being the 'discussant' during two sessions on the Portuguese in Canada organized by one of the editors at the Annual Meeting of the Canadian Association of Geographers (20–23 August 1997), and the second, for his support and encouragement over the past years. We also thank Peter Collins for his valuable editorial aid and Carolyn King for her assistance in drawing the maps.

We also appreciate the encouragement and input of the team from the University of Toronto Press – in particular, two anonymous reviewers; Virgil D. Duff, for believing in this project; Siobhan McMenemy, for being a great liaison between us and the rest of the team, and John Parry, for his thorough copy-editing. Also we would like to express our gratitude to Portuguese authorities in Canada and Portugal – in particular, António Montenegro, Chefe de Gabinete do Secretário de Estado das Comunidades Portuguesas, for his encouragement and moral support, and Eng. José Lello, Secretário de Estado das Comunidades Portuguesas, for the financial support provided to this project. Finally, we wish to thank all the Portuguese communities in Canada that we visited in the last two decades, for sharing with us their immigrant experience in Canada. We owe them this book!

Contributors

Onésimo Teotónio Almeida
Brown University, Providence, RI

Jean-Pierre Andrieux
St-Pierre et Miquelon

Peter Collins
York University

Victor M.P. Da Rosa
University of Ottawa

Manuela Dias-Tatilon
York University

Priscilla A. Doel
Colby College (Waterville, Maine)

Rena Helms-Park
York University

David Higgs
University of Toronto

Ilda Januário
OISE, University of Toronto

António Augusto Joel
York University

Gilles Lavigne
Université du Québec à Montréal

Manuela Marujo
University of Toronto

Edite Noivo
Université de Montréal

Manuel Armando Oliveira
Universidade Aberta – CEMRI,
Portugal

Maria Beatriz Rocha-Trindade
Universidade Aberta – CEMRI,
Portugal

Carlos Teixeira
University of Toronto at
Scarborough

John Warkentin
York University

THE PORTUGUESE IN CANADA

1

Introduction: A Historical and Geographical Perspective

CARLOS TEIXEIRA and VICTOR M.P. DA ROSA

This book is about the Portuguese in Canada – their history, problems, aspirations, and challenges and their impact on the receiving society. It aims at a better understanding of an important segment of the Portuguese diaspora. The origins of this project are associated with the celebration of the 500th anniversary of John Cabot's arrival in North America in Newfoundland in 1997. This event coincided with the 1997 Annual Meeting of the Canadian Association of Geographers in St John's, where two sessions examined the Portuguese presence in Canada dating back to the fifteenth century.

The contributors to this volume – many of them participants in the 1997 sessions – come from a variety of disciplines: sociology, anthropology, urban planning, geography, history, languages, literatures, and linguistics. As a result, they use a diversity of disciplinary/interdisciplinary approaches. Moreover, by mixing contributions by scholars born in Portugal and Canada, the editors hope to give readers a deeper understanding of Portuguese Canadians from both 'insider' and 'outsider' perspectives. Even though the Portuguese form a significant segment of Canada's heterogeneous population, the number of studies dealing with this group is very limited (see Teixeira and Lavigne 1998). We hope that this publication will help to fill this gap in the study of the Portuguese presence in Canada.

Historical Contacts and Migration

Portugal's history has been deeply influenced by lands beyond the sea. In the fifteenth century, three hundred years after the founding of Portugal in 1143, the period of its discoveries and its colonial empire began. The Atlantic Ocean became the main route for its explorers and navigators of the fifteenth and sixteenth centuries to reach other parts of the globe. This ocean, which transformed Portugal into a commercial and naval power, became in the nineteenth and twentieth centuries the main route for a massive exodus of its population to other countries and continents. Indeed, emigration has been a constant of the Portuguese people (Higgs 1990; Rocha-Trindade et al. 1995; Garcia 1998). In the last hundred years, some four million people have left the country – an exodus that affected the islands (Madeira and the Azores) first and foremost, followed by the northern, and then the central, regions of mainland Portugal (Figure 1.1).[1]

For most of this century, successive Portuguese governments did not hinder this emigration, recognizing, first, that the future transfer of emigrants' remittances back home was essential to the country's balance of payments[2] and, second, that the exodus eased the problems of unemployment and its attendant social tensions. The origins of this emigration lay primarily in the underdevelopment of the country and its lack of resources. Other contributing factors included high population density, inadequate housing, poor use of land, and scarcity of jobs. As the Portuguese sociologists Almeida and Barreto observed some twenty-five years ago: 'Hunger, misery, life's oppressions and total insecurity bring about emigration' (1974: 251). This no longer applies to the majority of Portugal's population, including those in Madeira and the Azores islands. However, even today thousands of citizens live far below the poverty level according to European Union standards (Bacalhau 1984; Leeds 1984; Feldman-Bianco 1992; Manuel 1998).

Modern Portuguese immigration to Canada began in the early 1950s (Table 1.1). However, historical contacts with Canada date back to the fifteenth century, when Portuguese navigators are believed to have reached the Atlantic coast (Allen 1992). While the Portuguese did not settle the land, their presence is preserved today in place names along this coast (Brazão 1964; Alpalhão and Da Rosa 1980; Mannion and Barkham 1987). Names of Portuguese origin dot the capes, headlands, offshore islands, and large harbours. For example, 'Labrador' probably derives from the Portuguese explorer João Fernandes, a 'Lavrador' (farmer) of the island of Terceira (Azores). Other place names of Portuguese origin in the region include: Bacalhaos (Baccalieu Island), Cabo de S. Jorge (Cape St George), C. Rei (Cape Ray), Fogo (Fogo Island), Frey Luis (Cape Freels), Ilha Roxa (Red Island), S. Maria (Cape

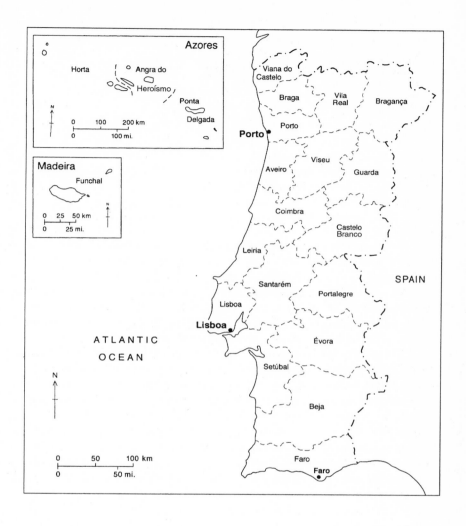

Figure 1.1. Districts of mainland Portugal, the Azores, and Madeira

TABLE 1.1
Portuguese immigration to Canada, 1950–92

1950–9	17,114
1960–9	59,677
1970–9	79,891
1980–9	38,187
1990–2	16,712

Sources: Canada, Department of Citizenship
and Immigration, *Report of Immigration
Branch*, 1955, 1957; information from Canada, Employment and Immigration Canada,
for years 1960–92.

St Mary's), and Terra Nova (Newfoundland) – all testimony to the historical presence of the Portuguese in the northwestern Atlantic.

However, as noted in Table 1.1, the early Portuguese settlers in Canada arrived mainly during the 1950s, when Canada was promoting
this immigration in order to meet its need for agricultural and railway
construction workers (Anderson and Higgs 1976). Sponsorship and
family reunification accounted for the acceleration of the process
mainly through the 1960s and 1970s. From the mid-1970s on, numbers
diminished considerably, partly because of changes to Canadian legislation in 1973. Another factor may have been Portugal's accession to
the European Community. This created prospects of better and more
remunerative jobs and a higher standard of living for the Portuguese at
home. With respect to the Azores, geographical position and strong
historical and family contacts with the United States and Canada
explain the attraction of Azoreans to these areas. Therefore North
America rather than Europe will probably continue the preferred destination for Azoreans.

In fact, 60 per cent to 70 per cent of Portuguese living in Canada
came from the Azores, particularly from the island of São Miguel, or
are descendants of Azorean families. The lack of disaggregated data
concerning the regions of origin of Portuguese immigrants makes it
difficult to determine the percentage of Azoreans and their descendants in Canada. Similarly, estimates on the number of Portuguese in
Canada vary. The Portuguese consulate in Toronto estimates between
300,000 and 500,000. The 1991 Canadian census recorded 292,185; of
them 84 per cent were entirely and the rest partially of Portuguese ori-

TABLE 1.2
Number of people of Portuguese ethnic
origin (single origin), by census metropolitan
areas (CMA), Canada, 1991

CMA	Number
Toronto	124,325
Montreal	32,330
Kitchener	13,755
Hamilton	9,625
Vancouver	9,255
Winnipeg	7,970
Ottawa-Hull	6,580
London	6,330
Edmonton	4,685

Source: Data from Statistics Canada.

gin. A reasonable estimate would probably be between 350,000 and 375,000 (Teixeira 1999).

Settlement

Today, four decades after the arrival of the first immigrants in Canada, we can find Portuguese communities from coast to coast. Most Portuguese Canadians live in Ontario (202,395), Quebec (42,975), British Columbia (23,380), Alberta (9,755), and Manitoba (9,530) (Figure 1.2).

It has been a long and harsh journey from Portugal (particularly the Azores and Madeira) to rural Canada and later to the major cities (see Anderson and Higgs 1976). A major characteristic of the Portuguese in Canada is their urban nature (Table 1.2). Most of the contributions to this volume deal with Portuguese in Canadian urban settings. Curiously, despite their rural roots in Portugal, there is a notable lack of large Portuguese-Canadian settlements in rural areas (see Joy 1982; Cole 1997, 1998). The Portuguese urban settlements are of recent origin; consequently their concentration in particular immigrant neighbourhoods is not surprising. Today, in Toronto, Montreal, Vancouver, Winnipeg, and Edmonton we can identify a 'core' or 'centre' of the Portuguese communities.[3] These communities, particularly in the above-mentioned cities, are self-contained and self-sufficient. Their high degree of 'institutional completeness' is demonstrated by their appreciable number of social, cultural, and religious institutions, as

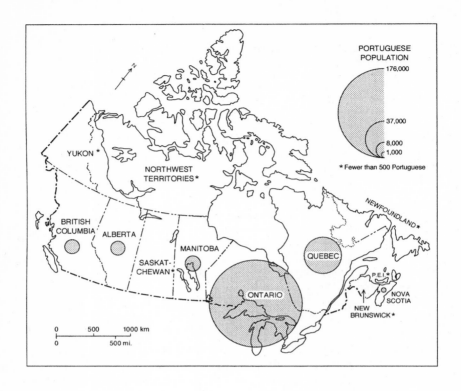

Figure 1.2. Population of Portuguese ethnic origin, by province and territory, Canada, 1991. *Source*: Data from Statistics Canada

TABLE 1.3
Portuguese-Canadian institutions, by region, Canada, 1993

Type of institution	Western Canada	Ontario	Quebec and Atlantic provinces	Total
Businesses	365	3,500*	750†	4,615
Clubs/associations	65	111	22	198
Community schools	10	32	5	47
Churches	7	26‡	5	38

Sources: Portuguese consulates in Montreal, Toronto, Winnipeg, Edmonton, and Vancouver and the Portuguese embassy in Ottawa.
*Federação Luso-Canadiana de Empresários e Profissionais.
†Aliança dos Profissionais e Empresários do Quebec.
‡Guia Comercial Português (Portuguese Telephone Directory), 1993.

well as by their wide range of ethnic businesses (Table 1.3). Portuguese settlement showed distinct spatial patterns, which translated into spatial and social isolation from the host society. This segregation was a barrier to the blending of first-generation immigrants into Canadian society. By 1981, Portuguese Canadians were among the most segregated groups in these cities (Bourne et al. 1986; Balakrishnan and Hou 1995).

In the last two decades, residential patterns have changed (Teixeira 1996), and the Portuguese are spreading over a larger territory than ever before, spurred by the improved economic positions of some Portuguese families and their wish to acquire the 'dream' house, preferably in the suburbs. The slow dispersion of the Portuguese Canadians is a fairly recent phenomenon, with the movement out of the 'core' being clearly reflected in the 1976, 1981, and 1991 censuses. If this trend continues, the next censuses may show a weakening of their concentration within the 'core.' Within this context lies the dilemma of the Portuguese in Canada – communities in transition.

Introduction to the Essays

This collection of essays is an attempt to examine comprehensively the Portuguese presence in Canada – from the early Portuguese explorers, through the later Portuguese fishery on the Grand Banks and the Portuguese cultural impact on the people of Newfoundland, to the state of contemporary Portuguese immigrant communities in Canada. The perspective is at once broad and particular, ranging from historical analysis of the Portuguese diaspora over centuries to the stories of individual Portuguese immigrant women in Montreal and Toronto.

Maria Beatriz Rocha-Trindade (chapter 2) presents an overview of the historical antecedents, as well as the nature and causes, of emigration from Portugal and the situation of the Portuguese diaspora today. She does not forget the new phenomenon of return migration by Portuguese nationals and the significant increase in the number of African immigrants settling in Portugal.

The Portuguese maritime presence in Atlantic Canada was renewed in the twentieth century with the annual sailing, from the 1930s to the 1970s, of the famous 'White Fleet' to the fishing grounds of the Grand Banks. This friendly armada and the relations of its members with Newfoundland and its people form the subject-matter of part I. Priscilla A. Doel (chapter 3) examines the history of the Portuguese codfishing fleet. In particular, she discusses the use – by government and corporate authorities – of icons of nationalism aboard key ships of the White Fleet to assert state control over these fishermen. Jean-Pierre Andrieux (chapter 4), who has spent his life commuting between St-Pierre and St John's, provides us with an insightful view, by a contemporary observer, of how Portuguese state and business interests colluded in the organization, and eventual destruction, of the White Fleet. Finally, the cultural and social impact of the White Fleet on the people of Newfoundland is examined by Peter Collins (chapter 5), a young Canadian literary scholar, who still remembers with great 'saudade' the presence of the White Fleet in his native St John's. He discusses the representations of the Portuguese in Newfoundland literature and journalism and concludes the volume's treatment of the singular 'moment' in Portuguese-Canadian relations that was the White Fleet.

The history of the Portuguese in Canada today is a story of immigration – the subject of part II. As we stated above, the majority of these migrants came from the Azores. In these islands, as in many other regions, emigration is not an individual decision. It is a phenomenon intimately linked to the political and social structure of the country of origin and to that country's position within the world economic order. It is within this context that Manuel Armando Oliveira writes (chapter 6) on the emigration from Pico Island to Canada, dealing with the eternal struggle of emigrants to 'belong' somewhere. If it was so difficult to move from the Azores to the American continent, it was no less of a challenge for Portuguese women to overcome the numerous barriers created by this process. Ilda Januário and Manuela Marujo share with the reader case stories (chapter 7) in which they examine how learning to survive in a society where one's mother tongue is a foreign language – as well as getting a job, facing a harsh climate, and coming to terms with totally different social values – produces innumerable personal and family tensions for women. Value conflicts are also the main theme of Onésimo Teotónio Almeida (chapter 8), where he compares and contrasts the Portuguese in Canada and those in the United States in terms of the struggles for cultural adjustment and adaptation between communities. This contribution is a testimony to Almeida's active community involvement and knowledge of the Portuguese diaspora.

The essays in part III deal with issues of language and identity. Rena Helms-Park (chapter 9) studies heritage language education in Canada and how language retention is associated with the maintenance of an ethnic identity. Manuela Dias-Tatilon (chapter 10) describes the linguistic interferences between Portuguese and French in Montreal – a timely discussion in the context of the political uncertainties that Quebec is facing. Portuguese identity is also the subject of Edite Noivo's contribution (chapter 11). She reviews major theories on diasporic identities and formulates a theoretical framework to look at three generations of Portuguese Canadians.

In part IV, Carlos Teixeira, in association with Gilles Lavigne or Victor M.P. Da Rosa, or by himself, describes 'Little Portugals' in Canada – in Montreal (chapter 12), in the province of Quebec (chapter 13), and in Toronto (chapter 14), respectively. The three chapters challenge the long-held assumption about the immutability of these communities. Political and economic changes taking place in Canada in general, and in Quebec and Ontario in particular, are affecting the new Canadians' view of Canada. The changes that the Portuguese communities will experience within the near future will be critical to the survival and integrity of the group – its cohesion, culture, and traditions.

Part V examines the literature and sense of history of Portuguese Canadians. António Augusto Joel (chapter 15) writes about new works of Portuguese background in Canada, such as Erika de Vasconcelos's *My Darling Dead Ones*. David Higgs, a true pioneer of Portuguese studies in Canada, closes this work (chapter 16) with a professional interpretation of the sense of history among Portuguese Canadians. We could not find a more appropriate way to conclude this volume.

12   Carlos Teixeira and Victor M.P. Da Rosa

Some twenty years ago one of the editors wrote that Portuguese immigrants have brought to Canada, in addition to their labour, certain cultural values destined to become an integral part of Canadian heritage. As we did then, we must reiterate now our hope that the Portuguese presence in Canada be both a guardian of the past and a beacon for the future.

NOTES

1 Portugal has an area of 91,985 square kilometers. Its population of approximately 9.5 million (1997) is distributed among eighteen continental and four island districts. Madeira has one district (Funchal). The islands of the Azores are divided into three districts: Angra do Heroísmo (islands of Graciosa, São Jorge, and Terceira), Horta (Corvo, Faial, Flores, and Pico), and Ponta Delgada (Santa Maria and São Miguel) (see Figure 1.1).
2 According to Portuguese authorities, the remittances of Portuguese from the diaspora are, even today, very sizeable. In the last four years approximately 2.420 million contos (1 conto = 1,000 escudos) arrived in Portugal from immigrants living abroad (Ribeiro 1998). (In May 1999 Can$1 = 128 escudos.)
3 The areas identified as 'core' or 'centre' of the Portuguese communities reflect relatively homogeneous and compact socio-spatial units within these cities, where a large number of Portuguese live and where most of their institutions, businesses, and services are located.

Allen, J.L. 1992. 'From Cabot to Cartier: The Early Exploration of Eastern North America, 1497–1543.' *Annals of the Association of American Geographers* 82 no. 3: 500–21.
Almeida, C., and Barreto, A. 1974. *Capitalismo e emigração em Portugal*. Lisbon: Prelo.
Alpalhão, J.A., and V.M.P. Da Rosa, 1980. *A Minority in a Changing Society: The Portuguese Communities of Quebec*. Ottawa: University of Ottawa Press.
Anderson, G.M., and Higgs, D. 1976. *A Future to Inherit: The Portuguese Communities of Canada*. Toronto: McClelland and Stewart.
Bacalhau, M. 1984. 'Regional Distribution of Portuguese Emigration According to Socio-Economic Context.' In T. Bruneau, V.M.P. Da Rosa, and A. Macleod, eds., *Portugal in Development: Emigration, Industrialization, the European Community*, 53–63. Ottawa: University of Ottawa Press.

Balakrishnan, T.R., and Hou, F. 1995. *The Changing Patterns of Spatial Concentration and Residential Segregation of Ethnic Groups in Canada's Major Metropolitan Areas, 1981–1991.* London: University of Western Ontario, Population Studies Centre.

Bourne, L.S., Baker, A.M., Kalbach, W., Cressman, R., and Green, D. 1986. *Canada's Ethnic Mosaic: Characteristics and Patterns of Ethnic Origin Groups in Urban Areas.* Toronto: University of Toronto, Centre for Urban and Community Studies.

Brazão, E. 1964. *La découverte de Terre Neuve.* Montreal: Les Presses de L'Université de Montreal.

Cole, S.C. 1997. 'Género e família na construçao das identidades portuguesas no Canadá.' *ANTROPOlógicas* 1:3–19.

– 1998. 'Reconstituting Households, Retelling Culture: Emigration and Portuguese Fisheries Workers in Canada.' In S. Ilcan and L. Phillips, eds., *Transgressing Borders: Critical Perspectives on Gender, Households, Culture,* 75–92. Wesport, Conn.: Bergen and Garvey.

Feldman-Bianco, B. 1992. 'Multiple Layers of Time and Space: The Construction of Class, Ethnicity, and Nationalism among Portuguese Immigrants.' In N.G. Schiller, L. Basch, and C. Blanc-Szanton, eds., *Towards a Transnational Perspective on Migration,* 145–74. New York: New York Academy of Sciences.

Garcia, J.L. 1998. *A emigração Portuguesa: Uma breve introdução.* Lisbon: Secretaria de Estado das Comunidades Portuguesas.

Higgs, D. 1990. 'Portuguese Migration before 1800.' In D. Higgs, ed., *Portuguese Migration in a Global Perspective,* 7–28. Toronto: Multicultural History Society of Ontario.

Joy, A. 1982. 'Accommodation and Cultural Persistence: The Case of the Sikhs and the Portuguese in the Okanagan Valley of British Columbia.' Doctoral dissertation, University of British Columbia.

Leeds, E. 1984. 'Salazar's "Modelo Económico": The Consequences of Planned Constraint.' In T. Bruneau, V.M.P. Da Rosa, and A. Macleod, eds., *Portugal in Development: Emigration, Industrialization, the European Community,* 13–51. Ottawa: University of Ottawa Press.

Mannion, J., and Barkham, S. 1987. 'The 16th Century Fishery.' (Plate 22). In R.C. Harris, ed., *Historical Atlas of Canada. Volume 1. From the Beginning to 1800,* 58–59. Toronto: University of Toronto Press.

Manuel, P.C. 1998. 'The Process of Democratic Consolidation in Portugal, 1976–1996.' *Portuguese Studies Review* no. 1: 33–47.

Ribeiro, M.A. 1998. 'Remessas de Imigrantes.' *Correio Português,* 15 June: 5.

Rocha-Trindade, M.B., et al. 1995. *Sociologia das migrações.* Lisbon: Universidade Aberta.

Teixeira, C. 1996. 'The Suburbanization of Portuguese Communities in Toronto and Montreal: From Isolation to Residential Integration?' In A. Laperrière, V. Lindstrom, and T.P. Seiler, eds., *Immigration and Ethnicity in Canada*, 181–201. Montreal: Association for Canadian Studies.
– 1999. 'Portuguese.' In P.R. Magocsi, ed., *An Encyclopedia of Canada's Peoples*. Toronto: University of Toronto Press, 1,075–83.
Teixeira, C., and Lavigne, G. 1998. *Os Portugueses no Canadá: Uma bibliografia (1953–1996)*. Lisbon: Direcção-Geral dos Assuntos Consulares e Comunidades Portuguesas.

2

The Portuguese Diaspora

MARIA BEATRIZ ROCHA-TRINDADE

Migration within the Global Context

Analysis of emigration movements was originally rooted firmly in demography. Wherever researchers noted a significant population flow between a country of origin and a country of destination, they counted the people in transit and duly classified them according to gender, age group, educational level, and professional profile. Later, more economically oriented studies of emigration patterns explored the reasons underlying emigration through analysis of the differentials of demographic pressure, economic level, and job opportunities between the two ends of the journey. This led to the formulation of theories that were based on the dual concept of attraction and repulsion.

However, such indicators were not in themselves sufficient to explain the complexities of collective movements, and so researchers began to consider other aspects of migration relating to sociology, social psychology, and cultural anthropology. These aspects were linked to issues concerning motivation, the circulation of information, and the sometimes stereotypical images constructed about both the country of origin and the country of destination. This approach was developed in the large receiving countries, where it was extended to the analysis of settlement and integration of the various waves of immigrants. In contrast, governments in the countries of origin were concerned more with securing guarantees in terms of employment, social insertion, and respect for the rights of the workers and families settled abroad.

Today, the globalization of communications and the continuing international circulation and settlement of peoples render the study of emigration and immigration movements of particular importance in government, social, and urban planning. Spatially dispersed diasporas – such as that of the Portuguese – can have a cultural and economic impact on a global level by linking such otherwise disparate societies as Canada's and Brazil's. Thus the study of the historical migrations of this group serves as a good example of the value of migration studies to our understanding of contemporary societies.

This essay first looks at Portuguese emigration up to the nineteenth century. Second, it examines emigration in this century. Third, it analyses return migration and immigration to Portugal. Finally, it presents characteristics of this diaspora as a synthesis of the remarks and arguments presented in this chapter.

Historical Antecedents

Colonial Emigration

Situated in the extreme southwestern corner of Europe, in close contact with both the Mediterranean and the Atlantic, Portugal has been a stopover on journeys of peoples throughout history. Visited by Greeks and Phoenicians, occupied by Romans, invaded by 'barbarians' from northern and eastern Europe, conquered by Moors, and made independent by its first Christian king in the twelfth century (1143), Portugal possesses the oldest frontiers of any country in Europe. The multiple ethnic and cultural influences that have been the products of this historical process, leading to what is today an extremely homogeneous national culture, may be one explanation for the Portuguese inclination to seek contact with other peoples and places.

This predilection has in fact characterized the whole of Portuguese history over the last five centuries. In the fifteenth and sixteenth centuries, Portuguese overseas expansion established a trade network and military domination on a world-wide scale, extending from the north and west coasts of Africa to India and from the Straits of Malacca to China and Japan. In the Western Hemisphere, possession of the Atlantic archipelagos reinforced Portuguese military and economic power over the South Atlantic and Brazil.

Accompanying this overseas expansion were the first waves of emigrants from Portugal. Some sources (see Serrão 1971) refer to the departure of about 2,400 individuals per year, to the fortified towns of the Indian Ocean, in the early sixteenth century. This movement grew in the second half of the century with emigration to Brazil, which received some 3,000 emigrants a year. As a result, the Portuguese population resident in that colony, estimated at some 57,000 in 1576, quadrupled between 1580 and 1600.

At the end of the seventeenth century, departures for Brazil increased, owing to the discovery of mines of precious metals and gems, which led to a massive migration, primarily from northwest Portugal. Improvements in the shipping connections to Brazil also account for the annual departure at this time of over 2,000 Portuguese – who set sail from the ports of Viana, Oporto, and Lisbon – heading for Pernambuco, Baía, and Rio de Janeiro. This flow of people was made up of those seeking to make their fortunes quickly, especially in trade, since agricultural tasks 'would continue for some time still to be done by slaves of African extraction.' These emigrants included not only 'individuals of the humbler classes' but also 'nobles and men of letters invested with official or officious duties' who, once there, became involved in liberal professions (Sérgio 1956).

The subsequent decline in Portuguese power in India and southeast Asia led to larger contingents of emigrants being sent to Brazil, thereby encouraging a colonial policy that essentially transferred the focus of emigration from the Indian to the Atlantic Ocean.[1] The fact that interest in Brazil persisted is clear from the high number of annual departures (between 8,000 and 10,000) recorded during the first two-thirds of the eighteenth century. Although figures dropped off slightly late in the eighteenth century, they picked up again during the nineteenth, following the transfer of the Portuguese crown to the colony (in 1807). After Brazil's independence (1822) ended the Portuguese colonial presence in that region, demographic movements from Portugal to the new country became in effect international – as opposed to colonial – emigration. Although the Portuguese empire survived until recently in India (1961), Africa and Timor (1975), and Macao (20 December 1999) – this in spite of its becoming progressively more limited and weakened – the movement of people to these colonial destinations never reached a scale comparable to the Portuguese migration to Brazil.

The Nineteenth-Century Transatlantic Emigration Cycle

Following the pattern of the previous century, the Portuguese in the nineteenth century settled primarily in northeastern Brazil, in Pernambuco and Baía, where they were involved in the growing of cotton and sugar cane. Later, there was a movement towards the centre of the country, thanks to the growth of the mining industry after the discovery of large deposits of gold and precious stones. This led to the spread of Portuguese settlement as far as Goiás, Minas Gerais, and Mato Grosso. Some settlers quickly acquired spectacular wealth, which was responsible for the birth of the 'O Mineiro' (Miner) figure in Portuguese folklore; an image that faded only with the impoverishment of the gold and diamond beds and a consequent sharp drop in emigration.

The next phase of the Portuguese emigration to Brazil, which occurred in the second half of the nineteenth century, was connected to new economic conditions (extensive coffee and cotton plantations in the São Paulo region) and social and political changes (independence in 1822 and an end to slavery through progressively liberating legislation, culminating in the Áurea Law, which in 1888 decreed its abolition in Brazil).[2]

Meanwhile, territories populated and colonized earlier by the Portuguese – primarily the Atlantic archipelagos of Madeira, the Azores, and the Cape Verde Islands – changed from 'receiving' to 'sending' regions when many of their natives left in search of a better life beyond national borders. Initially they headed for Brazil (settling particularly in the coastal areas of the southern states: Paraná, Santa Catarina, and Rio Grande do Sul) and for Africa (Mozambique and the Angolan Plateau). At the end of the last century, Madeirans also headed for the Pacific (the Sandwich Islands, now Hawaii)[3] (Felix and Senecal 1978; Dias 1981; Rocha 1983), as well as for British Guiana (Demerara) and the Dutch Antilles (Curaçao) – all places that could be reached only by a long and hazardous voyage.[4] The Azoreans, however, preferred the American continent. In the words of Martins: 'The [Portuguese] colony in California is Azorean, for American whaling ships go to the Azores to recruit seamen. Whaling ... is to a part of the Azorean people what Brazil is to people from the northern Minho province' (1956: 234). For these migrants, after fishing as an employee on someone else's boat or as a self-employed fisherman, jobs in factories and on farms were the most common occupation; the former were mostly on the east coast (Massachusetts and Connecticut), and the latter largely in California, particularly in the San Joaquin Valley.

Another North American destination – Canada – is insufficiently documented in this period. While the role played by Portuguese navigators in the discovery of Newfoundland, Labrador, and the eastern seaboard of continental Canada is widely recognized, there are only a few isolated references to the Portuguese names of families settled there since the sixteenth century. This is unusual, since the intensive fishing activity carried out by Portuguese boats in these regions is well known and would naturally have given rise to a fair, though limited, number of settlers (Moura 1992). However, Canada seems to have become a major important destination for Portuguese emigration only after 1950.

In general, all these tides of transatlantic emigration became geographically specialized streams, providing a clear example of the demarcation of geographical destination zones, which lasted throughout the following decades.

Contemporary Emigration

Transoceanic Destinations

The two main destinations for Portuguese emigrants in the Americas – Brazil and the United States (Tables 2.1 and 2.2) – have one characteristic in common, namely that they both maintained these permanent regular streams of emigrants during the first half of the twentieth century, except during the two world wars. During the First World War, the almost total suspension of departures from Portugal was mainly a result of Portuguese involvement in this conflict, which absorbed many in both the young and adult population. During the Second World War, the total insecurity of the Atlantic sea crossing, owing to attacks by German submarines, ended shipping.

During peacetime, emigrants of Azorean origin dominated the migration to the United States, primarily because of family members' having settled there since the previous century. The main settlement areas continued to be the northern part of the eastern coast, as well as California, where the immigrants enjoyed significant prosperity (Pap 1981; Baganha 1990).[5] A great impetus to this emigration occurred in 1958, with passage of the Azorean Refugee Act – after an initiative taken by Senator John F. Kennedy of Massachusetts – which allowed entry to persons displaced by the eruption of Capelinhos Volcano in the archipelago. In the 1960s and 1970s, Portuguese emigration exceeded 1,000 people a month on average, with more than half of them coming from the Azores. In the next two decades, however, these numbers fell to some 2,000 to 3,000 annually.

TABLE 2.1
Emigration from Portugal, by country of destination, 1966–92

Year	Germany	South Africa	Australia	Brazil	Canada	United States	France	Nether- lands	Luxem- bourg	United Kingdom	Switzer- land	Venezuela	Other countries	Totals
1966	9,686	4,721	288	2,607	6,795	13,357	73,419	1,308	462	597	205	4,697	2,097	120,239
1967	2,042	1,947	347	3,271	6,615	11,516	59,415	401	205	631	191	4,118	1,803	92,502
1968	4,886	921	381	3,512	6,833	10,841	46,515	467	215	537	176	3,751	1,417	80,452
1969	13,279	713	446	2,537	6,502	13,111	27,234	420	361	783	276	3,044	1,459	70,165
1970	19,775	702	360	1,669	6,529	9,726	21,962	393	269	506	362	2,927	1,180	66,360
1971	16,997	339	435	1,200	6,983	8,839	10,023	338	175	303	344	3,500	924	50,400
1972	14,377	274	249	1,158	6,845	7,574	17,800	149	529	309	527	3,641	652	54,084
1973	31,479	359	672	890	7,403	8,160	20,692	394	2,870	586	1,246	4,294	472	79,517
1974	3,049	452	643	729	11,650	9,540	10,568	278	2,123	666	735	2,550	414	43,397
1975	1,072	217	256	1,553	5,857	8,975	2,866	44	649	630	123	1,903	666	24,811
1976	346	212	213	837	3,597	7,496	1,780	19	137	299	94	1,833	630	17,493
1977	210	209	441	557	2,335	6,822	1,417	34	198	201	238	3,681	883	17,226
1978	112	159	500	321	1,868	8,176	1,604	25	185	145	212	3,575	1,777	18,659
1979	76	164	231	216	2,805	8,177	2,159	19	512	177	30	3,934	2,074	20,574
1980	69	162	320	230	2,334	4,999	1,867	38	448	99	40	2,734	4,731	18,071
1981	41	422	1,420	228	2,196	4,295	1,565	50	188	46	50	2,484	3,528	16,513
1982	25	142	1,462	187	1,484	1,889	546	12	92	27	48	2,827	1,535	10,276
1983	23	101	867	197	823	2,437	665	15	49	24	45	1,376	474	7,096
1984	25	150	1,045	121	764	2,651	668	17	15	16	31	661	392	6,556
1985	18	125	1,121	136	791	2,783	1,180	13	23	16	27	631	285	7,149
1986	23	27	1,015	91	977	2,725	924	17	13	19	56	160	224	6,271
1987	32	27	1,345	28	3,400	2,644	167	7	12	11	92	81	262	8,108
1988	38	26	889	21	5,646	2,110	370	5	28	6	115	81	205	9,540
1989	12	4	317	17	1,006	255	153	4	21	2	18	2	10	1,821
1990	12	27	329	12	569	377	120	3	59	4	21	9	12	1,554

Source: General Directorate for Consular Affairs and Portuguese Communities, Ministry of Foreign Affairs, Portugal.

TABLE 2.2
Portuguese living abroad, by country, 1997

Country / territory	No.	%	Country / territory	No.	%
Europe			*Americas*		
Andorra	9,000	0.19	Antilles, Dutch	2,540	0.05
Austria	441	0.01	Argentina	16,000	0.35
Belgium	38,000	0.82	Aruba	500	0.01
Denmark	450	0.01	Bermuda	2,500	0.05
France	798,837	17.25	Brazil	1,200,000	25.91
Germany	170,000	3.6	Canada	515,000	11.12
Greece	300	0.01	Chile	112	0.00
Holland	9,230	0.20	Ecuador	300	0.01
Italy	5,655	0.12	United States	500,000	10.80
Luxembourg	51,800	1.12	Mexico	300	0.01
Norway	652	0.01	Panama	500	0.01
Spain	63,717	1.38	Uruguay	1,200	0.03
Sweden	2,553	0.06	Venezuela	400,000	8.64
Switzerland	155,104	3.35	Other	708	0.02
United Kingdom	60,000	1.30	Total	2,639,660	56.99
USSR	600	0.01			
Other	361	0.01	*Asia*		
Total	1,366,700	29.51	Saudi Arabia	149	0.00
			Bahrain	100	0.00
Africa			Un. Arab Emirates	325	0.01
Angola	20,000	0.43	Hong Kong	20,700	0.45
Botswana	240	0.01	India	6,000	0.13
Cape Verde	500	0.01	Israel	250	0.01
Congo, Rep. of	111	0.00	Japan	350	0.01
Congo, Dem. Rep. (ex-Zaire)	400	0.01	Pakistan	860	0.02
Guinea-Bissau	800	0.02	Thailand	260	0.01
Lesotho	200	0.00	Other	277	0.01
Malawi	200	0.00	Total	29,271	0.63
Morocco	1,000	0.02			
Mozambique	11,668	0.25	*Oceania*		
Namibia	794	0.02	Australia	55,339	1.19
Kenya	497	0.01	New Zealand	120	0.00
S. Tomé e Principe	451	0.01	Total	55,459	1.20
South Africa	500,000	10.80			
Swaziland	884	0.02	Total for all	4,631,482	100.00
Zimbabwe	2,200	0.05			
Other	447	0.01			
Total	540,392	11.6			

Source: Ministry of Foreign Affairs, Portugal.
*Estimate.

Brazil remained the chosen destination for the majority of Portuguese emigrants from the northern half of Portugal. The vast colony of people of northern Portuguese origin in Brazil attracted them, as did language and cultural affinity, which facilitated integration.

However, significant movements to other countries began in the second half of the twentieth century. In the case of Canada, Portuguese emigration became significant only after 1953. This was the year when 550 Portuguese – all male – were recruited from the mainland, the Azores, and Madeira, in a process coordinated by the Portuguese and Canadian authorities. Ever larger contingents followed in subsequent years, until the maximum annual figure of 16,300 was reached in 1974. Today, it is estimated that the number of residents of Portuguese origin in Canada is half a million (Table 2.2), of whom about 60 to 70 per cent come from the Azores. The largest Portuguese community is in Toronto (where more than half of the total reside), with significant numbers also in Quebec, British Columbia, and Manitoba (Da Rosa and Teixeira 1996; Teixeira 1996).

Another new destination in the late twentieth century has been Venezuela, as a result of the surge of wealth created by the oil-fields in the southern part of the Gulf of Mexico. Family migration to Venezuela came primarily from the district of Aveiro, in north-central continental Portugal, and from Madeira. Several large Portuguese communities sprang up, which prospered in the wholesale and retail trade and in the service industry, especially urban and inter-city transport. Despite the international oil crisis of the 1970s, and the internal economic crisis in Venezuela in the late 1980s, the community has grown and prospered and is now estimated at 400,000 people.

Although it was much smaller, there was also an emigration to Argentina in the postwar period, which expanded on an initial nucleus of Portuguese who had settled there in the 1920s. This new group came mainly from the eastern half of the Algarve province in the south of Portugal (Ferreira 1976; Borges 1997), as well as from the Cape Verde Islands, then under Portuguese sovereignty (Poteca 1993). Given the sea-faring background of these emigrants, it is not surprising that they devoted themselves above all to fishing, boat-building, and ship-fitting. The community in Argentina is estimated at some 18,000 people.

The case of Portuguese emigration to South Africa is distinct from the flow to most countries because of its 'accidental' origins. The largest group of such immigrants hailed originally from Madeira, which was on the sea route between Britain and its colonies in Africa; Madeirans were carried along by the stream of Britons, both public officials and colonists, heading for South Africa. Once there, the Madeirans dedicated themselves to farming, trade, and services.

South Africa also enjoyed a temporary migration of Portuguese colonists from Mozambique who moved there to find work in the mines. Because Mozambique shared a common border with South Africa and had easy access to it, when the Portuguese colonies of Angola and Mozambique became independent in 1975, there followed a massive exodus of Portuguese of European origin not only back to Portugal, but also to South Africa. In the following decades, the tide of emigration from Madeira to South Africa continued, and even intensified, until today the total number of people of Portuguese origin in the country is estimated at some 800,000.[6]

Australia completes this story. Japanese occupation of Timor and the island's subsequent liberation by the Allied armies (of which the Australians were a part) brought to Australia many of the Portuguese who had been serving or living in the Portuguese colony, and many settled there permanently. Others followed, primarily from the Portuguese territory of Macao in southeast China. Australia continues today to be a destination favoured by the Portuguese, given its rapid growth, low population density, numerous job opportunities, and chances to prosper. The community is estimated at 65,000 people.[7]

Intra-European Emigration

After the Second World War, northern Europe experienced a period of explosive economic growth. This led to the creation of new jobs, especially in the industrial (primarily construction) and service sectors. The movement of local workforces to the more highly skilled and better-paid jobs created a vacuum in the supply of manual labour, which was filled by foreign workers from the Mediterranean basin including – besides the Portuguese – Spaniards, Italians, Yugoslavs, Turks, Greeks, and North Africans. While competing with these others, the Portuguese found open markets – in France, Germany, and other countries – which were hungry for unskilled labour. In the 1960s and 1970s, when more than one million Portuguese emigrated, over half of them moved within Europe. Most destination countries, except West Germany, which accepted only legal immigrants,[8] received undocumented immigrants who had crossed the border illegally. Indeed, clandestine emigration, which was not new to Portugal, was predominant in this flow. The fact that one could travel from Portugal to any European country by land made it relatively easy for emigrants to cross borders, by interrupting the journey by rail or road and then walking; generally at night and away from places where lines of communication crossed borders (Almeida and Barreto 1974: 184–9).

Although the movement towards France began slowly, it grew steadily, and it soon overtook emigration to Brazil (in 1963). The Portuguese colony in France in the 1990s is estimated at around one million. Other European destinations have been Germany (which now has about 170,000 Portuguese) and – with fewer emigrants – Belgium, Britain, Holland, and Scandinavia (Table 2.2). In Luxembourg, Portuguese account for almost 15 per cent of the population and one-third of its workforce.

The Swiss have always had a policy of temporary, rather than permanent immigration, and many Portuguese worked there on a yearly or seasonal basis. However, some flexibility in recent legislation allowed long-term temporary workers to be given permanent work permits. Thus Switzerland has become, after France, the European country with the highest number of Portuguese immigrants.

The entire European pattern of emigration–immigration changed suddenly in the 1970s, with the onset of a widespread economic depression, which not only halted the progress and pace of development of European countries, but also severely affected the flow of imported labour, which until then had been a major economic support. Among working populations, immigrants were at the bottom of the pyramid of professional skills. Formerly considered productive and useful, they soon came to be seen as dispensable and an excess burden. Thus, their *host* countries came to be referred to as *receiving* countries (with a somewhat negative connotation).

Thus the oil crisis of 1973–4 changed the fate of the human pieces on the chess-board of international interests, with consequences that lasted throughout the 1970s, which saw widespread unemployment in Europe (Perez 1981; Kubat 1984; Ferreira and Clausse 1986; Rocha-Trindade et al. 1988). At first, European governments found a rather simplistic, pragmatic solution: they would send foreign workers home, together with their families; sending immigrants back to their countries of origin would ensure the financial survival of domestic companies which claimed that they could not keep employment at its former high levels. Foreign workers would therefore be the first target in staff reductions. However, as we now know, many jobs taken by imported labour are not the type that host nationals would ever accept. This, together with the political unpalatability of forced repatriation, led to alternative, more moderate solutions.

In countries of origin such as Portugal, closing of borders to new emigrants caused concern, aggravated by the failure of recent attempts to open up new markets for Portuguese emigration. The lack of security in Portuguese-speaking Africa (a possible alternative destination) limited the number of emigrants to those countries, who were mostly people who signed short-term cooperation agreements. Other countries with strong demand for qualified technical personnel (the Maghreb countries and the Middle East) generally offered only fixed-term contracts, as well as living conditions unlikely to attract family emigration.

In the end, only the traditional non-European destinations (the United States, Canada, and Venezuela) continued to show some permeability, and of the new destinations only South Africa and Australia were significant. The virtual end of emigration within Europe did not rule out two possibilities – short- and mid-term temporary emigration (agricultural work, construction, and the hotel industry, especially in Switzerland and France) and the reunification of families, which, though severely restricted, still led to a significant number of departures. Portugal's entry into the European Community (EC) in January 1986 changed the legal status of Portuguese residents in member countries, as well as that of those seeking a new labour market, from 'economic emigrants' to 'resident EC citizens.' Later, 1988 saw full implementation of the principle of free circulation of persons within the EC.

This change in status removed entries and exits from Portugal to EC countries from migration statistics, making Portuguese intra-European migration difficult to estimate. The only reliable measure will be the difference between the 1990 national census and the upcoming results of the next one, in 2000.

Immigration and Return Migration to Portugal

We have so far focused on the departure of Portuguese from their European territory to two distinct types of destination – first, dependent territories (Brazil up to 1822 and the colonies in Africa, Asia, and Oceania up to 1975) and, second, the same territories after independence, as well as other countries. Strictly speaking, the first situation was one of internal migration.

We can now analyse the three types of movements in the opposite direction (from other countries to Portugal) in a similar perspective. First, if immigrants were residents of former Portuguese territories, who retained Portuguese nationality after independence, their departure for Portugal is the equivalent to a *return of nationals*. Second, if they were foreign citizens, then we have *international immigration*. Third, if they were immigrants or born in a foreign country, but held Portuguese nationality, then their movements constitute *return migration*. There are numerous examples of all three in recent history, but they are not always easy to identify and classify.

The Return of Nationals

The return of nationals, as a result of Portuguese decolonization in Asia and Africa, began in 1960 (Rocha-Trindade et al. 1987, 1995). India's occupation of the Estado da Índia (the Portuguese state of India – Goa, Damão, and Diu) began this process. It led to a sudden influx of refugees (of both European and Asian origin) into continental Portugal and Mozambique. The outbreak of wars of liberation in Angola, Mozambique, and Guinea-Bissau also produced a significant influx of residents of European origin, as well as young Africans whose academic training Portugal wished to encourage. Labourers from Cape Verde also arrived to occupy jobs left by Portuguese doing military service (mainly overseas) or by emigrants and came to make up the oldest and largest Portuguese-speaking African community in Portugal (Carreira 1977).

The collapse of Antonio Salazar's long-time dictatorship in Portugal in 1974, and the end of the colonial war in Africa and the ensuing rapid decolonization, helped reverse population movements in and out of Portugal. The turbulent emergence of the new African states in 1975 led to repatriation of at least half a million Portuguese – perhaps as many as around 800,000, or about 8 per cent of the country's population. Of returnees, 61 per cent came from Angola, 33 per cent from Mozambique, and 6 per cent from the other former colonies (Pires et al. 1984: 38). Of those who returned, 60 per cent were born in continental Portugal, with the remaining 40 per cent including not only their descendants but also a number of African born or people who had been granted Portuguese nationality.

Those returned nationals from East Timor and Macao are in Portugal because of unusual circumstances. In legal terms, both territories are still under Portuguese administration, although East Timor has been occupied by Indonesia and Macao will revert to China on 20 December 1999. The political and social instability which resulted from the civil war that raged throughout East Timor in the summer of 1975, and the subsequent occupation of the territory by Indonesia, lasting until October 1999, led many Timorese to move to Portugal. As for the Macanese of Chinese ancestry in Portugal, it is difficult to assess the size of their community. However, arrivals were expected to increase as transfer to China in late 1999 approached.

The fact that these newcomers of several decades have Portuguese nationality makes estimates of numbers problematic. Whatever their ancestry, their full citizenship rights have led to almost complete integration within Portuguese society.

International Immigration

International migration to Portugal from Portuguese-speaking countries is closely related to the return of nationals, which actually induces and creates a precedent and stimulates the emigratory options of citizens living in those former colonies. Their knowledge (good, fair, or poor) of the language and the possible presence of family and acquaintances in Portugal facilitate such moves. According to information provided by the Portuguese border-control and immigration authorities, by the end of 1996, 81,176 foreigners from Portuguese-speaking African countries resided in Portugal, representing 47 per cent of authorized foreign residents.

As a reverse image of the former Portuguese emigration to Brazil, many Brazilians are now emigrating to Portugal for the same reasons of linguistic and cultural affinity. This immigration consists mostly of young people, some with qualifications, and even specialists who work in various professions in Portugal (dentistry, design, marketing and advertising, tourism and professions related to show business). Another less qualified group finds more modest jobs in industry and commerce. Today the Brazilian immigrant community ranks second in size among foreigners residing in Portugal.

However, the geographical origin of foreigners settled in Portugal is not limited to Portuguese-speaking countries in Africa and Brazil. The number of immigrants from North America, Britain, France, Germany, and Spain is also significant. Their socioeconomic status, however, is higher than that of the majority of African immigrants. The underlying motivation for this category of immigrant appears to be the renaissance of political, economic, and social life that followed consolidation of Portuguese democracy, which attracted new foreign investment aimed mainly at tourism, trade, agriculture, and the service sector. These investments were promoted mainly by Americans and Europeans, some of whom have settled in Portugal.

Return Migration

As a rule, transoceanic Portuguese migration tended to lead to permanent settlement, except in two extreme situations – first, complete failure to reach the objectives sought, because of bad health or simply bad luck; and second, significant success, encouraging return to the country of origin. In cases of family emigration with children born and brought up in the receiving country, however, such a return has sometimes been difficult because of opposition from descendants.

With intra-European migration, close proximity allows for regular trips back and forth, and no final decision on permanent residence is necessary. Indefinite postponement of the final decision is common, even though the desire to return to Portugal persists and becomes, in the end, a utopian dream (Rocha-Trindade et al. 1983). Serious economic crises and higher unemployment, as occurred in much of Europe during the oil crisis, or outbreaks of xenophobia, as took place particularly in France and Germany in the early 1990s, could make necessary a definitive decision.

However, advances in transportation technologies allowing for inexpensive mass transit over long distances permit temporary return on holidays. This constitutes a new way for Portuguese to retain links with their origins and to live their migratory experience.

Characteristics of the Portuguese Diaspora

Analysis of the various migratory movements of Portuguese has revealed a series of trends. The first relates to the regular and constant flow of departing Portuguese, beginning in the fifteenth century and continuing until present times, which led historian Magalhães-

Godinho (1974) to characterize emigration as 'a structural phenomenon of Portuguese society.' A second characteristic is its extreme
dispersion among numerous countries, on all continents where the
Portuguese have settled, living in relative harmony with a vast variety
of races, cultures, and religions.

Related to this second point is the Portuguese ability to integrate into
different cultural contexts, learning the local language, adopting daily
practices, and very often intermarrying with people from the majority
society. The first generation has usually reached a reasonable level of
social insertion into the receiving country after only a few years, and
the generation continuum of their descendants may generally consider
themselves integrated *ab initio*. In such circumstances, the Portuguese
and Luso-descendant communities that have sprung up in foreign
countries firmly reject any tendencies to self-segregation. However,
their integrationism seems to coexist with a deep feeling of identification with their roots – with Portugal – and, particularly among the first
generation, with the region of the country whence their progenitors
came. There is a need to visit Portugal, to locate family, and to maintain
permanent contact with acquaintances in the faraway country of origin.
Many emigrants recall or re-create types of behaviour and cultural features evocative of their ancestral legacy, which is thus continued and
renewed, sometimes in hybrid and syncretic forms.

Even when the Portuguese language has been lost, there still
remains a tendency to seek the company of other people of the same
origin, in associative groups that take different forms, in each place
and in each period, and have varied purposes and types of activities. It
is through such associations that groups of people of Portuguese origin
have sought to identify interests that lead them back to their original
common reference points and that enable them to construct symbols
capable of lending form and expression to such references. Intertwin-
ing the flags of the distant country with that of the present one is possibly the most frequent symbol and no doubt the one that best represents
these 'hyphenated Portuguese' shared feeling of belonging (Rocha-
Trindade 1989).

Likewise with immigration into Portugal, numerous immigrants'
associations are springing up almost explosively. Given their characteristics of economic immigration of unskilled or semi-skilled workers,
and their relatively recent arrival, these organizations play a crucial
role in defending the rights of the respective communities and establishing dialogue and negotiation with the Portuguese authorities.[9]

Immigration comes mostly from Portuguese-speaking Africa and has led to progressive establishment of a sizeable associative movement. The community of Cape Verdean origin is the most visible, having begun to arrive in the late 1960s and being quite large. Brazilians also have a significant presence. But above all it is the Timorense who have best used their associations as an operational tool in their political struggle for self-determination for East Timor.

The similarities between the associative movements of Portuguese emigrants abroad and those of immigrants in Portugal are not merely coincidental. From this perspective, the flows and counter-flows of people, through their physical, emotional, and cultural intermingling, are but two moments, forever being renewed, of the same wave. Portugal remains, as a country and a national identity, profoundly defined by the realities of migration. Whether this be emigration or, more recently, return migration, the Portuguese migrant has been a constant of Portuguese history to this day.

NOTES

1 Many Portuguese writers at the turn of the century turned their attention to what was then considered 'the emigration problem.' Among these were Herculano (1879), Costa (1911) and Silva (1917), who left a rich store of information about the phenomenon, situating it within the national and international economic and political context of their times through descriptions that not only indicate the origin of the flow of emigrants but also represent its size. Using macroscopic approaches, they link up the social variables that underlie the causes, growth, and characteristics of emigration. Their works became reference points for the writers who once more took up the theme of global analysis of emigration in the 1960s and 1970s : Serrão (1971) and Magalhães-Godinho (1974).

2 The abolition of slavery marks the end of one phase and the beginning of another in the immigration process in Brazil. The Aurea Law, or Law of Redemption, which abolished slavery in 1888, was preceded by a series of laws that progressively traced out the path to freedom. First came the Law of Free Womb, known also as the Law of the Unborn, which in 1871 made the children of slave mothers free. The Law of the Sexagenarians in 1885 gave freedom to slaves over sixty years of age.

3 The Sandwich Islands were one of the destinations preferred not only by emigrants from the Atlantic Portuguese archipelagos, in particular

Madeira, but also by a significant number of people from the district of Serpa in the Alentejo (centre-south of Portugal). In 1910 and 1911 close to one thousand Portuguese fled drought and the disastrous consequence of a weak attempt at agricultural reform. On one single voyage an English ship carried 500 to Hawaii. As the newspaper *Diário de Notícias* wrote at the time, it was the exodus of the starving. This was the first large-scale emigration from the Alentejo (*Boletin da Câmara Municipal de Serpa*, April–May 1977). Dias (1981) wrote a text about the Portuguese presence in Hawaii and also produced a video about their presence, in both Portuguese and English versions. The images that illustrate it are based on the text of Felix and Senecal (1978).

4 The technical features of international means of transport profoundly affected the voyages made by emigrants in this period.

5 The writings of many scholars, novelists, and journalists of Portuguese origin – some resident in the United States, others already back in Portugal – provide data on Portuguese emigration to that country, letting us trace chronologically the long and lasting route that connects the two sides of the 'Atlantic River' (Almeida 1997). These analyses present the Luso-American way of life in L(USA)lândia (see Almeida 1987) and link the two reference points – a forever-present origin and a totally adopted destination that they do not want to abandon. Among other writers see, for example, Dias 1981, Chaplin 1990, and Freitas 1990.

6 Official Portuguese and South African statistics indicate a smaller number (600,000), since the Portuguese who suddenly took refuge just at the time of the independence of Angola and Mozambique were not properly counted.

7 Today both Australia and Canada clearly restrict immigration in terms of age and professional profile.

8 This was legal immigration but was intended to be temporary. For this reason, migrants have always been known there as *Gästarbeiter* (guest workers), which in practice was not the case.

9 The legal existence of associations constitutes not only recognition of the presence of immigrants in their new country but also allows them as a group to present legitimate complaints, which, on an individual basis, might not have been heard by decision-makers. Their creation has generally been supported by the authorities of the country of origin, who, through them, establish a connection with the immigrants for political and economic reasons. Portuguese governments after the 1974 revolution have supported these associations of immigrants; in 1996 the government set up a high commissioner for immigration and ethnic minorities, attached to the prime minister's office.

REFERENCES

Almeida, C., and Barreto, A. 1974. *Capitalismo e emigração em Portugal*. Lisbon: Prelo.

Almeida, O.T. 1987. *L(USA)lândia: A Décima Ilha*. Angra do Heroísmo: Direcção de Serviços de Emigração.

– 1997. *Rio Atlântico*. Lisboa: Edições Salamandra.

Baganha, M.I.B. 1990. *Portuguese Emigration to the United States, 1820–1930*. New York: Garland.

Borges, M.J. 1997. Portuguese in Two Worlds: A Historical Study of Migration from Algarve to Argentina. Doctoral dissertation, Rutgers University.

Carreira, A. 1977. *Migrações nas Ilhas de Cabo Verde*. Lisbon: Universidade Nova de Lisboa.

Chaplin, M.L. 1990. *Retalhos de Portugal dispersos pelos Estados Unidos da América: Mulheres migrantes de descendência portuguesa*. Farmingdale, NJ.

Costa, A. 1911. *Estudos de economia nacional I: O problema da emigração*. Lisbon: Imprensa Nacional.

Da Rosa, V.M.P., and Teixeira, C. 1986. 'O Multiculturalismo canadiano e o futuro dos Açorianos no Quebec.' *Arquipélago* 9 and 10: 217–37.

Dias, E.M. 1981. *A Presença portuguesa no Havai*. Lisbon: Separata do Boletim Cultural da Assembleia Distrital de Lisboa.

Felix, J.H., and Senecal, P.F. 1978. *The Portuguese in Hawaii*. Honolulu: Centennial.

Ferreira, E.S. 1976. *Origens e formas da emigração*. Lisbon: Iniciativas Editoriais.

Ferreira, E.S., and Clausse, G, eds. 1986. *Closing the Migratory Cycle: The Case of Portugal*. Breitenback. Social Science Studies on International Problems, No. 11, Saarbrücken.

Freitas, V.A. 1990. *Jornal da emigração: A L(USA)lândia reinventada*. Angra do Heroísmo: Gabinete de Emigração e Apoio às Comunidades Açorianas.

Herculano, A. 1879. 'A emigração – 1873–1875.' In *Opuscullos*, 105–294. Lisbon: Viúva Bertrand e Ca. Sucessores Carvalho & Ca.

Kubat, D., ed. 1984. *The Politics of Return. International Return Migration in Europe*. Rome: Centro Studi Emigrazione/Center for Migration Studies.

Magalhães-Godinho, V. 1974. 'L'émigration portugaise du XVe Siècle à nos jours: histoire d'une constante structurale.' In C.E. Labrousse, ed., *Conjoncture économique, structures sociales: Mélanges en honneur*, 253–68.

Martins, O. 1956. *Fomento Rural e Emigração*. Lisbon: Guimarães.

Moura, M.A. 1992. *Les Portugais dans l'exploration et la colonisation de l'Est du Canada au XVIe Siècle*. Montreal.

Pap, L. 1981. *The Portuguese-Americans*. Boston: Twayne Publishers.

Pérez, J.C., ed. 1981. *Emigracion y retorno: Una perspectiva europea*. Madrid: Instituto Español de Emigración.

Pires, R.P., et al. 1984. *Os retornados: Um estudo sociográfico*. Lisbon: Instituto de Estudos para o Desenvolvimento.

Poteca, M.M. 1993. 'Los immigrantes caboverdeanos en la Argentina, una minoria invisible.' *Museo* 1 no. 1: 40–6.

Rocha, R. 1983. *Apontamentos sobre a comunidade portuguesa de Hawaii*. Lisbon.

Rocha-Trindade, M.B. 1989. 'A Presença dos Ausentes.' *Sociedade e território: Revista de estudos Urbanos e regionais* 3 no. 8: 8–16.

Rocha-Trindade, M.B., et al. 1983. *O regresso imaginado*. Lisbon: Instituto de Defesa Nacional.

– 1987. *O fenómeno migratório na Região Centro: Regresso e reinserção na Diocese de Coimbra*. Coimbra: Comissão de Coordenação da Região Centro/Secretaria de Estado das Comunidades Portuguesas/Caritas Diocesana de Coimbra.

– 1988. *População escolar directa e indiractamente ligada à emigração*. Lisbon: Projecto Universidade Aberta.

– 1995. *Sociologia das migrações*. Lisbon: Universidade Aberta.

Sérgio, A. 1956. *Antologia sociológica*. Lisbon: Edição Autor.

Serrão, J. 1971. *Emigração portuguesa: Sondagem histórica*. Lisbon: Livros Horizonte.

Silva, F.E. 1917. *Emigração portuguesa*. Lisbon: Tipografia Universal.

Teixeira, C. 1996. 'The Suburbanization of Portuguese Communities in Toronto and Montreal: From Isolation to Residential Integration?' In A. Laperrière, V. Lindstrom, and T.P. Seiler, eds., *Immigration and Ethnicity in Canada*, 181–201. Montreal: Association for Canadian Studies.

PART ONE

NEWFOUNDLAND AND THE WHITE FLEET

3

The White Fleet and the Iconography of Control

PRISCILLA A. DOEL

This essay looks, first, at the history of the codfishing fleet up to 1950; second at the golden age of the White Fleet, through the 1970s; third, at the iconography of its pride and joy, the *Gil Eannes*; and fourth, at the decline of the fleet and at historical conservation efforts.

Historical Introduction

The Early Years

Cod ... *bacalhau*. For centuries, salt cod was the staple of many a poor country's diet, including Portugal's. Cod was the fish found in almost unlimited quantity from the time that John Cabot in 1497 reported taking them up in abundance by means of weighted baskets. 'Bacalhau' was the fish that brought the Portuguese codfishing schooners ('bacalhoeiros') of Portugal's Great White Fleet to the Grand Banks of Newfoundland – and particularly into St John's harbour – where the fishing captains sought shelter from hurricanes spawned in the Caribbean or for supplies or repairs from the 1940s until the early 1970s.

A 1529 reference to cod in *Tierra de los bacallaos* states that 'up until now nothing of value has been found with the exception of codfish which are held in little esteem' (Cortesão and Da Mota 1960: V). Although the cod seemed not to have had value at that time or to that cartographer, three years later another cartographer noted of Tierra Nueva de los Bacallaos that 'this land was discovered by the Portuguese ... there is nothing of value here except for the cod which is a fish and a very good one. Here the Corte Reales were lost' (Cortesão and Da Mota 1960: V). The charts of the day spread the news that the

Portuguese were in these areas and that codfish was abundant and good to eat.

Portugal's codfishing on the Grand Banks continued on a regular seasonal basis until Portugal, having been annexed by Spain in 1580, was forced to contribute all vessels above a minimum size and burthen to Spain's grandiose preparations in gathering together and outfitting an 'Invincible Armada' to do battle against England (Martin and Parker 1988). Although one of the staples in the diet of the seamen who trained on these ships was cod or tunny (served on Tuesday, Friday, and Saturday) (Valadão do Valle 1991), it was to become scarce, for the British defeat of the Armada dealt such a blow to Portuguese maritime activities that significant distant-water sailing stopped for 300 years.

Modern Organization

Not until the 1830s does there appear to be any sizeable effort to organize long-distance codfishing to the Grand Banks. At that time the Companhia de Pescarias Lisbonense (1830–57) approached Britain for help in organizing, outfitting, and buying six schooners for the Grand Banks fishery (Moutinho 1985). This venture probably taught the Portuguese handlining techniques and the use of various tools, and possibly the dory. The dory and tools, some with names of English origin,[1] were to be used in the North Atlantic codfisheries until 1974, when the last codfishing schooner left St John's harbour, bound for Portugal (Doel 1992).

During the period 1866–1901 two companies controlled all Portuguese codfishing on the Grand Banks with a total of twelve ships. Since these vessels viewed certain tax considerations, the fleet could not be augmented without tax penalties being levied. Mariano e Irmãos (1866–1903) operated three vessels, and Bensaúde & Ca. nine. The name of the latter, founded in 1866, changed in 1902 to Parceria Geral de Pescarias (Moutinho 1985).[2]

From 1900 to 1950

The Portuguese codfishing fleet continued to sail to the northwest Atlantic on its yearly campaigns for cod through the First World War, the Great Depression, the Second World War, the forty-year dictatorship of Salazar and his Estado Novo (New State) corporatism (1926–

66), and the '25 de Abril para sempre' (April 25th forever) revolution, until present times. During this century, the politics surrounding the economics and the administration of the fisheries underwent many changes. What started out as a small endeavour on the part of a few fishing companies trying to stay afloat while dealing with problems of supply and demand, foreign competition, taxes, and government instability became a strong and visible presence in Newfoundland by the 1950s. By that time, although the fleet had grown, it had not kept abreast of technological advances in ship design. Portugal was slow, among fishing nations of the world, to introduce a significant number of trawlers, relying instead on handlining. During the First World War era, the necessity of organizing and protecting the growing industry was recognized and discussed. Between 1903 and 1914 the number of *bacalhoeiros* had grown from sixteen to thirty-four. By the end of the war there were eleven, but the fleet expanded steadily until, by 1922, it consisted of sixty-five vessels (Manso and Cruz 1984).

The early twentieth century brought about growth in the size and carrying capacity of the fleet as new companies entered the fisheries, but development continued along unstable administrative and economic lines (Doel 1992). The 1930s saw struggle as the industry, in addition to fighting hard times in general, had to face fisheries-related issues such as low catches and workers' protest against the lack of reasonable contracts and insurance policies.[3] The 1930 campaign to the Grand Banks was so unproductive that the captain of the *Santa Mafalda* decided to set out, without charts, in search of the fabled banks of Greenland. Although the courageous captain was unsuccessful, he had sown the seed of hope. The following year his vessel was accompanied by the *Santa Isabel*, the *Santa Joana*, and the *Santa Luzia*, with their captains from Ilhavo making their way through the fields of ice to the rich Banks of Greenland. From this time on, the Greenland trip became an integral part of the yearly campaign.[4]

As the Estado Novo attempted to upgrade the fisheries in the 1930s, organizational structures emerged in keeping with its corporative policies. The Comissão Reguladora do Comércio de Bacalhau (CRCB), Regulatory Commission of the Codfish Industry) was founded in 1934 and then restructured so as to more effectively control and protect Portuguese interests in its codfishing industry. It regulated prices paid to the supplier, built refrigerated warehouses, stabilized market prices, regulated imports of cod, modernized ships, and sent the first trawler, the *Santa Joana*, to the Banks in the late 1930s. In addition, the Grémio dos Armadores de Navios de Pesca do Bacalhau, or GANPB (Guild of Shipowners of Codfishing Vessels) was formed in 1935, followed by establishment of its insurance company (Mútua) one year later. The first trip of the first hospital supply ship, the *Carvalho Araújo*, took place in 1923, followed by the earliest voyage of the first *Gil Eannes* in 1927.

Organizational efforts during the following decade brought a serious labour problem to a head when recruitment for the 1937 campaign erupted in a famous strike; a state decree forced all those men participating in the 1936 campaign to enrol immediately for 1937; those who did not sign up were to be considered deserters. Violence and protest erupted but were immediately put down. According to the opinion of the day, the well-being of the Estado Novo – the Portuguese nation – was at stake (Moutinho 1985).

By 1938 the codfishing fleet was in desperate shape as it suffered financial, labour, and physical woes. Any significant growth during the Second World War was difficult because of the scarcity of materials and lack of interest by shipowners. In 1942, forty-five ships duly authorized by the CRCB, and full-fledged members of the GANPB, set out for the Grand Banks and Greenland (Manso and Cruz 1984).

Despite the dangers involved in sea travel during the Second World War, Portugal continued sending ships to the northwest Atlantic; but they now travelled in convoy, strictly observing blackouts and radio silence. Sailing ships of different hull speed and motor capacity, trawlers, and the hospital supply ship *Gil Eannes* all crossed in silence. 'The term [White Fleet] was coined during World War II by the convoy skippers. Portugal, who remained neutral during that conflict, had a pact with Germany not to attack its fishing fleet. It was agreed that all the hulls would be painted white with the ships' name in huge letters amid-ships, plus the flag. Prior to the war, our fleet (Parceria Geral de Pescarias, I mean) had oxblood hulls. They continued to be painted white after the war, however' (Frantz 1989).

During the war the Estado Novo very deliberately began to define and celebrate the role of the brave and God-fearing Portuguese doryman labouring on the Banks for the good of the Portuguese people (pátria) and for his own family (família). The first concrete example of this type of propaganda was the book written by the Portuguese journalist and photographer Jorge Simões (1942). The Grémio invited him to accompany the fleet on its 1941 campaign aboard the *Groenlândia* and the *Gil Eannes*. Through photographs and exciting accounts of storms, a fire aboard, encounters with Inuit, a meeting with Pinto Hans, a collision, and many more adventures, *Os grandes trabalhadores do Mar* (1942) gives the *campanha* the visibility and respect that it needed to become an acceptable part of the Estado Novo's social and economic policies.

Codfishing on the Grand Banks continued to prosper after the war, and Salazar, through politics and propaganda, controlled Portuguese society both at home and on the Banks. His Estado Novo was clearly a dictatorial form of government; being a contemporary of Hitler, Mussolini, and Franco, he used similar authoritarian and undemocratic policies. The life of the doryman both at home and on the Banks had been characterized by misery, poverty, and repression, as had been the life of many Europeans and Americans during the Great Depression and the two world wars. Patriotism, religiosity, and family all intertwined as Portuguese society became more and more centred in the state, the church, and the family (Pátria, Deus, Família) (Doel 1992).

The Golden Age and the *Gil Eannes*

Given Newfoundland's new status as a Canadian province in 1949, the 1950s marked the beginnings of restrictive Canadian policies and resource protection in territorial waters. By the early 1950s the International Commission of Northwest Atlantic Fisheries (ICNAF) was established, and the cod-abundant waters bordering Newfoundland (Canada) and Greenland (Denmark) were to be studied and evaluated with an eye towards resource protection. Concomitantly, national territorial rights to the sea were extended from three miles to twelve, and later to two hundred. At the same time, however, technological innovation with the requisite capital inputs significantly increased the exploitative capacity of the fishery of most nations. Of particular note was the introduction of dragger fishing.

The 1950s also marked the move of the Portuguese codfishing fleet into international visibility and fame through Alan Villiers's (1951) book, *In Quest of the Schooner Argus*, followed by prominent articles in *National Geographic*. Villiers, a celebrated writer and a respected man of the sea, had been invited by the Portuguese ambassador in Washington to sail to Newfoundland and Greenland aboard one of the bacalhoeiros. This he did in 1950, aboard the beautiful and modern *Argus*, owned and managed by Portugal's oldest codfishing company, the Parceria Geral de Pescarias. His book took the story of the Portuguese

White Fleet to the English-speaking world with a highly romanticized vision of the life of the humble, hard-working, God-fearing Portuguese fisherman. Meanwhile, through the visual and written propaganda of state and church ceremonies, newspaper articles, and the indispensable magazine *Jornal do Pescador*, the dictatorship at home continued to define and celebrate the role of the Portuguese codfisherman for himself and for the rest of Portugal.

As Canada began to exert its territorial claims to the waters around the Grand Banks, Portugal, at home and abroad, continued to emphasize both the importance of her codfishing fleet on the Grand Banks and its traditional fishing rights in these waters. Without a doubt, it intended the launching of the new hospital supply ship *Gil Eannes* in 1955 to enhance and ensure its place in the Grand Banks fisheries. The editorial 'Welcome to the Portuguese' in the *Evening Telegram* (St John's) remarked that 'this year also marks the fifth century of the discovery of the Grand Banks by the Portuguese and the fourth century of their participation in the fisheries there.'[5] The new ship, whose medical services were rendered free to all fishers on the Banks, was a majestic symbol of Portugal's past, present, and future presence in these cod-rich waters. It was fitting that the new *Gil Eannes* graced the period 1950–65 – Portugal's Golden Age in the Grand Banks fisheries.

Of all the vessels on the Banks and in Canadian ports, the *Gil Eannes* best symbolized Portuguese pride, having been built in Viana do Castelo with domestic materials by native shipwrights and craftsmen. The glistening-white, new ship of state embodied the Estado Novo's principles regarding state, church, and family, and her name evoked Portugal's glorious days of exploration and discovery – the days of Gil Eannes rounding Cape Bojador in 1434. The vessel was a symbol of state control over the reorganized long-distance fisheries. This 323-ft, 4,854-ton, state-of-the-art, steel-hulled vessel watched over some four thousand to five thousand fishers from the coastal villages of Portugal and the Azores, who were launched from some sixty to seventy vessels to fish in their one-man dories under the watchful eyes of their captains and officers. Although all ships were privately owned, all were united under the Grémio.

The *Gil Eannes* was designed for multiple functions. In addition to being a sea-going hospital ship, she carried supplies for the fleet: food, water, fuel, bait, and spare parts for repairs. She was also the fleet's communication control centre, with elaborate and powerful external and internal communication systems, and she carried an information-gathering bio-hydrographic laboratory. In addition, the ship housed a small chapel on the aft deck. The commander's quarters were the official space for meetings between the commander, representatives of Portugal, ship captains, and dignitaries of other nations in ports of call. Wherever she went, the *Gil Eannes* was the symbol of Estado Novo ideology, reinforcing Portugal's traditional presence in North Atlantic waters, assisting its handlining fleet, and solidifying relations with Canada.

Moreover, while the captain of each ship worked for the owner of that vessel and had great latitude in the determination of where and when to fish on the Banks, how to treat or discipline his crew, and how to respond to emergencies related to the well-being of ship and crew, he was always subject to the authority of the commander of the *Gil Eannes*. The commander was Portugal's official representative in the North Atlantic – a figure to be respected and feared – a symbol in uniform of the Estado Novo.

When the new *Gil Eannes* came through the Narrows and entered the harbour of St John's in May of 1955, Newfoundland was ready to greet her. One reporter described her arrival as 'probably the most colourful and historic sight that St. John's had ever seen.'[6] On both sides of the Atlantic, every detail of pageantry and ceremony had been minutely planned to showcase the Portuguese fisheries on the Grand Banks of Newfoundland. On 27 May, four thousand Portuguese fishermen, clad in their colourful checkered shirts, walked fifteen to twenty abreast up the hilly streets of St John's to the Basilica of St John the Baptist, bearing the three-and-one-half-foot-high statue of Our Lady of Fátima, their gift of gratitude and friendship. Our Lady was to be a holy link between the two peoples, and, even today, worshippers pray before her in the specially prepared alcove to the left of the main altar. The six thousand men and women who filled the cathedral, along with those who lined the streets, were part of 'one of the most colourful, inspiring, and solemn events ever to take place in St. John's.'[7]

State Icons on the Gil Eannes

Given constraints of time and distance related to management of the long-distance fisheries, it was difficult for the Estado Novo to maintain total control over the men of the Portuguese fleet. Fishing vessels moved from one fishing area to another and had frequent contacts with people from other nations in Canadian ports, where fishers and captains alike experienced a less rigid, more democratic way of life – a challenge to Estado Novo systems of control.

In order to solidify unwavering commitment to Deus, Pátria e Família, the new *Gil Eannes* incorporated symbols of these concepts into her decorative motifs. The state commissioned the Azorean artist Domingos Rebelo to paint two murals for the ship: one to grace a long wall of the commander's quarters, the other to enhance the altar of the little chapel on the aft deck. In accordance with the Estado Novo's use of moral symbols that justify the institutional arrangements of its political system, 'skill groups [such as artists] ... define and promulgate official images of the world and what is happening in it, official "definitions of the situation"' (Gerth and Mills 1953: 212–13).

The commander's quarters displayed Rebelo's colourful mural. Within the narrative frame of a state-sponsored mural, the artist visually reconstructs the epic story of the life of the Portuguese doryman so as to suppress other versions of that life, which was widely known as one of hard work, sacrifice, deprivation, and physical and psychological abuse (see Figure 3.1). Most viewers probably did not analyse structure, style, or content but merely reacted to symbols that they had internalized. Domingos Rebelo, however, guides the viewer/reader through the three narrative scenes surrounding the fisherman. For example, if we start with the fisherman in the foreground, we meet his gaze straight on. We become anchored to the mural with the oar that he holds with both hands. Then the circular motion of his arms lifts our eyes to the top of the oar and then directs our view to the left, letting us see family life at home in Portugal. The right-hand corner of the crib at bottom left redirects our eyes over the head of the boy and his teacher to the iceberg in the background behind the fisherman. We look from left to right and then return, directed by the oar to the other scene at home, where all fishermen, active or aged, are cared for. Through the integration on canvas of different artistic spaces and geographical places, the artist presents the life, idealized through memory images, of a typical Portuguese dory fisherman on the Grand Banks.

As we consider the images, we must ask who is this stalwart, emotionless man dressed in the typical plaid flannel shirt who meets our gaze head on? The message is clear. He is an anonymous fisherman – the stereotype of the good, humble, obedient, stable fisherman. He is father and husband. He is all the fishermen on whom rest the responsibility for the well-being of Pátria e Família. He is the faithful Zé Pescador, the central figure in a national mission.

The paternalistic role played by the Estado Novo in the life of the

Figure 3.1. Mural from the commander's quarters on the *Gil Eannes*, by Domingos Rebelo (courtesy of Priscilla A. Doel)

fisherman's family during his six-to-seven-month absence each year is seen to the left, where we see buildings representing health, education, and welfare programs administered by the Estado Novo, through the Junta Central de Casas de Pescadores. Prominent in the foreground is the son – the future fisherman – receiving instruction at the school of fishing and navigation. With his teacher, he is studying a model of a sailing vessel. Behind the boy is a young girl learning to sew so as to fulfil her future role in the Estado Novo as mother and homemaker. Motherhood and family clearly dominate this scene, with one expectant mother holding an infant, another mother holding her baby, and yet another infant resting in a crib. The Estado Novo took great pride in its programs promoting nutrition, good hygiene, and health services, as symbolized by the large, official two-storey building. Other social programs included day-care centres and construction of new homes for the fisherman and his family, as seen in the background.

The scene to our right again shows the protective arm of the Estado Novo as it cares for the active fisherman when he is at home or for the aged fishermen. The Estado Novo, under the iron hand of Commander Henrique dos Santos Tenreiro, government representative to the Grémio, oversaw many programs that provided care and services: transportation (the Volkswagen), equipment (foul-weather gear, line), health care (the operating table), and homes for the aged (the scene on the far right).

The scene in the background at the horizon shows three evocative memory images of the Grand Banks cod fisheries: the extremely large iceberg in the centre, the large fog bank approaching to the left, and the famous and beloved *Gazela* (now owned by the city of Philadelphia) to the right. All icons are white. The artist does not narrate anything about this scene in detail. It is precisely the hardships that underlie these icons that are absent from this mural – the realities of life on the Banks.

In considering this mural as grand symbolism for the place of the humble fisherman in the Nation, we must ask one remaining question. Who saw this mural hanging in the saloon of the commander's quarters? Fishermen certainly did not enter this space, but officials of state, visiting dignitaries, and captains of the fishing vessels were entertained here or held meetings here. As we have seen above, through the examples of the *Gil Eannes* and the commander of the fleet – whose official title was Representative of the Ministry of the Navy and Chief Officer of Assistance and Supply Services to the Portuguese

Cod Fleet – management of symbols within the authoritarian system of the Estado Novo was essential in defining and reinforcing its ideology. Visiting foreign dignitaries would probably bring with them their own internalized symbols, which would be counter-symbols to the authoritarian regime. Also, and of utmost importance, Portuguese captains, most of whom were well educated and spoke English, would be exposed in their travels and personal and professional contacts in Canadian ports to counter-symbols of a more democratic political and social system. So those who might be tempted to consider other systems of state as more viable were controlled through visual imagery in the commander's quarters of the ship of state. The symbols used in this mural also served to evoke Portuguese pride in the doryman and the campanhas.

As if to corroborate the role of *Gil Eannes* as the icon of Portuguese nationalism and Rebelo's mural as the icon of family and social systems, yet another icon of Estado Novo ideology aboard the *Gil Eannes* represented the presence of *Deus* (omniscient, omnipotent, omnipresent) in the form of a chapel on the aft deck (see Figure 3.2). With the chapel doors opened wide, the viewer sees that this small place of worship contained another mural by Rebelo that effectively portrayed the central role of religion (Deus) in the relationship between bacalhau, the dorymen at work on the Banks, and the family at home in Portugal – all united through the mother of God.

The Virgin, arms extended to accept all those paying homage to her, is the focal point of the triangular arrangement of the space. To the viewer's left, two dorymen pay their respects to God through the Virgin. One is dressed in the typical flannel shirt, heavy pants, and rubber boots and carries foul-weather gear as he moves towards the Virgin. The other man, dressed in warm sweater and working apron, kneels as he prays with hands in symbolic gesture and eyes closed. At the feet of the standing fisherman is a representation of an enormous cod – his reason for being on the Banks and away from family and home. To the viewer's right, mother and child (wife and son) in Portugal pray to the Virgin for the well-being and safe return of husband and father. A satchel on the ground, perhaps containing her handiwork or their few items of clothing, complements the bacalhau. The colours worn by mother and son are sombre, suggesting a mood of mourning, while those worn by the men on the Banks suggest warmth and protection against the elements. The colours

Figure 3.2. Mural from the chapel on the *Gil Eannes*, by Domingos Rebelo (courtesy of Priscilla A. Doel)

surrounding the Virgin – blues and white – separate her from the four worldly figures.

In this state artwork of the Estado Novo era, we have seen that idealized myths surrounding Portugal's postwar cod-fishing industry were based on three basic symbols. First, the *Gil Eannes* was representative of Pátria in the modern world, with its advanced technology and social welfare being a source of nationalistic pride. Second, Rebelo's mural symbolized the interrelationship between the Portuguese codfishing industry and Família, the foundation on which the welfare system rested. Finally, the chapel with its other Rebelo mural symbolized the presence of Deus – long the unifying icon of Portuguese overseas expansion.

However, between the myth of the Estado Novo as it idealized the doryman and the reality of life on the Banks there lay a vast chasm. Within the collective memory of the Portuguese doryman, there still remained memories of earlier periods of virtual slavery; such as those described by Alan Villiers through a conversation he had with his shipmate Pierre Berthoud in 1929, when their ship crossed the outward-bound course of a small fleet of Portuguese schooners headed for the Banks: '"A tough life, you say?" The Frenchman looked fiercely at us. "A dog's life", that's what it is! My God there is no harder life upon the sea! All fishing is tough, but that's the toughest, hardest way to make a living that I know. Those fellows will be lucky to be back home six months from now. Aye, and some of 'em won't be coming. I warn you, shipmates, things are tough all over Europe now, but don't ever ship in one of them! Those Portuguese use one-man dories. Keep out of them!' (Villiers 1951: 17).

Decline and Restoration

In 1972, the *Novos Mares*, the last handling sailing vessel, left the Banks, never to return. The age of the one-man dory had finally ended, and it was clear that the *Gil Eannes* was no longer needed. With the 25th of April revolution of 1974 and the collapse of the Estado Novo, the already floundering fisheries suffered further blows, from which they never recovered.

Finally, in 1986, following the lead of its European neighbours, Portugal joined the European Community (EC). Until that time, Portugal had dealt directly with Canada in setting up bilateral agreements establishing its fishing quotas and access to certain areas. Now, as a member of the EC, it was part of Europe and could deal with Canada only through the bureaucratic channels of Brussels. Portugal continued to fish on the limited basis allowed her by European quotas, but the Canadian government banned its ships from Canadian ports, accusing them of overfishing and violating their quota allocations. Times had changed, and, with them, the very special relationship shared by the people of Newfoundland and their friends of the Portuguese cod fleet came to an end.

Knowing that codfishing, as a viable economic endeavour and as a way of life, will never return to the Grand Banks of Newfoundland, both Portugal and Newfoundland are moving towards different goals, each guided by new political, economic, and social systems. That these systems colour the manner in which the two peoples perceive their common past, linked by cod, is evident in the way in which each chooses to incorporate its past into its present and future collective memory.

While the fancy façades of brick and glass in downtown St John's appear to turn their backs on the inactive port beneath them, Canadian officials carefully monitor and study the depleted resources of the Grand Banks and surrounding waters. Resource protection and the assurance of a national sustainable fishery are their prime concern. For most of the inhabitants of St John's, the seasonal presence of Portugal's codfishing fleet is but a remote memory, and they, like the bronze statue of Gaspar Corte Real that graces their city, turn their backs on the port as they look in other directions for development and well-being. The little Lady of Fátima, a beloved icon, still graces the basilica, where she continues to receive the prayers of worshippers, some of whom know her story, others who do not. The small Portuguese immigrant community is well integrated into the city, since its children have grown up there as Canadians, and old customs have given way to new.

On the other side of the Atlantic, however, the age of cod is being carefully recorded and celebrated for future generations, as the famous captains of Ilhavo and their families work side by side with government and museum officials to document and thus to preserve their rightful place in Portugal's centuries-old seafaring heritage. The famous Rebelo murals, used by Salazar's state to reinforce the values of Pátria, Deus, and Família, were removed from the Gil Eannes in the early 1980s and now serve as icons for a new generation, constituting, as it were, new cultural texts that evoke responses from people who will share the collective memory without having experienced it. The chapel on the aft deck of the Gil Eannes was completely removed and is now a part of the permanent codfisheries exhibit at the Museu da Marinha in Belém, just outside Lisbon. It is fitting that the mural be housed close to the banks of the Tagus River, the point of departure not only for the ships that sailed to Newfoundland in search of cod but also a major point of departure for all Portuguese seafaring endeavours.

The mural that once adorned the commander's private quarters is now a permanent part of the museum in Ilhavo, a place that was home to many captains of cod and to many of the fishermen who rowed and sailed the dories in search of cod. The museum not only houses most of the archival material related to the codfisheries but also offers a hands-on experience of codfishing on the Banks through life-size replicas of fishermen and crew engaged in many typical activities, now part of Portugal's collective memory.

Although Rebelo's murals were removed from the *Gil Eannes* in the mid-1980s, the ship lay for some thirteen years alongside a quay in Lisbon, virtually abandoned and neglected as she deteriorated into a forgotten and disdained past. Plans to renovate her as a restaurant or a cruise ship never materialized. Fortunately, other plans to sell her for scrap never materialized either. Recent news, however, brings positive reports that – through the efforts of many individuals and groups – this once-proud ship of state will return to the shipyards of Viana do Castelo, where she was built and launched, to be renovated. Berthed in Viana, the hospital supply ship that served not only Portuguese fishermen but also those of other nations will once again enter service, this time as a museum (*O Ilhavense* 1997). With new purpose, *Gil Eannes*, like the icons in Rebelo's murals, will return to her former glory and become a part of the collective memory of past, present, and future generations.

NOTES

1 Moutinho (1985) suggests various words such as 'biguane' (a big one); 'levas' (livers); 'picefoque' (pickfork); 'suevlo' (swivel); 'troteiro' (throater).
2 This firm, having modified and modernized its operations, has headquarters on Rua de Ouro in central Lisbon. It maintains a limited number of codfishing vessels, which use St Pierre as their port of call.
3 An account of these problems is found in 'The Life of Those Who Go Fishing for Cod,' by doryman Marcelino Pires (1932).
4 An interesting account of this voyage, based on an original log-book entry, was written by Cachim and appears as a chapter in his book *Os Ilhavos, o Mar e a Ria* (1988), 65–71. This account was translated into English by Priscilla Doel and appears in a yearbook issue of *National Fisherman 76*, no. 12 (1996), 56–9.
5 *Evening Telegram*, St John's, 26 May 1955, 4.
6 *Newfoundland's National Weekly*, St John's, 31 May 1955.
7 *Evening Telegram*, 28 May 1955, 4.

REFERENCES

Cachim, A.E. 1988. *Os Ilhavos, o Mar e a Ria*. Estarreja: Câmara Municipal de Ilhavo.

52   Priscilla A. Doel

Cortesão, A., and da Mota Teixeira, A. 1960. *Portugaliae, monumenta cartographica*. Vol. v. Lisbon.

Doel, P.A. 1992. *Port O'Call: Memories of the Portuguese White Fleet in St. John's, Newfoundland*. St John's: ISER Press.

Frantz, B.B. 1989. Correspondence with author.

Gerth, H., and Mills, C.W. 1953. *Character and Social Structure*. New York: Harcourt Brace.

Manso, F., and Cruz, O. 1984. *A epopéia dos bacalhaus*. Porto: Distri Editora.

Martin, C., and Parker, G. 1988. *The Spanish Armada*. New York: W.W. Norton.

Moutinho, M. 1985. *História da pesca do bacalhau*. Lisbon: Imprensa Universitária.

Newfoundland's National Weekly. 31 May, 1955. 'Welcome to the Portuguese.

O Ilhavense. 1997. 'Gil Eanes em Bom Porto.' 17 Dec.

Peres, M. 1932. 'The Life of Those Who Go Fishing for Cod.' Republished in *Comércio da Póvoa de Varzim*, 4 May 1935.

Simões, J. 1942. *Os grandes trabalhadores do Mar: Reportagens na Terra Nova e na Groenlândia*. Lisbon: Oficinas Gráficas da Gazeta dos Caminhos de Ferro.

Valadão do Valle, E. 1991. *Bacalhau: Tradições históricas e económicas* Lisbon: Edição do Autor.

Villiers, A. 1951. *The Quest of the Schooner Argus: A Voyage to the Banks and Greenland*. New York: Charles Scribner's Sons.

4

Portuguese Fishermen
in Newfoundland

JEAN-PIERRE ANDRIEUX

Since the early sixteenth century, Portuguese fishermen have followed in the wake of early Portuguese navigators and travelled to the New Found Land in search of cod (Morison 1971; Abreu-Ferreira 1995, 1995–6).[1] They adopted the Virgin Rocks, one hundred miles east of St John's, as their traditional fishing ground. Portuguese fishing methods changed little in this time; continuing a long tradition of labour-intensive fishing methods. Even after 1945, when all other nations fishing in Newfoundland waters gavev up traditional handlining operations and converted to modern trawlers, Portugal – because of policies of the Salazar dictatorship – maintained the traditional system in parallel with the new, more efficient trawlers (Doel 1992).

This new technology, in particular the invention of the stern factory trawler, brought scores of nations to the Grand Banks. These intense harvesting methods transformed the fishery, and led to rapidly diminished cod stocks. In the face of such competition, the Portuguese attempted to modernize their ageing and antiquated fleet. However, the three- and four-masted handliners, in spite of being converted from wind power to engines and being fitted out with fish loops, radar, and more modern equipment, were clearly obsolete. Fortunately for the owners, fires of unknown origins would sometimes start aboard these old ships on calm days, and they would go to the bottom in Newfoundland waters. Insured owners could then convert to modern trawlers capable of harvesting fish in deeper waters as the old cod stocks were becoming exhausted (Andrieux 1996).

This essay is an account of this transitional 'moment' in the Portuguese fishery in Canadian waters. Based on conversations with Portuguese fishermen of the White Fleet, and using photos from this era, I attempt to shed light on a shadowy area of the history of the fisheries. Portuguese shipowners subsidized modernization of their fleets through insurance money from a long string of accidents and fires aboard their vessels. Primarily, however, this is the story of the Portuguese fisherman and his struggle to wrest a precarious living from the waters of the North Atlantic. It first offers a brief history to the late 1940s; second, looks at the 'golden age' of the White Fleet; and third, considers its strange demise.

The Portuguese Fishery: A Brief History

The first recorded voyage by the Portuguese to Newfoundland dates back to 1500, when the intrepid navigator Gaspar de Corte Real arrived hard on the heels of John Cabot. With a charter from the king of Portugal, he claimed this new land as Terras dos Labradores (Brazão 1964, 1965; Alpalhão and Da Rosa 1980). Immediately after this voyage, fishing companies were founded in Aveiro, Viana do Castelo, and Terceira for the purpose of sending vessels on codfishing expeditions to the Terra Nova. It seems that these vessels were sailing as early as 1504. This effort was so profitable that King Emanuel established a tax in the ports of the Douro and the Minho regions on the fish brought back from the Newfoundland Banks.

Portuguese fishermen crossed the Atlantic in sturdy fishing vessels on the spring east wind, to fish on the Grand Banks some two thousand miles from home. They used hook and line and filled their holds with cod, always in a race with the fierce seas of late autumn and winter off the coast of Newfoundland. Fog, gales, and freezing weather took their toll each year, yet fishermen still sailed. Cod had come to mean the difference between food and hunger in much of southern Europe (Simões 1942; Moutinho 1985).

The number of vessels engaged in the Newfoundland codfishery grew rapidly. In 1550 Aveiro alone had 150 fishing vessels sailing to Newfoundland, with equal numbers sailing from Oporto and other ports. These vessels sheltered in harbours close to the Bonavista area. In 1620 they were chased out of these ports by the British in a violent encounter. The Portuguese then shifted their fishing effort to the Grand Banks, where they have maintained a presence ever since.

In the last hundred years, however, the Portuguese fleet has become more active in the Newfoundland fishery. The fleet of the early twentieth century consisted of three- and four-masted schooners, whose decks were filled with one-man fishing dories. These Portuguese fishermen who went to the Newfoundland banks had passed on their traditional operations from generation to generation. However, political changes in Portugal would transform its fishery. In a military coup of 1927 António de Oliveira Salazar, a young professor from Coimbra University, was asked to put the finances of the country back in order. He soon rose to the presidency and installed a dictatorial government (Wheeler 1993).

The government took control of fishing policies, as the industry was an important part of the economy. For example, like their European counterparts, Portuguese owners started to introduce trawlers within the handlining fleet. However, as the number of trawlers grew, it became national policy, dictated by Admiral Henrique Tenreiro, who was in charge of fishing activities, to keep both fleets operating in parallel. This kept large numbers of workers employed in the older, labour-intensive fleet. Thus, while other nations converted exclusively to trawlers, Portugal maintained both methods.

During the Second World War, Portugal remained neutral, and its vessels were able to continue harvesting cod on their traditional fishing grounds. Initially they painted their name and their country of origin in large letters on the side, along with a replica of the national flag. Soon, however, the government forced the vessels, which had been painted in various colours, to be repainted white and to sail with full navigational lights during the night, to identify them to German submarine raiders as being neutral. Thus the vessels became known as the Portuguese 'White Fleet,' a name that remained long after the war (Andrieux 1996; Doel 1992).

At the beginning of the war all Portuguese fishing vessels travelled individually, but this, and their neutrality, did not necessarily guarantee them safe passage. There were, in fact, two casualties during the war (Rower 1983). The first was the *Maria da Glória*, a three-master owned by the fishing captains Silvio Ramalheira and Belo Morais. On 5 July 1942, she was on her way up from the Newfoundland Banks to Greenland for the summer fishery. She sighted a submarine, and her captain got on his radio set and told the other Portuguese vessels travelling with him that he had seen this submarine – a fatal mistake. The submarine, despite the vessel's neutrality, immediately sank her and even fired on the crew. The Germans then tried to sink all her dories with cannon fire. The vessel sank so quickly that the Portuguese had no time to get food supplies. Some men died in a storm that followed;

others went insane because of lack of water. After seven long days only two dories of survivors were sighted off the Labrador coast by a Canadian warplane.

Three months later, on 11 September 1942, the three-master *Delaes* was sent to the bottom by U96. This submarine had had a successful twenty-four-hour hunt, having torpedoed three other vessels. Why U96 had decided to sink a neutral vessel is unknown. Probably the *Delaes* had been in the wrong place at the wrong time, near an Allied convoy. As a result of these sinkings Portuguese fishing vessels no longer sailed alone to the Banks but were organized in convoys according to their speeds, as some lacked engines.

The war also brought another significant change. Two vessels made a port call in Halifax to pick up bait. So successful was this new bait (herring) that all the White Fleet started calling, after the cessation of hostilities in 1945, at St John's for this bait, known in Portuguese as *sardinha*. They changed later to squid (*lula*) and even later to mackerel (*cavala*), which also proved very good.

The Golden Age of the White Fleet

The postwar years marked the high point of the White Fleet fishery off Newfoundland. St John's welcomed thousands of Portuguese fishermen every summer. It was not an easy life on the White Fleet (Simões 1942; Villiers 1951). The days were hard and long amid the treacherous winds and waves of the North Atlantic (see Figure 4.1). What the men looked forward to most, besides returning home to their families (Cole 1990; Doel 1992, 1997), was their next visit to St John's.[2] When they were in port they could best be described as colourful, happy, and remarkably well-behaved (Doel 1997). These brave, hard-working seamen went about their business and leisure in an unassuming, quiet manner so that their presence did not interrupt residents' lives (see Figure 4.2).

When the fleet was in St John's, harbourside was a forest of masts, the rigging festooned with yellow oilskins, buoy markers, drying stockings, rubber boots, woollen underwear, plaid shirts, and dory sails. While in port the fishermen spread everything on deck to air and dry. On the piers they gathered to mend their sails, stretch and repair long lines of hooks, patch their shirts, or just sit and smoke or drink Portuguese wine (see Figure 4.3). They were always noted for their friendliness.

Figure 4.1. Stormy day on the Grand Banks (courtesy of J.P. Andrieux)

Figure 4.2. Portuguese White Fleet in St John's harbour (courtesy of J.P. Andrieux)

Few spoke English, but this wasn't a barrier. They would go to the stores and point out what they wanted or carry a note from someone who knew English. Or they might bring a page from an Eaton's or Simpson's catalogue with the item in question on it. Hundreds of fishermen could be seen on Water and Duckworth streets, carrying loads of merchandise. Indeed, given the size of their presence in St John's, it is a tribute to them that their demeanour during these frequent, friendly invasions has kept them in high standing as very welcome visitors.

By the early 1950s other nations had phased out dory fishing operations, which gave way to modern trawlers. In Portugal, however, sailing vessels were still setting out each spring for the Newfoundland Banks. Although time had brought changes in size, shape, and gear, the hardy fishermen were still facing most of the same hazards that their ancestors had. The Salazar government had decided, for political reasons, to keep the handlining dory vessels of the White Fleet operating in parallel with the more modern trawlers (see Figure 4.4). This, of course, did not please the fishermen of the White Fleet, who had harsh and crowded living conditions on board, often sleeping two to a bunk (see Figure 4.5). Toilet facilities were non-existent or basic. Fresh water

Figure 4.3. Portuguese White Fleet seeks refuge from Hurricane Blanche: St John's, 1969 (courtesy of Ian Brookes)

Figure 4.4. A handliner of the White Fleet on the Grand Banks of Newfoundland (courtesy of J.P. Andrieux)

was rationed, and no showers could be taken. Men had no water to wash themselves or their clothes. Financial rewards were few. Most men would have preferred, if they had a choice, to be on the trawlers, but signing on the White Fleet for a seven-year term got men out of compulsory military service.

The Sinking of the White Fleet

In 1955, Portuguese fishermen, despite their use of older fishing techniques, led European nations in volume of catches on the rich Banks of Newfoundland (Moutinho 1985). A major change would soon revolu-

Figure 4.5. Portuguese fishermen of the White Fleet (courtesy of J.P. Andrieux)

tionize the fishing industry and ultimately lead to its demise. The British arrived on the Banks with a new ship, a stern trawler called *Fairtry*, which had a self-contained factory that would catch, process, and freeze fish at sea. The USSR immediately copied this technology. The capabilities of this type of vessel spelled trouble for everyone. As more and more vessels of this type started fishing, stocks were being ravaged.

In order to protect these stocks, in 1964 Canada extended its fisheries limits from three to twelve miles. This change, and competition from the new factory trawlers, made the White Fleet less and less profitable. In September 1965 the Portuguese ambassador to Canada, Dr Eduardo Brazão, visiting St John's for the unveiling of the statue of Gaspar de Corte Real, predicted the end of the famed White Fleet and that its three- and four-masters would gradually give way to modern fishing vessels. What he failed to say was how this replacement was being undertaken.

Following a 'gentleman's agreement' between the insurers, the own-

Figure 4.6. The *Luiza Ribau* on fire at the Virgin Rocks off Newfoundland's coast on 23 August 1973 (courtesy of Capt. Francisco Marques)

ers, and the Portuguese government, much of the White Fleet succumbed to accidental fires during this period. It was said that the owners did not pocket the actual money from the loss but that it would go towards construction of a new vessel. The rest would be financed by the Foundation for the Renovation and Outfitting of the Fishing Industry (FRAIP) – a government body that lent money at low interest rates over a certain number of years to owners wishing to build modern vessels.

It was rumoured that most of the so-called accidental fires were actually deliberate, started by creation of a short-circuit in the engine room. The generators would soon be affected, resulting in the electrical supply's being cut off, making it impossible for water to circulate to fight the fire. Soon the vessel would have to be abandoned (see Figure 4.6) (Andrieux 1996, 1997).

The fishermen would often know, or sense, that their vessel's days were numbered. Consequently, they took few clothes or personal belongings when they left Portugal. If they sensed during the fishing campaign that something was bound to happen, particularly if fishing was very poor, they would leave their belongings with friends in St John's. In St John's there was the same feeling among local people who had a connection with the White Fleet. For example, the Harbour Pilots, who were familiar with the handlining fleet, would make comments and bets among themselves as to which vessel would next succumb to an engine-room short-circuit or some other imaginative scheme.

There were many ways in which fishermen could tell which vessel would next go down. Vessels of the White Fleet by tradition fished together, and their catches would not greatly vary from one vessel to another. Vessels had instructions from their owners to declare their catches by radio each week so that these could be progressively insured. In case the vessel went down, the owner would be compensated according to the fish reported to be on board. The airwaves were unscrambled, and the weekly messages could be intercepted. If a single vessel declared unusually high catches for two or three weeks in a row, listeners realized that the vessel in question would soon go down. Within a few days they would have to answer yet another distress signal and welcome shipwrecked countrymen on their already crowded handliner. They would usually keep them on board until the hospital supply vessel *Gil Eannes* picked them up to take them to St John's; if she was not in the region they would head themselves to St John's to drop off the crewmembers, who would then be repatriated to Portugal (see Andrieux 1996).

The ship chandlers in St John's also had their own way of predicting disasters. The vessels of the White Fleet salted their catches of large cod and had little, if any, refrigeration equipment for meats, fruits, and vegetables. As a result, the *Gil Eannes* went back and forth from St John's to where the vessels were fishing, delivering these fresh staples to the White Fleet, as well as mail and fresh water. If a handliner did not place an order, it was taken for granted that she was the most likely candidate for sinking.

There was little risk of loss of lives from these accidental fires. It was generally agreed, accordingly to rumours of the time, that when plans were made to sink a vessel, weather conditions had to be most favourable. Usually, these fires occurred on a calm day, when the fishermen were in their dories fishing or were in a position to get off the vessel without difficulty. Another condition was that there be other vessels close by so that the shipwrecked men could quickly be rescued. Many of the dozens of Portuguese handliners that came to grief in Newfoundland waters sank at the Virgin Rocks, about one hundred miles south-southwest of St John's. The Virgin Rocks are a series of outcropping shoals covering about ten square miles; the water around them ranges from two to nine fathoms deep, and the rocks were said to be the most profitable fishing grounds on the Grand Banks.

In the 1960s, it was felt that the new technology of factory freezer trawlers could be the only remedy for declining fish catches. No one seemed to realize that the Newfoundland Banks were not an inexhaustible fishing ground. By 1969 numerous non-traditional fishing nations (for instance, Bulgaria, East Germany, Japan, Poland, the USSR) had invaded the Grand Banks and surroundings, and it should have been little surprise to anyone that the fishery was collapsing. Foreign fleets were being blamed for exhausting the Labrador inshore fishery; they had fished 1,400 per cent more cod in 1969 than they had in 1958.

The following year, 1970, was pivotal for the Portuguese fishery. Major changes took place on two fronts. It was the year that Salazar died, and his successor, Marcelo Caetano, was perceived to be weak. The political system that fostered the labour-intensive White Fleet was crumbling, and more modern steel-hulled vessels were converted from their one-man dory operations to longlines and gill nets. The dories were being replaced by a handful of power boats. Steel-hulled vessels were suited for these conversions, but the older vessels were not. With these conversions, crews were reduced from one hundred per vessel to fifty-five.

These changes proved very successful. As a result, in the early 1970s additional vessels were converted to this new method of fishing, while the older, unsuitable vessels would continue to fish in their traditional fashion while awaiting their fate by fire. The White Fleet vessels were probably the only ones in the world that still used the 'one dory, one man' system of fishing.

By 1974 fire had decimated the rest of the wooden handliners, and only three of them left Portugal for the fishing campaign. Two days after they sailed, on 25 April 1974, a coup d'état was organized by General A. Spínola and by a group of army captains in Portugal. There was an explosion of popular joy among the Portuguese people, who placed carnations on the tips of the soldiers' rifles, in what became known as the Revolution of Carnations (Wheeler 1993), which ended decades of oppressive dictatorship.

Appropriately enough, the revolution took place in the dying days of the White Fleet, which had been kept alive by the regime and its fisheries minister, Tenreiro. As news of the revolution and their newly discovered freedoms spread among crew members of the White Fleet, there was great rejoicing. The men wanted to strike for higher wages, and the three handliners – the last of the White Fleet – headed for St-Pierre, the closest port. They remained there for a few days, until coerced by local authorities to leave.

Clearly the owners were unhappy with this situation. A few days later, on 26 June, the *Ilhavense* caught fire and went to the bottom. The *São Jorge* had a similar fate a couple of days later. She was the last vessel of the Portuguese handlining fleet equipped with dories to sink in Newfoundland waters. On 24 July, the last remaining member of the White Fleet, the *Novos Mares*, with her dories proudly stacked on her deck, sailed for the last time through the Narrows on her way back to Aveiro. She was the last remaining handliner of the fleet (Andrieux 1996). This event ended nearly five hundred years of traditional handlining in Newfoundland waters by Portuguese fishermen.

Conclusion

At the time of writing, February 1998, I stand on the nearly deserted docks of Gafanha (Aveiro), once the home of the mighty handliners of the White Fleet. It is with great nostalgia that I reminisce about the fleet that graced St John's and St-Pierre for centuries.

Much has changed for the Portuguese fishery in the twenty-four years since the White Fleet left Canadian waters for the last time. Handliners were replaced by modern factory freezer trawlers, which were harvesting fewer and fewer cod. The 200-mile limit, the withdrawal of codfishing privileges when Portugal joined the European Community in 1986, and quotas all combined to bring to its knees the once-mighty Portuguese fleet (Andrieux 1987). Dozens of old fishing companies have folded or are on the verge of folding. Their fish-drying facilities are empty for lack of cod and have a mournful appearance. Vessels have been sold to the European Union for scrapping purposes and for a handsome price for their fishing licences. It is speculated that, within a year or two, the surviving vessels will be concentrated in the hands of two or three owners.

The presence of the Portuguese in Newfoundland waters is now a historical one. They contributed socially and economically to the culture and history of Newfoundland – and particularly to St John's. The White Fleet now sails only in the memories of those Portuguese and Newfoundlanders who were alive in those hard, wonderful years. The persistence of its memory is a tribute to the warm relationship between the Newfoundlanders and the Portuguese of that era.

NOTES

1 I wish to acknowledge the contributions to this research project of numerous active and retired Portuguese captains, officers, fishermen, owners, ship chandlers, technicians, doctors, clergy, and merchants, who shared with me their recollections and experiences of the White Fleet. I gathered this information informally over a number of years on Portuguese vessels that visited the Grand Banks. During their port calls, my wife and I would be dinner guests on these vessels, where the stories of yesteryear would always surface. Many of the retired fishermen shared their stories during our numerous visits to Portugal.

   I was fortunate in having the assistance of Dr Anna Maria Lopes of the Museu da Marinha de Ilhavo, who supplied me with initial lists and positions of sunken Portuguese vessels in Newfoundland waters. Friends of the museum – Capt. Francisco Marques, Capt. Vitorino Ramalheira, Capt. Francisco Paião, and many others – had extensive knowledge of the fleet and were of great assistance, bringing light to many unanswered questions.

   Thanks also to Dr Manuel Lopes and his staff at the Museu Municipal de Etnografia e História (Póvoa de Varzim), the Canadian Department of Fisheries and Oceans, and many others who supplied me with photographs to illustrate these recollections.

2 See the exhibit catalogue *The Portuguese White Fleet, St. John's, Newfoundland 1969*, gallery of the Portuguese consulate of Toronto, 15–25 Feb. 1996. This photo exhibit by Ian Brookes, a retired geographer from York University, deals with twenty-nine ships of the White Fleet that in 1969 sought refuge in St John's from Hurricane Blanche. This exhibit was also presented at several museums in Portugal, as well as at the Annual Meeting of the Canadian Association of Geographers in St John's, 20–23 August 1997.

REFERENCES

Abreu-Ferreira, D. 1995. 'The Cod Trade in Early-Modern Portugal: Deregula-

tion, English Domination, and the Decline of Female Cod Merchandise.'
Doctoral dissertation, Memorial University of Newfoundland.

– 1995–6. 'The Portuguese in Newfoundland: Documentary Evidence Examined.' *Portuguese Studies Review* 4 no. 2: 11–33.

Alpalhão, J.A., and Da Rosa, V.M.P. 1980. *A Minority in a Changing Society: The Portuguese Communities of Quebec.* Ottawa: University of Ottawa Press.

Andrieux, J.P. 1987. *Newfoundland's Cod War: Canada or France?* St John's: O.T.C. Press.

– 1996. *Marine Disasters & Shipwrecks of Newfoundland and Labrador,* Vol. 3 1940–1980. St John's: OTC Press.

– 1997. 'The Portuguese White Fleet in Newfoundland Waters.' Paper presented at the Annual Meeting, Canadian Association of Geographers, St John's, 23 Aug.

Brazão, E. 1964. *La découverte de Terre-Neuve.* Montreal: Les Presses de l'Université de Montréal.

– 1965. 'Les Corte-Real et le Nouveau Monde.' *Revue d'histoire d'Amérique française* 19 no. 1: 3–52; no. 2: 163–202; and no. 3: 335–49.

Cole, S.C. 1990. 'Cod, Cod, Country and Family: The Portuguese Newfoundland Cod Fishery.' *MAST* 3 no. 1: 1–29.

Doel, P.A. 1992. *Port O'Call: Memories of the Portuguese White Fleet in St John's, Newfoundland.* St John's: ISER Press.

– 1997. 'The Spatial and Geographic Identity of the Portuguese White Fleet Fisheries.' Paper presented at the Annual Meeting, Canadian Association of Geographers, St John's, Newfoundland, 23 Aug.

Morison, S.E. 1971. *The European Discovery of America: The Northern Voyages.* New York: Oxford University Press.

Moutinho, M. 1985. *História da pesca do bacalhau: Por uma antropologia do 'Fiel Amigo'.* Lisbon: Editorial Estampa.

Rower, J. 1983. *Axis Submarine Successes, 1939–1945.* Annapolis, Md: Naval Institute Press.

Simões, J. 1942. *Os grandes trabalhadores do Mar: Reportagem na Terra Nova e na Groenlândia.* Lisbon: Oficinas Gráficas da Gazeta dos Caminhos de Ferro.

Villiers, A. 1951. *The Quest of the Schooner Argus: A Voyage to the Banks and Greenland.* New York: Charles Scribner's Sons.

Wheeler, D.L. 1993. *Historical Dictionary of Portugal.* Metuchen, NJ: The Scarecrow Press.

5

Remembering the Portuguese

PETER COLLINS

Records of the Portuguese presence on the eastern coast of Canada – associated largely with the White Fleet, which harvested cod on the Grand Banks of Newfoundland from the 1940s to the 1970s – are surprisingly rare, with few primary documents, and little secondary research, existing on the subject (see Teixeira and Lavigne 1998). This absence is particularly notable with regard to the Portuguese fishermen and their impact on Newfoundland, especially on St John's, even though thousands of them might be in port at one time during the summer fishing season.[1] Priscilla Doel, whose book *Port O' Call* represents a singular exception to this scholarly oversight, notes with astonishment the lack of any substantial documentary evidence of 'this elusive Portuguese presence' (Doel 1992: 5).

In the course of rediscovering these 'elusive Portuguese' for this paper, I found that a Portuguese word recurred again and again – *saudade* – generally translated as a longing, a homesickness, a nostalgia for something lost, with those who experience this feeling being *saudosistas*.[2] Although the term appears most frequently with respect to the Portuguese fishermen's longing for home and family during months at sea, saudade has broader resonance in English writing – particularly postcolonial and on emigration, where it may be read as a metaphor for the emigrant experience and the attempt to reconstruct the past.

As Salman Rushdie observes: 'writers in my position, exiles or emigrants ... are haunted by some sense of loss, some urge to reclaim, to look back ... But if we do look back, we must also do so in the knowledge ... that we will not be capable of reclaiming precisely the thing that was lost; that we will, in short, create fictions, not actual cities or villages, but invisible ones, imaginary homelands' (1991: 10). Rushdie

(12) uses the terms 'fictions' and 'imaginary' in reference to 'the partial nature of ... memories' that characterize the history, the story, of the emigrant experience. He notes that even 'precise' scientific reconstructions of the past, through history, geography, or archaeology, are always provisional and that therefore the recovery of stories – of past 'voices' – becomes an essential complement to the quotidian, statistical analysis of the world around us.

Rushdie's argument goes to the heart of the problem confronting research into the cultural impact of the Portuguese presence in Newfoundland: namely, the lack of documentary evidence. Configuring this argument in terms of the subject at hand – the Portuguese of the White Fleet – we may argue that while an accounting of the number of Portuguese fishing vessels, the dates of their sailing, the size of their crews and catches, and so on is of obvious use in our task, so too is reclamation of the cultural history of the Portuguese presence, of those 'voices evoking memories' – to use Doel's Rushdiesque language – 'expressed, more often than not, with *saudade*' (Doel 1992: 34).

Moreover, such an exercise serves as more than a sentimental record of a fading past. As Rushdie (1991) argues, such reconstructions are 'not merely a mirror of nostalgia' but are also 'a useful tool with which to work in the present' – to explicate the workings in 'nation[s] of immigrants [such as Canada!] ... of the phenomenon of cultural transplantation, [by] examining the ways in which people cope with a new world' (12, 20). Therefore, in studying the 'cultural transplantation' of these Portuguese fishermen into the landscape of Newfoundland, I first present my own recollections, next examine the extant documentary record – largely newspapers and journal articles – and finally supplement these sources by examining the representation of the Portuguese in local St John's theatre, as well as in the recorded 'memories and voices' of Newfoundlanders and Portuguese Newfoundlanders. Through 'close reading' – a mode of literary analysis that 'foregrounds' subtexts and subtextual contradictions – of these texts, I hope to illuminate this 'moment' in the centuries-old cultural cross-pollination between Portugal and Canada.

Figures in a Landscape

This paper has its origins almost a generation ago, in the mental landscape of a young boy growing up in St John's in the late 1960s and the 1970s. His world was rather small, limited to his working-class downtown neighbourhood, his school, and the nearby Bannerman Park. The figures in his landscape were ethnically and culturally homogeneous – generally poor, Irish-Catholic – save for the few Chinese families, which mostly kept to themselves, running their restaurants and laundry.

And then there were the Portuguese.

It is difficult to convey a sense of the place that the Portuguese fishermen, who seasonally visited St John's with the White Fleet, occupied in the boy's world. He would see them at Mass every Sunday morning, in the Basilica of St John the Baptist, clustered together near the statue of Our Lady of Fátima, to the right of the main altar. On Sunday afternoons, and indeed most every afternoon in the summer, he would see them playing soccer ('football') in Bannerman Park, the closest open space to the St John's waterfront.

To be a Portuguese fisherman, he knew, was synonymous with being poor. This was common knowledge in St John's, deduced from the fact that many of the fishermen could not afford even the cheap running shoes – 'Portuguese sneakers,' schoolchildren called them – that could be bought at the inexpensive Arcade store downtown, and would play soccer barefoot even on gravel and concrete. Yet despite their often darker skin, their foreign language, and their differences, in a strange way the Portuguese 'belonged.' The park had trees, the bandstand, the swimming pool, and the Portuguese ... always the Portuguese ... playing soccer rain or shine, very much a part of the landscape of the city.

In the years that followed, at some point when the growing boy was not looking, the Portuguese seemed to disappear from St John's. Later, as a young academic, he ... I moved to the Canadian mainland and became aware of the complex tapestry that is the story of the Portuguese migration and presence in Canada. However, in researching the cultural impact of the Portuguese on the life of St John's, I found that the memories of the Portuguese from a St John's boyhood would reappear to inform and shape the research. While this 'privileging' of subjective memory could be regarded as marring an 'objective' reconstruction of a historical moment, it may be argued that such works are inevitably 'broken mirrors, some of whose fragments have been irretrievably lost' (Rushdie 1991: 11).

Perception, interpretation, and the assigning of significance are, as Rushdie (1991) observes, all informed by our subjectivity: 'Human beings do not perceive things whole; we are not gods but wounded creatures, cracked lenses, capable only of fractured perceptions ...

Meaning is a shaky edifice we build out of scraps, dogmas, childhood injuries, newspaper articles ... It would be dishonest to pretend, when writing about the day before yesterday, that it was possible to see the whole picture' (12–13).

So it is too with my reconstruction of the Portuguese presence in St John's. The Portuguese shown here in the landscape of St John's – whether in memory, newspapers, or drama – are 'representations' from the point of view of Newfoundlanders. This situation presents an opportunity to perceive an annual ethnic 'invasion' – a term indicative of the scale of the Portuguese fishing effort off Newfoundland, which at its height employed dozens of ships and thousands of men – from the perspective of a host culture. Perhaps the most astonishing thing about this meeting of cultures was the warm and friendly atmosphere in which it was conducted, which may be seen to have its roots in a shared experience of poverty and an uncertain livelihood determined by proximity to the ocean.

Memories: Journalism

Newfoundland newspaper accounts of the relationship between the men of the White Fleet and Newfoundlanders again and again attest to the existence of a 'special relationship.' An article by G.A. Frecker in the *Evening Telegram* is representative of these expressions of the shared romance with the sea – the source of life, and all too frequently of death, for those who fished the North Atlantic from their precariously small dories. Frecker writes: 'I was born at the doorstep of the sea and ships are in my blood ... The Portuguese fishing fleet has a special interest for me because it is more than an agglomeration of individual ships; it is a floating community, a society of people who share in common the development of one of Portugal's great industries – the cod fisheries.'[3] The writer goes on to observe that the Portuguese are 'very welcome [in St John's] for they not only bring business but also colour and a cosmopolitan flavour to our city.'

This sense not only of economic ties but of an intimate cultural bond finds echoes several years later in newspaper editorials on the occasion of the Portuguese fishermen's gift of a statue of Our Lady of Fátima to the Catholic basilica. Two editorials in the leading local newspaper – 'Welcome to the Portuguese'[4] and 'Reflections on Portuguese'[5] – note both the size and the friendliness of the seasonal Portuguese invasion: 'Only on few occasions have so many foreigners, in the strict sense of the word, trod our shores at one time. Today we have over 3,000 Portu-guese fishermen in port from 40 banking vessels and trawlers ... Although speaking a different language, the Portuguese are regarded here as friends.'[6] The editor's choice of words is significant – the Portu-guese are 'foreigners' only 'in the strict sense of the word.'

The newspaper accounts of the Portuguese presence also suggest a popular local interest in, and knowledge of, things Portuguese. New-foundland journalists would sometimes even be sent on assignment to Portugal to report on conditions of daily life in the homeland of the fishermen who arrived on these shores in their thousands every sum-mer.[7] From St John's to Baccalieu, the coast of Newfoundland bears the inscription of generations of early Portuguese navigators (see Seary 1971, 1989), and there seems to have been a recurring interest by Newfoundland journalists in the theory that it was the Portuguese, not Cabot, who first discovered Newfoundland in the modern period.[8] Newspaper writers also display a close knowledge of the Portuguese fishermen themselves, noting how 'many of them are from Portugal's possession the Azores, [and] are trained in early youth for their ardu-ous calling.'[9]

This sympathetic representation is evident even in the controversy over the barring of Portuguese fishermen from Canadian ports for alleged overfishing in the 1980s. Newspaper accounts note how the Portuguese 'incurred the wrath of federal officials,' yet 'City [of St John's] officials, including Mayor John Murphy ... expressed concern over ... the unofficial ban on the Portuguese vessels.'[10] Years later, in an interview that the author conducted with Murphy, the former mayor recalled how 'very, very reluctant' he had been to accept the ban.[11] He observed that the Portuguese fishermen, invariably 'extremely cordial' individuals, were always distinct from the fishing fleets of other nations in their appeal to Newfoundlanders.[12] This representation of Newfoundlanders' differential view of the Portuguese recurs in earlier newspaper accounts of relations between the two peoples.[13] New-foundlanders perceived the Portuguese not as they did the Russians or the Spanish, who also fished the Grand Banks and contributed to the economy of St John's, but rather much more intimately.

Mayor Murphy, whose family owned the Arcade store downtown, noted as well that only Portuguese fishermen traded with Newfound-landers. They conducted this personal, under-the-counter trade largely in liquor from Portugal, but also in their handmade arts and crafts such as 'ornate lace tablecloths' and ship models, examples of which

Murphy purchased and still possesses.[14] This entrepreneurship is one example of a gap in 'respectable' journalism on the relationship, which invariably mentioned official trading ties, leaving unofficial ties undocumented. To rectify this lacuna, a researcher must look to other sources, particularly regarding perhaps the two most prominent aspects of the non-economic relationship – soccer and sex.

Over the decades-long presence of the White Fleet on the Grand Banks, there is not a single mention in Newfoundland papers of what remains perhaps the most defining characteristic of the Portuguese for the people of St John's: their love of soccer.[15] It is not until 1995, years after Canadian waters closed to Portuguese fishing vessels, that a newspaper article takes note of this passion. A flotilla of tall ships arrived in St John's harbour, and, although only the *Gazela* was of Portuguese origin, onlookers had memories only of the fishermen of the White Fleet. The headline reads, 'Tall Ships Evoke Memories of Soccer on the Waterfront,' and the article, consisting of interviews with members of the crowd, is dominated by their recollections of the Portuguese fishermen's love of the game. One man recalled: 'In the '40s when I was in school, when someone in your class said "The white ships are in the harbour!" after school you'd run right down to see them.' Another observed: 'All the Portuguese wanted was a bit of music and a game of soccer ... They played soccer right out on the harbour front. I don't know who could kick a ball better.' Yet another recalled: 'They used to go up on the hill with us and play soccer ... The Portuguese were excellent soccer players. They'd all go up in the meadows and take off their shoes and it'd be a game of barefoot soccer.'[16]

This article is representative of the memory not only of the author, but of almost everyone over thirty whom I informally questioned. The first, primary association that people who lived in St John's during those years have of the Portuguese is their love for soccer.[17] The sight of sailing ships, most of which were not Portuguese, evoked memories of the White Fleet long after it had vanished from Newfoundland waters.

Note that this single recorded mention takes the form of a transcription of popular memories. We can only speculate as to why journalists of the 1940s, 1950s, and 1960s ignored the subject. Perhaps soccer was then regarded as a sport of the working classes and so not worthy of note? Perhaps personal contact between ordinary Portuguese and Newfoundlanders seemed less significant than the economic and political dimensions that dominate newspaper accounts.

A Play

The silence of the journalistic record on relationships between the fishermen of the White Fleet and the women of St John's is perhaps more understandable. Fortunately, the city's theatrical community fills that gap with the play *Terras de bacalhau* (Land of Cod), a 'collective' creation by eight artists of Newfoundland and Portuguese descent produced originally in 1980, when memories of the White Fleet were still fresh in the collective memory (see Anonsen et al. 1996). The play, a mingling of Portuguese songs and music with the wry social comedy characteristic of Newfoundland theatre, is set in the 1960s and is primarily the story of a Portuguese boy's coming of age when he makes his first voyage with his father on the White Fleet and of their bittersweet romantic and sexual relations with women in St John's. The sensitivity of this issue – given both the frankness and the sympathy with which it deals with the unhappiness of the wives whom the fishermen leave behind in Portugal, as well as adultery and clashes of cultures – suggests why there is sparse discussion in other media.

In the play's most poignant moment, the Newfoundland girl who is the love object of the young Portuguese sailor has a confrontation (act 2, scene 5) with her father.

CECIL: What do you think I'm runnin' here? A flop house for common whores who run around with Portuguese sailors?
KAY: (*angry*) I am not a common whore and I don't run around with Portuguese sailors! I just happen to be going out with a guy from Portugal and (*emotional*) I, I think that I'm in love with him!

The memories of members of the Portuguese-Newfoundland community from this time support the notion that their sexual relations, like so many other types of their relations, were more than just 'economic.' The Portuguese, both in literature and in memory, are represented as very attentive, romantic lovers. Indeed, often when Portuguese sailors went absent without leave, and their ships returned to the Banks without them, Canadian immigration authorities found that a fisherman had done nothing more than sleeping in after a long night with a Newfoundland girlfriend.[18]

Terras de bacalhau makes effective comic use of the confusions that inevitably accompany contacts between different cultures, without any trace of prejudice or resentment. Act 1, scene 6, set in the Arcade, opens with a passing reference to the cheap 'Portuguese sneakers' and details the attempts by several Portuguese fishermen to buy lingerie for their wives back home:

VOICEOVER: In our Arcade shoe department, downstairs, brandname sneakers. Out they go, while they last, at the incredibly low price of three for a dollar.
...
RITA: What size do you want? 34, 36, 38, 40? What size?
CARLOS: Wife size.
RITA: Is your wife a big woman or is she small like you?
CARLOS: Sim, sim, 93–56–93!
RITA: She must be deformed! You're going to have to go into yardgoods to get something to fit her.
CARLOS: Não, não, não, 93–56–93, like you, smaller. Like you.
RITA: Like me! Smaller! I don't have to take that from you ... And me after starving meself all day. Do you know what I had to eat all day? A piece of dry toast and a cup of weak tea, that's all.
KAY: Rita, I think he's talkin' in kilometres or something!

Indeed, the play often presents the Portuguese as confused spectators of Newfoundlanders' well-intentioned attempts to communicate. In act 1, scene 7, Kay takes her new Portuguese boyfriend, João, home to meet members of her family, who are engaged in a typical, argumentative card game:

RONNY: Dad, sure she just said he don't speak any English.
VANYA: What difference is it, b'y? Sure, cards are a universal language.
...
AGNES: Kay, where did you meet him?
KAY: At the Basilica.
AMBROSE: They goes up there all the time.
AGNES: The Basilica, the Basilica?
RONNY: Dad, he don't know what you're saying. Dad, Dad? He don't speak English.
CECIL: If you shut up, I can explain it to him.

Much as the scene in the Arcade reflects popular memory of Portuguese shopping habits, so this scene gives form to the memory of the frequent presence of the Portuguese in the basilica. Moreover, Kay's father, Cecil, may be seen to embody the comic aspect of the play's representation of the relationship between the two peoples. Even when he criticizes his daughter for dating a Portuguese man, he is angry more out of concern for her than from any bigotry or cultural prejudice.

However, *Terras de bacalhau* also attempts to recreate the perspective of the Portuguese fishermen. The songs that they sing are often political, critical of the dictatorship at home and of the Portuguese merchants who exploit them. In act 1, scene 1, we hear:

MANUEL: (singing) 'Only a Fisherman.'
   I'm only a fisherman, and I do whatever I can,
   I don't like to take from my brothers and sisters,
   Who are just as poor as I am.
   ...
   Workin', workin', workin' for the rich man.
   Portugal was fascisto for years,
   People shed their tears for freedom,
   For a better way, they had their say,
   Like Mozambique, like Angola, they cried out.
   They said, 'No, no, no, to oppression.'
   Yes, I'm only a fisherman, and I do whatever I can,
   I don't like to take from my brothers and sisters,
   Who are just as poor as I am.

The poverty of so many of the fishermen, and their exploitation by merchants back home, must have evoked their own plight for many Newfoundlanders and made them identify so strongly with the Portuguese. However, this theatrical re-creation may also serve as a document of the forces that drove Portuguese emigration for much of this century.

And in the End ...

In the Introduction to the published edition of *Terras de Bacalhau*, the editor contends that one of the play's main themes is the relation between 'self and other' (Peters 1996). As this essay has shown, however, the Portuguese were never really 'foreigners,' never 'other,' to the people of St John's. Rather, in the context of their representation in the memories and writings of Newfoundlanders, they seem to occupy an ambiguous 'liminal space' between 'self' and 'other,' indicative of the shared cultural values of the two peoples and of a common experience of economic deprivation and life defined, to a great degree, by the ocean.

Clearly both the absence of substantial documentary evidence and the complexities of the relationship between Newfoundlanders and the Portuguese of the White Fleet necessitate an approach that supplements media with memory (in the forms of literature and interviews). It is an exercise imbued, for the author as much as for the often-homesick fishermen whom he has been researching, with saudade. As Salman Rushdie writes, 'The past is a country from which we have all emigrated' (1991: 12).

In this sense, perhaps both Portuguese and Newfoundlanders are saudosistas – emigrants from a past that was materially poorer but culturally richer. This essay, then, can be seen not only as part of the story of Portuguese fishermen in the New World, but perhaps also as a reflection on a unique moment of cross-cultural exchange that has, sadly, been lost to everything save memory.

NOTES

1 Anon., 'Welcome to the Portuguese,' St John's *Evening Telegram*, 26 May 1955, 4.
2 The two key Portuguese words recurring in this chapter are usually translated in English as follows: '*saudade* (f.): longing, yearning; homesickness, nostalgia; heartache ... *saudosista* I. (a.) of or pertaining to one who yearns or longs for the past. *II*. (mf.) one who yearns or longs for the past, die-hard.' See *The New Appleton Dictionary of the English and Portuguese Languages* (1967), 546–7.
3 Frecker 1953, 13.
4 *Evening Telegram*, 26 May 1955, 4.
5 Ibid., 1 June 1955, 4.
6 Ibid., 26 May 1955, 4.
7 White 1948, 8.
8 Anon., 'Portugues [sic] Discovery Celebration Begins: New Hospital Steamer Arrives from Portugal,' *Daily News*, 27 May 1955.
9 Anon., 'Reflections on Portuguese.' *Evening Telegram*, 1 June 1955, 30 May 1955.
10 Anon., 'Portuguese Vessels Are Barred from Entering Canadian Ports,' ibid., 6 May 1986, 3.

11 Mayor John Murphy, interview with the author, 2 Jan. 1997.
12 Ibid.
13 See Frecker, 1953, 13; Anon., 'Warm Welcome Extended Portuguese Ambas-
    sador,' *Daily News*, 11 June 1948, 4.
14 Murphy interview.
15 Here memory again serves to complement the documentary record. On the
    occasion of the Annual Meeting of the Canadian Association of Geogra-
    phers in St John's in August 1997, the author took a visiting Portuguese-
    Canadian academic on a tour of the city by cab. The taxi driver, on over-
    hearing the author's recalling the Portuguese and their love of soccer,
    began talking of how he himself had played with them in his youth; his
    recollections of their skill and sportsmanship had largely defined his high
    regard for them through the intervening years of Portuguese–Canadian
    quarrels over fishing rights.
        Certainly this perspective on the Portuguese passion for soccer is
    shared by almost every Newfoundlander of my acquaintance, which
    makes its almost complete absence from the newspaper record all the
    more puzzling.
16 Tompkins 1995, 3.
17 This informal survey consisted of responses from ten people – three rela-
    tives or friends of the author and the others chosen at random from the St
    John's population – in early August 1997. I did this, without making any
    claims that these data would be significant, to satisfy my personal curiosity.
    Of those asked, everyone who lived in St John's during the period studied
    responded with wistful memories of the Portuguese and, of course, their
    passion for soccer.
18 António and Kathy Duarte, interview with the author, 28 Dec. 1996.

REFERENCES

Anonsen, K., Boland R., Silva, J.E., Koop, J., Payne, J., Spence, J., Thomey, G.,
    and Walsh, M. 1996. 'Terras de Bacalhau (Land of Cod) 1980.' In H. Peters,
    ed., *Stars in the Sky Morning – Collective Plays of Newfoundland and Labrador*,
    131–76. St John's: Killick Press.
Doel, P. 1992. *Port O' Call: Memories of the Portuguese White Fleet in St. John's,
    Newfoundland*. St John's: ISER Press.
Frecker, G.A. 1953. 'The Fleet's In: Portuguese Fishermen in St John's Follow
    Ancestors.' *Evening Telegram*, 11 Aug.: 13.
Peters, H. 1996. 'Introduction.' In H. Peters, ed., *Stars in the Sky Morning: Collec-
    tive Plays of Newfoundland and Labrador*. St John's: Killick Press.

Rushdie, S. 1991. *Imaginary Homelands: Essays and Criticism 1981–1991*. London: Granta.

Seary, E.R. 1971. 'Some Portuguese, Spanish and Basque Place Names in Newfoundland.' An Address to the Canadian Association of Hispanists, May.

– 1989. 'The Portuguese Element in the Place Names of Newfoundland.' In *Vice-Almirate A. Teixeira da Mota: In memoriam*, vol. II: 359–64. Lisbon: Academia de Marinha.

Teixeira, C., and Lavigne, G. 1998. *Os Portugueses no Canadá: Uma bibliografia (1953–1996)*. Lisbon: Direcção-Geral dos Assuntos Consulares e Comunidades Portuguesas.

Tompkins, J. 1995. 'Tall Ships Evoke Memories of Soccer on the Waterfront.' *Evening Telegram*, 5 Aug.: 3

White, J. 1948. 'Portugal's Fishing Ties Reach Back to 1255: Fishermen May Have Been Here before Cabot.' *Daily News*, 1 Dec.: 8.

PART TWO

IMMIGRATION FROM
PORTUGAL TO CANADA

6

Immigrants Forever? The Migratory Saga of Azoreans in Canada

MANUEL ARMANDO OLIVEIRA

Located in mid-Atlantic between North America and western Europe – 1,400 kilometres from mainland Portugal – and spanning 600 kilometres from east to west, the Azorean archipelago is made up of nine islands, with a total land area of 2,300 square kilometres. Though probably discovered by other peoples (Godinho 1969), the islands were occupied by the Portuguese in the fifteenth century, at a time when Portugal had no more than one million inhabitants. The Portuguese authorities opened the archipelago for other Europeans to settle. Thus some people would arrive from the Brittany region, in northern France, to settle in the largest of the islands (São Miguel), whereas the Flemish went principally to two other islands (Fayal and Pico). The Spaniards also arrived, as did Jews from various parts of Europe. All these peoples joined the Portuguese already there and helped colonize the new territory.

Despite rich volcanic soil, some of the best pastures in the world, abundant fish stocks, geostrategic importance,[1] and a mild climate, the Azores have failed through the centuries to provide an acceptable standard of living. Thus, starting as early as the sixteenth century (Frutuoso 1939–64), many inhabitants left to settle in Brazil, while others went to different parts of the world. The great Azorean exodus targeted North America, especially the United States. When the American whalers, from the U.S. east coast, started visiting the archipelago more than two hundred years ago (Clark 1954),[2] they initiated a significant flow (much of it illegal) of emigrants. Between then and the early 1920s, when the United States clamped down on immigration, thousands of Azoreans left the islands, most of them never to return. Today, many islanders like to refer to the 'one million plus' Azoreans and their descendants who now live in the United States, at a time when the Azores have less than one quarter of that figure (234,000). Azoreans ended up developing a deeply emotional attachment towards the United States, which continues to the present day. That closeness to the American 'Eldorado,' plus the fact of so many relatives living there, made emigration there by far the biggest aspiration of most Azoreans – the true 'Azorean dream,' if one really exists.

Azorean emigration has been attributed to economic, psychological, family, and even political factors, along with demographic pressures and natural cataclysms, such as volcanic eruptions and earthquakes (Aguiar 1976; Serpa 1978). Most observers, however, emphasize economic factors – specifically an archaic distribution of land in the largest island (São Miguel) and the relative backwardness that long characterized the archipelago (Serpa 1978; Da Rosa and Trigo 1990). Many Azoreans have concluded that other peoples doubtless have been able to achieve much more with considerably less.[3]

Not many Azorean emigrants have returned to live in the islands,[4] which some scholars have seen as proof that Azoreans, unlike mainland Portuguese, leave their islands determined never to return. This view of Azorean emigration, strong in the islands (Oliveira 1996), is even more so on the mainland, where some Portuguese scholars have reinforced it (see, for example, Neto 1981). In contrast, people on the mainland tend to see non-return as an indication that emigrants' plans have changed.

One counter-example is given by the group of Azoreans examined in this essay. For this group, as for so many other Azoreans whom I have interviewed in Canada over the last two decades, failure to return for good was the result not of any pre-established plan or firm commitment but rather the consequence of a change in circumstances. All of them immigrated to Canada from Pontas Negras on the island of Pico. I take the personal experience of the first of those villagers to move to Canada – DaSilva is his name – to illustrate the migratory experience of so many like him, who emigrated with the dream of returning one day. Then, exploring the experiences of other Pontanegrese, I look at why, for most of them, that dream would never materialize.

The present essay draws on various data sources – namely, bibliographical research and ethnographic fieldwork done in Toronto, where seventy-five of the ninety-four Pontanegrese who emigrated to Canada have settled. Besides residing for two decades in that city, during which I was a careful observer of the day-to-day life of the Portuguese and their descendants, I was actively involved in research on the Pontanegrese for about three years up to 1995, during which period I was a direct and participant observer, as well as an informal interviewer. I also conducted research in the village itself, in the Azores, where I collected economic and demographic data on every household. After first looking at the village itself, I next present the story of the first Pontanegrese to emigrate, and then consider the situation and attitudes of Pontanegrese in Canada today.

Pontas Negras: A 'Typical' Azorean Village

Located on the southern side of Pico island, in the Azores, Pontas Negras is a small village of few more than fifty houses. At the beginning of the modern Portuguese emigration to Canada in 1953 it had 217 inhabitants – 108 males and 109 females. Most were peasants, the majority of them not owning enough land to feed their families. Most of the men spent their time cultivating the small land plots they owned and working irregularly in agriculture, construction, or fishing.

The scarcity of means and the harshness of daily life, coupled with the extraordinarily rosy picture of life in the United States, made 'going to America' the biggest aspiration of the locals, but by this time it was an unattainable dream. The obstacles raised by the American authorities blocked practically everyone, and the American whalers, which had provided an escape for so many Azoreans, were no longer to be seen in Azorean waters. After the American clampdown on immigration in the 1920s, only four villagers went to the United States – three brothers, of the Ramalho family, and another villager, from the Canarinho family. Only when something really unexpected happened, as when the Capelinhos volcano on the island of Fayal erupted in 1957, did American immigration policy change briefly.[5]

A Migratory Saga

A Place Called Canada

Suddenly, however, word spread that Canada was opening its doors to immigration. The year was 1953, and modern emigration from Portugal to Canada had begun, with the departure of the first group of 555

Portuguese to this country (Marques and Medeiros 1978). When the news broke, however, no one in the village seemed particularly enthusiastic. In reality, the name 'Canada' was unfamiliar, as was the term 'emigration,' since people in the Azores did not 'emigrate' but rather 'went to America.' This initial reserve was obvious throughout the Azores: in the parish of which Pontas Negras is part, for instance, only two people applied to emigrate;[6] from the municipality, fifty-two. Of these, fifty were subsequently to change their minds during an information meeting organized by Canadian immigration authorities in the Azores.[7]

Fear of the unknown accounted for some misgivings and for the fact that in Pontas Negras, for instance, only one villager decided to 'try his luck' in Canada. Above all, however, it was the incredibly optimistic image of the 'terra da América'[8] which everyone harboured that made other countries seem poor alternatives. No other place on earth aroused such intense interest and enthusiasm, because no other place could compete with the image of supposedly unparalleled material wealth. Although in the distant past Azoreans had emigrated to other parts of the world such as Brazil, no one in the village could remember anyone else who had done so, much less 'struck it rich.'

Finally, there were considerable financial costs associated with emigration. These included the boat trip between Pico and São Miguel, but above all the trip to Canada. Fare money had to be borrowed, even though there was no guarantee acceptance by the Canadian authorities in São Miguel.[9]

'Going to America'

None the less, it would be the image of the 'terra da América' that would motivate one Pontanegrese (DaSilva) to emigrate, that would give him the necessary courage to leave home in search of a better life. When it became known, from two elderly men – who had themselves once lived in the United States – that it was possible to 'cross over from Canada to America,' emigration to Canada suddenly looked completely different. It was as if geographical proximity to the United States were synonymous with a guarantee for success. It kept alive the hope of one's achieving the 'great Azorean dream' of 'going to America.' At that time, had the Pontanegrese received the slightest encouragement or support from relatives in the United States – for instance a slight hint that once in Canada they would be encouraged to cross the border – most of their misgivings would no doubt have dissipated. Besides, there would certainly have been no lack of financial support from villagers who would offer to lend a bit of money to pay for the trip and other necessary expenses. As one Pontanegrese put it, 'the entire village would, without a doubt, have simply taken off.'[10] No one, however, received any such encouragement, not even from U.S. relatives, and no one dared ask for help or even advice, fearful of what was then referred to as the usual 'America-here-is-not-what-we-think-of-there' excuse!

DaSilva, however, decided on a slightly different approach: he would still ask for help, but only after landing in Canada! Once confronted with that reality, he thought, relatives would have no alternative but to give him a helping hand. Even today, this first Pontanegrese – and one of the first Azoreans – to emigrate to Canada confesses that his plan was not to stay in Canada but to go to 'America.' That was what gave him the strength to face the unknown and made him want to do 'whatever it took' to make his dream come true. As he himself says: 'Once I made that decision, the way forward then became, for me, the only way out!'

In every sense, then, that Pontanegrese was 'going to America,' and it was the United States, not Canada, that motivated him. He had to make what he thought would be a short stop in another country – the price of 'going to America.' Like so many people over the years, he made Canada a stepping-stone to the United States. At twenty-seven, single and with no immediate plans to start a family, he was in a somewhat different situation from most other villagers. As soon as his decision became known, in Pontas Negras and surrounding villages, he instantly became the object of conversation: many other villagers wanted to express their support and encourage him. Temporarily a local hero, DaSilva must have felt considerable pressure, even if self-imposed, to go ahead, since for him to change his mind would have disappointed many people.

The entire village wished its first 'Canadian' well and admired his courage. There was a great deal of curiosity to see what awaited him in that strange land and how he would handle an uncertain future. Thus when he left for São Miguel, many showed up to say good-bye, to give him a final word of encouragement, and to wish him the best of luck. After the necessary medical exams and last-minute preparations in São

Miguel came a moment that he would never forget: at the Ponta Delgada harbour he boarded the ocean liner *Homeland* and headed west to Canada. The day was 22 March 1954.

'America,' Finally!

A few days later, on 27 March, after a five-day trip from Ponta Delgada, *Homeland* arrived in Halifax. On board, together with other early Azorean emigrants, was the first Pontanegrese to set foot on Canadian soil. For DaSilva, there was a certain feeling of 'pioneerism,' of being the first from his village and one of the very first from his islands to arrive in this strange land. Even today, he takes pride in having been 'the first to open the way to others ... to open the gates for those who'd come after me.' Above all, this moment represented the first step on the route to his dream – from this country 'you could walk to America.'

Once landed, these new immigrants met a religious group that distributed medals to everyone. Then they immediately proceeded to customs and immigration, where each received a tag; the colour of that tag, they later found out, indicated the province where they were to be sent. Quebec was to be DaSilva's destination. An old friend and companion, however, with whom he had travelled from Pico, was sent 'to the other side of Canada' – British Columbia. The two were from neighbouring villages and had known each other since early childhood.

From Halifax the two men travelled by train to Montreal, where they settled in temporary accommodation provided by the immigration authorities. Quebec farmers showed up in the next few days to 'choose and pick' from among those who appeared to be the best workers. 'We looked like Domingos Folião pigs!' DaSilva remembers; the farmers approached the immigrants and looked them over 'from top to bottom,' either picking one or passing on.[11] This behaviour was shocking, certainly not the sort of reception that they expected in Canada. The majority of farmers were interested in hiring only one immigrant each, but some would take two. 'I'll only go with one who takes two!' said DaSilva to himself. The idea of ending up in the 'middle of nowhere' in the vast Canadian territory, and having no one to speak to in his own language, 'worried me stiff,' he later said. For that reason, he initially refused the offers that some farmers made to him. He could not, however, continue to refuse indefinitely. By the third day, he decided to accept a job in Quebec.[12]

On the Farm

DaSilva remembers life on the farm vividly: 'Hard work day and night, not enough food, unfair treatment ... [and] all that you could imagine to make life miserable.' For a few months, he lived in terror of having to stay there for a long time. There was also 'the terrible problem of communication.' He had a hard time understanding his boss and making himself understood, which frequently led to uncomfortable, even embarrassing situations, and sometimes to conflict.

After four months he felt that he had reached his limit. He then decided he would run away. He planned to go to Montreal, and from there to Toronto, but he would wait until after Saturday – pay day. The next day – the first Sunday of August, 1954, a day he was never to forget – he took his old suitcase on his shoulders and 'took off.' His boss, who immediately understood what he was up to, started shouting at him and trying to intimidate him. 'Police' and 'Portugal' were then words he clearly understood, which left little doubt in his mind that he was being threatened with deportation. But no words could have stopped him. 'The only way out was the way forward' – an expression that he often uses with reference to his experiences in Canada. At about midnight he arrived at the bus station, only then realizing that his feet were bleeding badly. He was also hungry, but at that late hour, nothing was open. He leaned against a wall, smoking cigarette after cigarette, until the bus finally arrived.

In Montreal, he learned that there was work in Ontario, on the tobacco farms, but he could not leave right away, as he was not able to walk. He stayed in Montreal for two weeks and then boarded the train to Toronto. That city already had a few Portuguese around, some of whom he recognized as having travelled with him for São Miguel. A number had been there for some time, having run away from the farms. Shortly afterwards, he left for the tobacco farms in southwestern Ontario,[13] where he soon concluded that life there was not much easier that the one that he had left behind in Quebec. Perhaps the immigration officer, who had given that discouraging speech about life in Canada, had been right after all. This was a thought that constantly haunted DaSilva. Judging by his first six months in Canada, it seemed that the immigration officer had not painted life in Canada badly enough!

Then one day he received a reply from his godfather in San Diego,

California, to whom he had written of his plans to go to 'America.' But his godfather warned him that 'it would be better to stay there,' since in the United States 'things were not very good!' The tuna fishing industry in San Diego had seen better days, and his chances of finding a good job there were slim. Now all his effort seemed in vain. After two years of temporary jobs, however, he finally found work, in February 1956, at the De Havilland plane factory, in the suburbs of Toronto. He would stay there for many years to come.

The Big City

In Toronto, the first Portuguese immigrants congregated around the Kensington Market – a somewhat rundown area in the heart of the city, where rent was relatively low and where recent immigrants, as well as other low-income groups, would settle. They replaced earlier immigrants, who 'graduated' to the suburbs. Here Jews had congregated, established businesses, and settled, until economic conditions allowed them to move out. Then came the Italians, who gave way to the Portuguese in the 1960s (Teixeira 1995).

Having come to Canada usually as sponsored immigrants, the Pontanegrese naturally took up residence close to family members who had sent for them. During the early years they all felt the need to remain in close contact with other Portuguese, to feel the encouragement and support that the group never failed to provide. Life in Canada was more difficult, after all – far more than when they dreamed of travelling to Canada 'fazer uma América' (make it in America) – and return. As DaSilva well remembered, this expression had become part of local parlance in the Azores, referring to someone who is 'making it big.'

A Dream That No longer Is

With a single exception – that of a woman who left the village convinced that 'if Canada was good to make money, then it would probably also be good to spend it' – all the Pontanegrese adult emigrants, as well as many other Azoreans now living in Canada whom I have contacted over the years, left their island with a clear intention of someday, somehow, returning to live in their village. There they would live a quiet life, working the few plots of land that they would have bought with their earnings from Canada, plus having a little income provided by the remainder of those earnings. When asked about how long they had thought that it would take for them to achieve that goal in Canada, the answers were surprisingly similar: 'about ten years' or 'something like a dozen years.'

Between 1954 – when the population of Pontas Negras was 217 – and 1976 ninety-four villagers left to Canada, of whom seventy-five settled in Toronto. As noted above, practically all adult villagers left with a clear intention – and hope – of return. For the large majority, however, that dream never came true. Would those immigrants like to return but cannot afford to do so, or could they easily afford it but don't want to do so?

They remain in Canada of their own will, they respond, and could easily return if they so wished. As to why the dream has not materialized, the answers are rather vague: 'I'd love to go, but all my children are here – how can I go?' 'Now that I'm getting old and no longer have my kids with me, how could I live there?' 'I couldn't get used to living there anymore.' 'It's OK to go there on holidays, but not to live permanently.' 'The way they treat us there? – not a chance!' The first question makes them reason in purely economic terms, and in that respect they have no doubts that they could return. If pressed, however, they think of the factors involved, which brings to mind all the complexity of the matter.

Upon their arrival in Canada and during the initial stages here, only one of those factors – the economic one – blocked their dream. Had they, in those early days, 'struck it rich,' not one of them would be here today (except for two young men whose only reason to emigrate was to avoid the military draft). Seven years later, on average, most of them had bought, and paid for, their own houses. By this point, however, not one of them would even consider returning home! As happens in so many other situations in people's lives, objectives set ever so clearly end up being redefined once they appear within reach. In the case of immigrants, such a situation leads to successive postponements of the decision to return. It is as if the immigrant, having reached a certain stage along his or her migratory cycle, could not set aside the idea of someday returning to the homeland, but at the same time could not muster the courage finally to do it. Other factors besides the economic had come into play.

For most of the Pontanegrese in Canada, one of the most important factors had to do with their children and the future that they now envisaged for them. Once they had convinced themselves of the indisputable superiority of things in their new land, they soon came to realize that their children's future lay in Canada, not in Portugal.[14] However, once they had paid for their houses, they started going back to the Azores for short summer visits, which produced mixed feelings. There was excitement, mixed with the disappointment that so many other immigrants before them had already experienced, once they came to face reality in the islands and see it against the image of the 'lost Paradise' they had so laboriously constructed in their minds over the years of their absence (Abou 1981).

Such return trips launched a radical change in individual perceptions that the Pontanegrese, like so many other Portuguese immigrants in Canada, would go through. The change affected the way in which they 'see' their motherland, their fellow countrymen back home, and sometimes even themselves as Portuguese and as immigrants. Later, as time went by, they felt more competent and relaxed in performing their jobs, their knowledge of the majority language improved, and the 'institutional completeness' (Breton 1964) of the local Portuguese community expanded. The majority of Portuguese immigrants began to feel more and more comfortable with the surrounding socio-cultural environment. They had finally reached the point of appreciating Canada and much of what life had to offer them here. Then, when asked about their initial dream of returning home, many flatly rejected the idea, while the remainder responded: 'Yes ... well, maybe ... perhaps some day later.'

Conclusion: Immigrants Forever?

In the end, then, the Pontanegrese who emigrated to Canada would find themselves in a situation that they would never have expected when they left their village. The years in Canada still have not made them feel true citizens; after all they 'are not Canadians,' they simply have 'Canadian papers,' as they refer to their citizenship documents. However, those years spent away from home have made them feel like strangers in their own country. This difficult and unexpected situation came about largely as a result of conflict among their perceptions of each of these three socio-cultural environments that are now relevant to their lives. Taken together, these make up what could well be termed the 'cultural triangle of the immigrant' – first, their homeland (Oliveira 1996) as it was when they left and as they still remember it; second, that same homeland as they see it today; and third, their present life in Canada.

Thus, in spite of their material success and comfort, they have never had in Canada the feeling of truly 'belonging' that they felt in their village. Hence the constant reminiscing about the past, which many of their children see as an exaggeration and about which they sometimes complain and even feel resentment. Parents then tend to mythologize that past, slowly to 'build' in their minds a homeland that does not exist and never existed. On returning to that homeland, so many of them become disillusioned – a feeling that grows stronger with each new trip back.

Just as shocking for these immigrants, however, is the realization that in the Pontas Negras of today many of them feel that they no longer belong. As a result, they keep away from the residents, with whom they feel they have less and less in common, and the locals tend to keep their distance, to give 'off-the-cuff' answers, and frequently to change topic when a 'Canadian' approaches a group of them. On returning from a holiday in the islands, many of these immigrants show satisfaction over some pleasant moments, coupled with disappointment and even anger at what they saw and at the way in which they were treated. Some say out loud, 'That was it!' They will spend their next holiday not in the Azores, not anywhere in Portugal, but in California, in Florida, in Cape Cod ... The majority of them, however, seem to not have learned the lesson of repeated trips to the Azores – however big the disappointments, these will soon be forgotten, and the cycle repeats itself. Again the mythologizing of the past, the village construed as the 'lost paradise,' the recycling of a certain state of mind ... until the next visit ...

People mythologize the past as a response to a present to which they do not belong, but it is customary to think that immigrants are affected by that alienation only while in the receiving country. The experience of the Portanegrese in Canada shows, however, that such alienation may come about equally in the immigrant's own country of birth. For these Azoreans, as for so many other Portuguese immigrants in Canada, this is the real drama – feeling 'Portuguese when in Canada' but 'Canadian when in Portugal,' they end up being, in a very real sense, 'immigrants forever.'

NOTES

1 Which led, for example, to the establishment, in one of the islands (Terceira) of an important U.S. military base.
2 According to Clark (1954), the first whaling ship originating on the U.S. east coast (Nantucket) arrived in the Azores in 1765.
3 As an example, some of the Azorean emigrants living in Bermuda (of which there are approximately 14,000 and from whom I have repeatedly heard about this subject) like to point out how a small island like Bermuda, with no natural resources to speak of and a rather high population density (more than 50,000 inhabitants on fifty-four square kilometres of land), manages to have one of the highest living standards in the world. 'If Bermuda can achieve this,' one of them told me, 'then the Azores, comparatively, should be a world superpower!' The reality, however, is that while many Azoreans, mostly from São Miguel, had to emigrate to Bermuda, in search of what their own land has denied them, 'no Bermudian is known to have emigrated to the Azores,' according to my informants. On this same subject, one Portanegrense living in Toronto expressed the opinion that 'our bad luck, as Azoreans, was that the *Mayflower* would miss us on her way to America.'
4 As an example, 147,005 Azoreans left the islands for the United States and Canada between 1960 and 1979 – more than half the resident population. During the same period, no more than 4,455 returned to live in the islands (Da Rosa and Trigo 1990: 74–7).
5 As a result of that eruption, the United States opened its doors to thousands of Azoreans not only from Fayal, but from some of the neighbouring islands as well. This action had a profound impact on Azoreans, touching them deeply. To this day, they refer to it as an example – one more, as many like to emphasize! – of American goodwill.
6 One was DaSilva, from Pontas Negras; the other was Manuel António Pereira, from the neighbouring village of Ribeira Seca.
7 As the meeting progressed – some still remember today – those present started leaving the room, one by one, until only two of the initial fifty-two remained. One of them was the candidate from Pontas Negras.
8 Literally, the 'land of America.'
9 In all, it was thought that approximately 15,000 Portuguese escudos (at the time about Can$500) were needed. In 1953, that represented, for the average Azorean worker, about 700 days of work (at the then-going daily rate of 20 escudos – approximately 75 Canadian cents). Not even the 'wealthy' families in the village had such a large sum, although, based on

the property they owned, some might have had access to it through a bank loan.

10 This of course would also imply a less rigorous selection of candidates for emigration.

11 Domingos Folião was a pig farmer from a neighbouring village who would walk from place to place selling his pigs. The way in which the locals approached and observed those pigs in each village suggested the comparison that DaSilva is making here.

12 Forty years later, DaSilva does not remember well the locale of the farm where he worked. All he can say is that it sounded something like 'Hornston,' and was north of Montreal.

13 In the suburbs of London, Ontario. As far as DaSilva can remember, the name of the nearest town sounded like 'Montbridge.'

14 This is especially true of the Azoreans. Portuguese from the mainland – some would say – tend to cling more to their homeland and to be a lot more demanding about their children retaining Portuguese language and culture and attending Portuguese classes, as if hoping that someday they will go back, or at least prepare for that eventuality. In the end, however, most mainlanders, like most Azoreans, stay in Canada.

REFERENCES

Abou, S. 1981. L'identité culturelle: Rélations inter-ethniques et problèmes d'acculturation. Paris: Éditions Anthropos.

Aguiar, C. 1976. 'Dominantes histórico-sociais do Povo Açoreano.' In Livro da segunda semana dos Açores, 139–63. Angra do Heroismo: Instituto Açoreano de Cultura.

Breton, R. 1964. 'Institutional Completeness of Ethnic Communities and the Personal Relations of Immigrants.' American Journal of Sociology 70 no. 2: 193–205.

Clark, R. 1954. Open Broad Whaling in the Azores: The History and Present Methods of a Relic Industry. London: National Institute of Geography.

Da Rosa, V.M.P., and Trigo, S. 1990. Contribuição ao estudo da emigração nos Açores. Angra do Heroísmo: Gabinete de Apoio às Comunidades Açoreanas.

Frutuoso, G. 1939–64. Saudades da terra. Ponta Delgada: Instituto Cultural de Ponta Delgada.

Godinho, V.M. 1969. L'économie de l'empire portugais aux XVe et XVI siècles. Paris: SVPEN.

Marques, D., and Medeiros, J. 1978. Imigrantes portugueses: 25 anos no Canadá. Toronto: Movimento Comunitário Português.

Neto, J.P. 1981. 'O contributo do emigrante para o desenvolvimento regional: Uma perspectiva sociológica e antropológica.' *Democracia e liberdade* 19: 1–18.

Oliveira, M.A. 1996. 'Mito e realidade na emigração açoreana.' Doctoral dissertation, Instituto Superior de Ciências Sociais e Políticas, Lisbon.

Serpa, C.V. 1978. *A gente dos Açores: Identificação, emigração e religiosidade, séculos XVI–XX*. Lisbon: Prelo.

Teixeira, C. 1995. 'The Portuguese in Toronto: A Community on the Move.' *Portuguese Studies Review* 4 no. 1: 57–75.

7

Voices of Portuguese Immigrant Women

ILDA JANUÁRIO and MANUELA MARUJO

During the selection of the 1953 contingent, 230 dependants left behind had been examined and one of the yardsticks of the initial immigration trial's success was the rate of application for their admission in Canada. The 952 men who came in 1954 left behind 1,223 wives and children ready to join them when they were ready to send for them.

Marques and Marujo 1993: 99

The Portuguese first arrived in Canada in 1953, recruited for heavy jobs on the railways and low-paid farm work (Marques and Marujo 1993). In that year, 186 men were granted visas, beginning a movement that would grow in the following years. For the first group selected, officials especially asked for single men. Those who were married and came later left their wives and children behind in Portugal. Although the policy of family reunification began at the end of the 1950s, it took years for most immigrant men to resume their family life.

The first books examining the Portuguese immigration to Canada (Anderson and Higgs 1976; Marques and Medeiros 1978) recounted men's lives and men's stories. More recently, however, there has been research on Portuguese women in Ontario and Quebec (Nunes 1986; Demers 1987; Giles and Januário 1987; Neal and Neale 1987; Anderson and Davis 1990; Grosner 1991; Noivo 1992; Aguiar 1994; Giles and Preston 1996; Marujo 1996; Giles 1997) and more particularly about their role in the labour force and as mothers and homemakers (for a comparison of first- and second-generation Portuguese-Canadian women and families see Noivo 1992; Aguiar 1994; and Giles 1997).

This essay first examines two stories – those of Lurdes and Izilda, who live in Toronto – that illustrate the experiences of pioneer Portuguese women of the 1950s. The second part interweaves other stories of women who arrived in Canada in the 1960s and 1970s with descriptions of their situation and conditions. This may help us to understand better the lives of many immigrant women who came mainly from rural backgrounds and whose lives in a foreign urban setting did not necessarily bring them the happiness and quality of life to which they aspired. In the second part, Idalina and Sofia of Montreal speak of work in the Azores and mainland Portugal, respectively; we are introduced to the stories of Adelaide (Montreal), Zaida (Montreal), Fátima (Toronto), in the context of work in Canada.

Both researchers for this essay constructed population samples from referral networks and collected life histories or 'récits de vie.' They conducted taped interviews with the women in Portuguese about their economic and family situation in Portugal and in Canada, both in Montreal (by Januário and Salvador)[1] and in Toronto (by Marujo). This essay makes no pretence at attempting a comprehensive analysis of the experiences of Portuguese immigrant women. Rather, it seeks to illustrate the unique challenges faced by these women, which have not received the scholarly treatment that they deserve.

Marujo collected her sample of pioneer women in the course of doing research for the book *With Hardened Hands* (Marques and Marujo 1993). She selected fifteen women, all in their sixties and retired, living in Montreal and Toronto, who arrived in Canada during the 1950s. All were of working-class background in terms of previously held occupation and level of formal education. Most came from the Azores and Madeira, with only five coming from mainland Portugal. The islanders and two of the mainlanders had been homemakers, artisans, or non-paid family help in the fields, whereas three of the mainlanders had already held jobs outside the house in an urban setting. All came to join their husbands after at least a year of separation. Marujo collected the story of Fátima, who immigrated in the 1970s, as part of a sample of fifteen Portuguese families for a qualitative research project about parental involvement in children's language maintenance in Toronto (Marujo 1990). It portrays how, for some women, life did not improve with immigration.

The Montreal group of twenty was part of a wider group of eighty immigrant women from four countries of origin (see Januário 1988; Labelle, et al. 1987). These Portuguese women were between eighteen and fifty-five; two-thirds were married, and all were of working-class background (as defined by occupation and education of both spouses). Almost all were from a rural background, although seven of the mainlander women had migrated to an urban setting or to other countries before Canada. Three women were from the Azores, and three from Madeira.[2]

Two Pioneer Women of the 1950s

Lurdes arrived in Toronto in 1954 from Madeira, where she had never worked outside her home. She could sew and embroider ('delicate work,' as she puts it). The couple had just bought a house with the help of the family, and her husband had worked in the hospitality industry. He had read in the newspaper *Diário da Madeira* that 'they' were asking for immigrants to Canada, and he had decided to come 'just for the emotion of travelling' (*só pela emoção de embarcar*): 'I cried many tears, but it wasn't worth anything. I was pregnant with my first child; in spite of that he decided to leave. The day before he embarked, my son was born. They took the baby to church to be baptized, I was too sick to be present. But he was baptized and one day old they took him to the harbour to say goodbye to his father. I had many problems with my husband leaving. I was sick, the baby was sick. I thought I would never be healthy again to see him. He wrote me every week, though, sometimes two letters; at that time he had many things to talk about.'

Lurdes's husband emigrated to work on a farm in Canada but could not adapt to the new country. He lost his job and went to Toronto, where she joined him from Portugal. She did not know that he was unemployed, since he had not told her. She arrived with a baby boy, who celebrated his first birthday on board ship. In recalling her initial disappointment, Lurdes evaluates her life in Canada:

'When I arrived at Toronto railway station, my husband was waiting. I immediately notice how badly dressed he was – no tie, the open collar, the wrinkled clothes. My heart sank – I had never seen him looking as badly dressed. I did not know about his lack of success. He lied to me in his letters. I would have come anyway, since I just wanted to be closer to him. Our life was hard. But we managed to buy a house, started having boarders, and very soon we paid for it. I worked in the factory, cleaned the rooms, did the laundry and the cooking for the men who lived as boarders. It was hard. I missed my family, my work in Madeira, the lovely tablecloths and other embroidery that I made – but if you ask me if I want to go back now – my answer is no. My two children are secondary school teachers, both married with teachers as well. They both speak Portuguese very well, but they are Canadians, they only like Madeira for holidays. I would never go back there. I have my grandchildren and I love them – I would never go away from my family. And I like it here now. After more than forty years one adapts.'

Izilda travelled to Canada in 1953 from Lisbon, where she had worked in a building as a superintendent. It was through her initiative that she and her husband started a little business in Portugal as door-to-door milk distributors. They were young and ambitious and wanted to go to Canada to become rich. He emigrated to work on the railway in Goose Bay, Labrador. She joined him in Canada soon afterwards but was unaware that she could not live with him and had to stay in Montreal. Very soon they understood how she could help him prosper. He sold his co-workers products that they needed, which she sent him from the big city – items such as toothpaste, shaving cream, and warm clothes. It was the beginning of a very successful business career. She learned both French and English out of necessity in the pursuit of better deals. Her new language skills were most useful when she started buying large trucks and other sophisticated machinery needed in Labrador City.

Their commercial activity actually made a significant contribution to the growth of Labrador City. They organized the city's garbage pick-up and landscaping and the cleaning of most of the city's offices. In due course they owned a shopping mall with a restaurant, a motel, and a disco. As Izilda put it: 'My husband and I did not like to have all our eggs in just one basket.' Despite this busy life (they had at one time thirty-seven employees), they had time to travel in winter. They visited several Caribbean islands, travelled to Europe several times, and even visited Angola, looking for sunshine and a warmer climate.

Their daughter chose to live in Toronto after marrying a Torontonian. Izilda's husband died very soon after moving to the 'big city' (Toronto), where they chose to retire and be close to their only child. Their daughter wanted the big, beautiful house that her parents had bought and suggested that her mother buy a condo for herself. So today Izilda spends most of her time at her daughter's home babysitting her grandchildren. The interviewer asked her if she was happy with the choices that she made in life. She stated that she loved her life in Canada with her husband. They had had a hard but very rewarding life. They had made the right decisions and had been economically rewarded. She had developed her potential, and her husband had considered her a partner in everything that he did.

Unfortunately they did not get to enjoy a leisurely life together after retirement. Her untimely widowhood cut short all her dreams of enjoying the fruits of their hard work with her companion. In the end, she was caught between her daughter's need to have her take care of the children and the beautiful condo where she spent little time because she felt too lonely. Portugal had come to mean nothing to her in her sixties, as she had no ties there.

Immigrants of the 1960s and 1970s

Economic Activities in Portugal

Most women in this study immigrated to Canada in the 1960s and 1970s. Half were already married, and most of these had children. Their economic contribution started as single women in Portugal, supplementing the parental family income. After marriage, their contribution to their own family became essential, unless the husband had emigrated. Fifteen of twenty of these women, like most Portuguese immigrants to Canada, lived under Salazar's dictatorship before they left the mainland. Up until the revolution of 1974 they were considered legal and economic dependants of their husbands. Like their husbands, they had little schooling – on average, three or four years. Women were and still are most of the non-paid family help in Portugal because of the work they do in the family farm or plot and private businesses such as shops and restaurants. As men migrated or found salaried work in industry, the women tended to take over the family farm or plot (Brettell 1986; Pina-Cabral 1986).

Most of our respondents, given their rural origin, fitted this pattern. Only five women had remained connected to agriculture after marriage, while they waited to join their husbands in Canada. Already, in pre-revolutionary Portugal, the small farm was on the decline. In the 1960s men emigrated in large numbers from Portugal because of this phenomenon, as well as the colonial wars and the lack of employment in industry, particularly the clothing industry, the main source of industrial work in rural areas. Emigration replaced migration, as 'white collar' jobs in Portugal's urban centres were accessible only to those with schooling and the ability to speak formal Portuguese well.

Among salaried respondents, three single women were factory workers from the rural mainland; two were married factory workers from mainland cities; two were married industrial homeworkers; four artisans were also single women (embroiderer, seamstress, weaver); and four single women were live-in domestics. The conditions and relations of work were marked by the absence of unions, salary discrimination based on sex (the average woman earned half of the median male salary before 1974, two-thirds after that), and few benefits. Patronage relationships determined access to work, and work relations depended on the family status or connections of the worker. Women had to endure personal intrusions in their lives to keep jobs such as those in domestic work. These young women were often not allowed to have a boyfriend and were forced to attend religious services and to keep 'a good reputation.'

Idalina, of Montreal, a woman from the Azores with relatives in Canada, reveals how she obtained her job in a hospital in Ponta Delgada, Azores. Her mother had to share her personal family story with the head nurse in order to obtain her daughter a job. In return, Idalina had to prove that she needed the money earned for necessities: 'At the hospital I was hired faster because my mother told them about being a widow and that I was the eldest child. I also had a brother but he was thirteen and although he was working, his salary did not cover expenses. So the chief nurse was very moved by my mother's situation, and, at the end of fifteen days, she called me to work ... Once I heard from the chief nurse that I should stay home because I really did not need to work because of the way I dressed. That I should give my place to a poor woman! And she threw in my face that she only hired me because I did not have a father; that if it was to feed my expensive habit she would not have hired me!'

As in other less industrialized countries, women in Portugal worked outside the home mainly between the ages of fifteen and twenty-four and tended to leave the formal labour market after marriage or the birth of children. Generally a return to the formal labour market was not the norm, as with the pre-war situation of women in Quebec and the rest of Canada. Almost all respondents who did not emigrate as single women became homeworkers or stayed on as artisans and family help before emigrating. While the artisans waited to join their husbands, their economic activity remained secondary to farm or household activities. The homeworkers, however, contributed substantially to the family budget and speeded up the immigration process, subordinating housework to homework.

Sofia, of Montreal, was an industrial homeworker who manufactured knitted gloves for a factory while her mother-in-law, with whom the couple lived, baked cakes for sale. Sofia had this to say, in 1980, regarding the importance of homework in their household in Portugal: 'It was a poor milieu. It was very rare that women worked, and men did not like it ... They thought it brought contempt at that time. The town of Alcanena could not employ women ten years ago. Those who wanted to work had to go outside, to the town of Minde ... When I made gloves at home, if my mother-in-law had wanted to associate herself to us, *we would have not gone abroad. Perhaps today I would still be doing that.* She was one of those people who made lots of cakes at home. She was very busy. She sold them on the market.'

Economic Activities in Canada

Until the mid-1970s, family reunification was the greatest determinant of Portuguese immigration to Canada. In general, the men arrived first, and the women entered as legal and economic dependants. Canadian immigration practices reinforced the politico-cultural model. Eight of twenty respondents immigrated as single women – three of them to join their families, and the rest as domestics. Women tended to work mainly in factories in Montreal. Our respondents were employed in clothing factories (seven) or started there (fourteen); or as cleaning ladies (ten); or in other services, such as a grocery, bakery, inn, or old people's home (four). There was great mobility between factories and service industries and a marked tendency towards the services as the women learned one of Canada's official languages. This movement meant less security and fewer benefits as workers, given the non-unionization of small enterprises. However, the women earned comparable pay under better working conditions, with more freedom and mobility and less stress.

Working conditions in the clothing industry were characterized by weak unions as well as sexual discrimination in wages and qualifications. This situation was both a cause and a consequence of high turnover in employment, aggravated by the workers' family responsibilities. These sectors were characterized by paternalism,[2] workers' lack of fluency in the official languages, and tensions among workers of Portuguese origin resulting from their concentration in certain factories and slow adjustment to the pace of industrial and piece work. Employers used these tensions to promote competition and productivity.

Adelaide, who had been a factory worker in Portugal, described the situation in a coat factory in Montreal:

I had a nervous breakdown here. I was really in bad shape, I even lost my memory ... I did piecework ... My workmates were very mean towards each other; they did not cheat each other only if they couldn't get away with it. We got stressed. Some of us wanted to do our work well, but there are always those who are not perfectionists. The one who is suffers the most. They were mean to each other, they were jealous of each other. The Portuguese cheat each other a lot. I have complaints mostly about the Portuguese.

In my work, I am the most senior; I showed them how to do the work out of goodness, I gave them my secrets. There are ways of making the work faster, and when you do piece work we must do it faster no matter how, and even at piece work rate, I showed them, do it this way. A couple of them, one from my village, I showed them all my tricks, they owed me so much, yet after a while they started to be mean to me, to sabotage the work, by fooling the ticket system. I did not want to lag behind, so I forced myself to the last drop of blood! From a ticket, they made it look like ten! Sometimes they found a coat with a ticket, and they put in a number and added a zero to it. At the end of the day that made for a lot of tickets!

But my character is not like that, I did not have the courage to do this or to denounce what I saw ... I could have 100 coats ready at the end of the day, and they had 120 by five p.m. But how could that be if I gave it all I could? Sometimes the work was not done by my arms, it was done in my head, I couldn't stand it any more, I was getting lost on the way home ...

I had a rest at home for several months, and when I went back I told them I would no longer work unless I was paid by the hour. The 'bossa,' because she knew my work, did not let me go. After that I was paid by the hour. But that also provoked jealousy, because they [the women to whom she revealed her 'secrets'] wanted the same ... But she did not let them be paid by the hour ...

To come to Canada, I spent the money I had in Portugal. I was so enthusiastic because I really wanted to come to Canada. I gave myself to work too much because I wanted to rebuild my lost savings. By doing piece work, I earned more than my husband at the end of the year!

In industrial homework, as in domestic work, relations of work are individualized; except in hiring, where referrals are important. The absence of unions results in a paternalistic style of negotiation of rights and salaries. Demand for these types of employment, however, was on the increase in Canada at the time of our research because the lack of factory work (Giles and Preston 1996).

There is no doubt that the economic contribution of women to the family economy intensified with immigration. But, for two-thirds of our respondents, this process had already started in Portugal. Research (see Lamphere 1987; Iacovetta 1992) has shown that intensification does not lead to a change of traditional roles in the household in Canada; women continue to do the bulk of child care and housework and change jobs to adjust to the family cycle. The principles of sexual division of labour continue intact, modified by the demands of the new setting and the lack of an extended family. Some of our interviewees responded to the harsh conditions in industry and the demands of motherhood by adopting shift work in coordination with their husbands – one working by day, and the other by evening or night – or by changing from factory to cleaning work and vice-versa.

Sofia worked after her children were born:

> I started work as a cleaning lady because my son left home at about eight or half past eight. I couldn't very well go to the factory at around seven and leave my son at the door. Cleaning [private homes] I could start at nine or half past nine. All I had to do was to stay longer in the afternoon. I worked as a cleaner for two years. The 'madames' lived far, in Côte-Saint-Luc. That was always a problem; I went into domestic service because of my son ... I also left it because of him.
>
> Afterwards, the opposite happened. He was going to school, near home, so I went to work in the factory so that I could come home to give him lunch. He used to finish at three and left at four. But in the meantime my husband arrived, so the child was always supervised. And this because I do not believe in putting my child in a babysitter. That is why I had to do all these contortions, for the good of the child. The child's development is very important. Now I am [an industrial] homeworker like in Portugal. I have been doing this since my daughter was born.

For many, in both Portuguese and Canadian contexts, domestic work was the only possibility, despite initial reluctance expressed by several women because of the low status of this occupation. The married 'Portuguese cleaning lady' was common in urban contexts in both countries, and attempts at legislating their benefits and work conditions were equally difficult to enforce in both countries. 'Living out' dilutes the patronage relations characteristic of the situation of being living-in domestics that some of the women had known in Portugal. This is the case particularly in Canada, with work by the day and for several employers.

Zaida, in Montreal, says that even in Canada such employment retains its paternalistic – in this case, maternalistic – ambivalence:

> I work at my boss's if as if they were my family. She considers me part of the family, and her children share that feeling ... They are so good to me, like a god! When I was sick and I had to have an operation, they needed me, but they waited for me. They are always afraid that I am not eating enough or tell me to leave earlier because my husband is waiting for me. What they eat, I eat, there is no difference. If they eat in the dining-room, I eat there too; if they eat in the kitchen, so do I, there is not difference whatsoever. If I weren't treated that way, I don't think I would be working there, believe me.
>
> It's not that I feel inferior, but I could not stand that people treat me like an inferior, that would go against my values. I don't do that to anybody, and I wouldn't accept that it would be done to me. My son got married, and they went to my son's wedding, as if they were part of my family, and they felt the same. I would like to find another type of work, maybe at the hospital, but I could not leave them unless they did not need my services any longer; they tell me they hope I never leave them ...
>
> When I started working there they told me I would start at half past eight and I would finish at half past two, [but] I start at nine and finish at four because of the children; she told me to, I don't like to come home after four. I work longer hours for her, and she pays me less than the other lady [from a different ethnic group]. It's hard to believe, but it's true!
>
> I prefer this type of work to working in a factory, store, or anything else. When the bosses or managers are there, you really have to work ... The way I work is completely different; I know what I have to do, I do it. If sometimes I have to go to the doctor's or something else, I called the boss and I tell her I have to leave at such and such a time and that's all.'

Another thread of continuity is between artisanal and industrial work. Several respondents, Lurdes among them, had learned sewing either as preparation for married life or to work as seamstresses/artisans. This skill served them well in Canada and facilitated their learning to operate industrial machines. Economic disruption was experienced by women, such as Lurdes, who were non-paid family help and artisans in rural settings or housekeepers in the city.

Fátima of Toronto, like the majority of Portuguese women in Canada, was born in the Azores. Fátima's story illustrates how a rural origin and a strong patriarchal ideology[3] in the household can impede integration and seriously impair the quality of life in the new country.

Fátima was born in the Azores and immigrated to Toronto to join her husband when she was eighteen. She left all her family behind. She and her husband had never visited the 'old country' since their arrival in Canada. Her husband works in construction, and she works in a factory.

At the time of the interview the couple had four children aged twenty, sixteen, fourteen, and eight. Her eldest daughter did not finish grade twelve and works in the same factory as Fátima. Her sixteen-year-old daughter dropped out of school and idles her time away at home. Her fourteen-year-old son has a learning problem and is in a special education class. Her eight-year-old girl does not understand any Portuguese and cries often when her father talks to her because she cannot understand what he says. The children never took Portuguese-language classes, and the parents never went to any classes in English as a second language. The father understands English words but cannot make a sentence because he has spent most of his work life with Italian bosses and Italian or Portuguese co-workers.

Fátima misses her family in the Azores, especially her sisters, but she would not like to go back. They were very poor, and she does not miss her hard life there, where they worked in the fields as non-paid family help. When her mother died, she was not able to go to the funeral because of the cost of travel. She would like to have English lessons, but her husband will not allow her to leave the house in the evening to take them. All her conversations with her children are in English, the only language they speak fluently. She would like to learn more and be able to understand her children. She asked the interviewer: 'Could you please ask my husband to let me attend English classes? He doesn't listen to me in spite of my begging for all these years.'

She obviously feared her husband, who did not listen to her requests. Fátima said that she loved Canada; she loved to go to the malls with her children and spend time window-shopping. She regretted not having a driver's licence, but her husband did not think that she needed to learn how to drive (although they own two vehicles – a van and a smaller car). Fátima's children seemed to love her very much and to fear their father. She could not, however, go to their schools and keep herself informed of their progress, in part because of her long work days and lack of language skills, but mainly because she did not have permission to leave the house. Fátima seemed to accept her situation.

Conclusion

The greater participation of Portuguese immigrant women in the Canadian economy in comparison to Portugal can be explained by the availability of jobs and the high salary rates, as well as by individuals' greater immersion in a monetary economy and the need to settle. Women enter the labour force as mothers and spouses, and it is as such that they justify their role as workers. As in Portugal, their economic contribution becomes more crucial in the urban setting.

Emigration to Canada is not only a substitute for rural–urban migration or a process of continuity. It is also a leap in time, historical development, and cultural space. It is as if married women who migrate from a Portuguese rural setting to a Canadian urban space skip a generation in time. They leave social relations and extended family behind, to live in relative isolation.

The lives of Portuguese-Canadian women are not very different from those of Italian and other first-generation immigrant women who arrived before them and who had to make a transition from a rural to an urban setting (Iacovetta 1992). A second generation of female professionals is slowly starting to develop, while the Portuguese cleaning woman has become a stereotype. To be a 'cleaning lady' is, for many women, one choice among a number of low-paying jobs. They can take their children to school before starting their work, and they can be home to welcome them to the familiar smells of a cooked meal. To them as women befalls the task of remembering and re/membering the culture and the family on foreign soil (Di Leonardo 1987; Giles 1997). Portuguese-Canadian women thereby help maintain strong families; children tend not to leave home until they get married, and grandchildren are supposed to receive care from their grandparents, especially the grandmother. A third generation of Portuguese Canadians owes its skill in Portuguese to grandmothers who cared for it, as part of the 'kin work' performed without any remuneration, as described by Di Leonardo (1987). 'Dollar stores' and shopping malls are a paradise for many women who find in them a substitute for the village square; the malls are a meeting place where they can chat with friends. Bargain stores satisfy, in a harmless way, the inevitable consumerism that they have grown to enjoy.

As we mentioned above, women who left the 'old country' do not feel the desire to relocate there permanently. They love holidays in Portugal, the good weather, the familiar language of their ancestors. But they will not exchange it for the economic sense of security given by Canadian pensions and social services and a health care system that they learn to appreciate as they get older. Above all, they will not go back because they value the company of the children whom they brought from Portugal or who were born in Canada. Those offspring grow up and belong in Canada, where they continue the processes that the mothers initiated in the first generation.

NOTES

Ilda Januário wishes to thank Maria Margarida Salvador, currently a teacher and a graduate student in archaeology living in Portugal, for permission to use the interviews that she collected for a project directed by Professors Micheline Labelle and Deirdre Meintel, Department of Sociology, Université du Québec à Montréal (UQAM).

1 Ours is the first formal research or the Portuguese women who settled in Montreal in this period. We used the referral method, which ensures better data because of the higher likelihood of establishing the level of trust required to get the women to talk freely in a single interview. It also produced a higher rate of mainlander women in this research and fewer of the more marginalized and oppressed women. Many of these would have been from the Azores, one of the more isolated regions of Portugal, with a strong tradition of immigration to North America (Da Rosa and Trigo 1994).

2 In these situations, the boss or the contractor, working alone or with his spouse, is also the supervisor. These highly personalized situations may create an ambivalence, where harassment may alternate with bestowing of gifts and favours. Workers are encouraged to negotiate individually with the boss

and to break ranks. This ambivalence in work relations can easily be turned against co-workers. See also Teal 1985 and Gannage 1986.
3 Menteil (1993) explains that, from an anthropological point of view, patriarchy is a specific form of social organization in which power and the distribution of economic resources favour the older male(s) of the household, to whom women and younger males are subject. Patriarchal ideology can permeate family and work relations even where patriarchy is not a viable form of social organization.

REFERENCES

Aguiar, M. 1994. 'The School and Immigration Histories of Women from the Island of São Miguel in the Azores Region of Portugal.' MA thesis, University of Toronto.
Anderson, G., and Davis, J.C. 1990. 'Portuguese Women in Canada.' In D. Higgs , ed., *Portuguese Migration in Global Perspective*, 136–44. Toronto: Multicultural History Society of Ontario.
Anderson, G., and Higgs, D. 1976. *A Future to Inherit: The Portuguese Communities of Canada*. Toronto: McClelland and Stewart.
Brettell, C. 1982. *We Have Already Cried So Many Tears: The Stories of Three Portuguese Migrant Women*. Cambridge, Mass.: Schenkman Publishing.
– 1986. *Men Who Migrate and Women Who Wait: Population and History in a Portuguese Parish*. Princeton, NJ: Princeton University Press.
Cock, J. 1980. *Maids and Madams: A Study in the Politics of Exploitation*. Johannesburg: Ravan Press.
Da Rosa, V.M.P., and Trigo, S. 1994. *Azorean Emigration: A Preliminary Overview*. Porto: Fernando Pessoa University Press.
Demers, S. 1987. 'Émigration, famille, travail et communauté : Rôle caché des femmes portugaises de Ottawa-Hull.' MA thesis, Université d'Ottawa.
Di Leonardo, M. 1987. 'The Female World of Cards and Holidays: Women, Families and the Work of Kinship.' Signs 12 no. 3: 440–53.
Gannage, C. 1986. *Double Day, Double Bind: Women Garment Workers*. Toronto: Women's Press.
Giles, W. 1997. 'Re/membering the Portuguese Household in Toronto: Culture, Contradictions and Resistance.' *Women's Studies International Forum* 20 no. 3: 387–97.
Giles, W., and Januário, I. 1987. 'The Lone Woman: The Migration of Portuguese Single Women to Montreal and London.' *Canadian Woman Studies/Les cahiers de la femme* 8 no. 2: 43–6.
Giles, W., and Preston, V. 1996. 'The Domestication of Women's Work: A Com-

parison of Chinese and Portuguese Immigrant Women Homeworkers.' *Studies in Political Economy* 51: 147–81.

Grosner, L.B.B. 1991. 'Azorean Portuguese Women in London, Ontario: The Construction of Gender.' MA thesis, University of Western Ontario.

Iacovetta, F. 1992. *Such Hardworking People: Italian Immigrants in Postwar Toronto*. Montreal: McGill-Queen's University Press.

Januário, I. 1988. 'Les activités économiques des femmes immigrantes portugaises au Portugal et à Montréal à travers les récits de vie.' MSc thesis, Université de Montréal.

Labelle, M., Turcotte, G., Kempeneers, M., and Meintel, D. 1987. *Histoire d'immigrées. Itinéraires d'ouvrières, colombiennes, grecques, haitiennes et portugaises de Montréal*. Montreal: Les Éditions du Boréal Express.

Lamphere, L. 1987. *From Working Mothers to Working Daughters: Immigrant Women in a New England Industrial Community*. Ithaca, NY: Cornell University Press.

Marques, D., and Marujo, M. 1993. *With Hardened Hands: A Pictorial History of Portuguese Immigration to Canada in the 1950s*. Etobicoke: New Leaf.

Marques, D., and Medeiros, J. 1978. *Imigrantes portugueses: 25 anos no Canadá*. Toronto: Movimento Comunitário Português.

Marujo, M. 1990. 'Parental Attitudes towards Language Maintenance among Portuguese Families in Toronto.' Qualifying research paper. Department of Curriculum, Ontario Institute for Studies in Education.

– 1996. 'Mulheres portuguesas dos anos 50: Retratos.' In J.M. Lopes and M.S.P. Lopes, eds., *Uma longa viagem: História da emigração portuguesa para o Canadá*, 23–6. Toronto: OISE Press.

Meintel, D. 1993. *Étudier 'les femmes': Perspectives théoriques*. Montreal: UQAM.

Neal, R., and Neale, V. 1987. 'As Long as You Know How to Do Housework: Portuguese-Canadian Women and the Office Cleaning Industry in Toronto.' *Canadian Women's Studies Journal* 16 no. 1: 39–41.

Noivo, E. 1992. 'Family Life-Worlds and Social Injuries: Three Generations of Portuguese-Canadians.' Doctoral dissertation, Université de Montréal.

Nunes, F. 1986. 'Portuguese-Canadian Women: Problems and Prospects.' *Polyphony* 8 nos. 1–2: 61–6.

Pina-Cabral, J. de. 1986. *Sons of Adam, Daughters of Eve: The Peasant Worldview of Alto Minho*. Oxford: Clarendon Press.

Rollins, J. 1985. *Between Women: Domestics and Their Employers*. Philadelphia: Temple University Press.

Teal, G. 1985. 'The Organization of Production and the Heterogeneity of the Working-Class: Occupation, Gender and Ethnicity among Clothing Workers in Quebec.' Doctoral dissertation, McGill University.

8

Value Conflicts and Cultural Adjustment in North America

ONÉSIMO TEOTÓNIO ALMEIDA

In 1986, I was invited to give a keynote address at a conference on the Portuguese community of Ontario, held in Toronto.[1] The organizers suggested that perhaps I could say something based on my experience with the Portuguese communities in the United States, not only in New England but also in California. Having written this essay with a particular Portuguese community in mind, it is not without hesitation that I submit a 'talk among family' to be reprinted in this volume. What follows is essentially my address with minor revisions, additions, and notations of factual changes.

The Portuguese communities in Canada are at least a hundred years more recent than those of the United States. However, this may be their biggest difference. At the deep level of cultural structures they seem to experience a similar struggle for adjustment and adaptation as people mostly of rural origin adapt to an urban, industrial society and as they try to reconcile southern European/Iberian, Catholic values and an Anglo-American world.

Fully aware of the complexities involving generalizations about cultural groups, with the inherent risks of stereotyping, I offer a broad look at the Portuguese communities in Canada based on my decades of extensive contacts with the Portuguese communities in the United States and my long-standing attempt to understand Portuguese culture. Thus the impressionistic observations in the first part of this essay are at least recurrent enough to confirm my sense that they run deep in our culture; there is indeed common ground. I attempt, second, to support these observations with others by researchers studying the Portuguese in the Americas and Europe. A basic assumption of this work is that one can talk about cultural backgrounds and that it is possible to detect the underlying structure of a value system and the hierarchy of values of a cultural group, however generalized this may be.[2] Third, I speculate about the future of the Portuguese on this continent.

A Caveat

The more I read about a group such as the Portuguese, be it in writings from outsiders (most of them non-Portuguese) or insiders (the Portuguese themselves), and the more contact I have with the Portuguese not only in Portugal, in the Azores, or in Madeira, but also in immigrant communities in the United States, Canada, Bermuda, France, and Venezuela, the more I become convinced of the existence of some basic values shared by the majority of the Portuguese. I say the 'majority,' for I do not believe that there exist homogeneous cultural groups. Of course there are differences among Portuguese, some of them quite significant. Who would deny that there are differences between the *lisboetas* and the *transmontanos* or the *açorianos*? But even within one of these groups one finds distinctions. Among the Azoreans, for instance, there are the *micaelenses*, who are distinct from the *picarotos*, and both in turn differ form the *terceirenses*.

The point is that one can go on finding differences until one reaches the individuality of each member of the group. But that happens only if we compare the elements of a group with each other. If we take the group as a whole and compare it with another group taken as a whole, it is then that we find the similarities shared by the members of each group. It is only when we compare the Spaniards as a group with the Portuguese that the differences between a *transmontano* and an *algarvio* become minimal and often unimportant.

By the same token, if we compare the Iberian peoples, taken as a unity, with the Germans, we will find quite a few striking differences. I recall here Roger Brown (1958: 365), the Harvard psycholinguist, who said: 'Sometimes a college student who has been talked out of his stereotypes in a psychology course is amazed to discover on his first trip abroad, that the Germans really are different from the Italians.'[3]

Common Ground

However, enough of these general considerations. Let me use a few lines taken from a newspaper clipping from my collection. It is from a story reporting a study of a Portuguese immigrant community made by a group of social scientists. As the reporter puts it, the Portuguese are discreet, not given to delinquent habits or to xenophobia, and seem absent from all the national debates on immigration. Lately, the Portuguese have joined forces to defend their language and culture, but their leaders have no visible profile outside the community. They are 'good immigrants,' and they have dozens of organizations and associations of all sorts. No other immigrant community has produced as many clubs, most of them mainly for soccer and religious feasts.

However, the reporter goes on to note, the young generation rejects such organizations, as they often do the Portuguese language and culture. The adults feel themselves divided between Portugal and their new immigrant home and visit Portugal as often as they can; but their children shy away from their past and the small world of their parents. They do not keep up ties, nor are they interested in bringing to the Portuguese community their own experience, which could both help to promote unification of its interests and give it visibility in the country at large, in the process attracting attention to some of its needs.

Now you are going to think that this must have been taken out of the *Toronto Star*, the *Globe and Mail*, or a French-Canadian newspaper. Wrong. Your next guess would be the *New Bedford Standard Times* or the *Providence Journal*, perhaps the *Boston Globe*, or even the *New York Times*. None of the above. It is French, yes, but from Paris. The newspaper was *Le Monde*, and the group described was the Portuguese community in France. But it certainly looks as if *Le Monde* is talking about us in Toronto or in the United States.[4]

Three Viewpoints

This false supposition serves to confirm my earlier statement that it is legitimate to speak about generic (in the sense of widespread) characteristics of a cultural group. Countless people familiar with the Portuguese, not to mention the Portuguese themselves, still would accept as roughly accurate the following characterization by the Portuguese anthropologist Jorge Dias in 1959:

> To describe the traditional national character in a phrase, we can say that the Portuguese is a mixture of dreamer and man of action, or better still, an active dreamer, who has a certain practical and realistic basis. Portuguese activity does not have its roots in cold-blooded will but is nurtured on imagination and is deeply reflective. They share with the Spanish the

aristocratic disdain for small-minded gain, for pure utilitarianism and comfort, and the paradoxical taste for ostentation of wealth and luxury. But they do not have a strong abstract ideal like the Spanish, or a pronounced mystic tendency. The Portuguese are above all, profoundly human, sensitive, loving and generous without being weak. They do not like to cause suffering, and avoid conflicts, but can be violent and cruel when pride is hurt ...

There is, in the Portuguese, an enormous capacity for adaptation to ideas and people, but this does not imply lack of personality ...

They do not have the exuberance and noisy spontaneous joy of the other Mediterranean peoples. They are more inhibited because of their great sense of the ridiculous and fear of the opinion of others. They are, like the Spanish, strongly individualistic, but have a profound basis of humanitarian feeling. The Portuguese do not have a strong sense of humor, but a critical and mocking spirit which can be sarcastic and destructive.[5]

To preclude the possibility of misunderstanding, let me say here that the great Portuguese ethnologist Leite de Vasconcelos (1958), in a three-volume work on Portuguese cultural traits and manifestations, noted that studies had shown that Portuguese children were as intelligent as their American, Belgian, and British peers. But he observed that a particular study showed that while they actually ranked higher than the American, Belgian, and British children in verbal and abstract intelligence, their practical intelligence, where long periods of concentration were necessary, was not as good. Portuguese children were quick in reaction, but worse at keeping their attention fixed for long periods. Accordingly, the Portuguese were quick in comprehension but showed little persistence in sticking to one thing. In Portugal the impartial spirit of inquiry has been rare; people have preferred to be either for or against something. The Portuguese, a poetic people who have considered themselves amorous, have liked to succeed without effort and to shine before their friends. Leite de Vasconcelos also observed that their lively intelligence was ruined by emotion and sentiment.

Although he deemed the Portuguese people as a whole to be gentle, sociable, and quiet, Vasconcelos also believed that irony, disenchantment, sadness, *saudades* (a melancholy yearning and nostalgia), and individualism were characteristic of them. Their volitional characteristics include patience, passivity, fatalism, a desire for profit, carelessness, and neglectfulness. Foreigners thought the Portuguese a hospitable, smiling, and docile people who worked as little as possible to make easy money and gain a superficial sense of importance. While northern Portuguese were hardworking and serious (at least more so than their compatriots), everywhere there was a non-European sense of time. Vasconcelos also noted that other observers added to the lot of national defects parasitism, extreme credulity coupled with a certain fatalism, megalomania; moral insensitivity, a spirit of indecision coupled with a proclivity to contradictory actions, and a spirit of routine coupled with a love of novelty and change. Finally, he also found that since the sixteenth century our fellow countrymen had a strong tendency to consider anything foreign, particularly French, better than anything indigenous, and were consequently imitative.[6]

A foreigner, Paul Descamps, does not seem to be off the mark when, commenting on some Portuguese cultural traits, he asserts that the Portuguese are lacking not in initiative but in perseverance. He thinks that they have no sense of time or of the consequences of their actions. Although he detects a tendency towards anarchic individualism, he concludes that the Portuguese are 'unstable communitarians rather than true individualists': their main bonds of social solidarity are based on family, clan, and patronage.[7]

These three portraits differ in many ways, but they overlap in a remarkable number of characteristics. It goes without saying that none of those characteristics need be linked to genetics. There are many powerful theories that have been circulating for a long time which offer plausible reasons for their existence. Some of them reach back to the Greeks. Aristotle, for one, attributed to the Mediterranean sun and pleasant climate a strong power over the emotions of the region's people. But we do not have to get into such explanations at this moment.[8] It suffices to stress here that no single theory can account for the diversity of cultures. Attempts at identifying the differences aim simply at mapping them out. One can often identify connections and underlying structures. In some cases it may seem possible to glimpse the roots of a particular characteristic of a culture.

'A Great Coherence'

After extensive research in various regions of Portugal, some contemporary Portuguese anthropologists have found 'a great coherence' in the Iberian world. In a debate following a conference on Iberian identity held at the University of California, Berkeley, in which the Portuguese anthropologists João de Pina-Cabral and Rui Feijó participated, Pina-Cabral stated: 'I am convinced that if we look at the different ways in which people organize their lives, we could find something that would amount to an Iberian ethnographic region ... I think it is important that the Iberian Peninsula, the Portuguese Atlantic Islands, the Balearics, the Languedoc, and the French Pyrenees are all areas that, from a sociological point of view, present great coherence. This is something which people who, in Portugal, are concerned with regionality, such as Rui Feijó or myself, cannot ever forget.'

Rui Feijó responded: 'We came to look for Iberian identity, and we came out with an idea that there are different levels and different meanings of identity in Iberia, and this is quite important. But if we have come up with this idea of diversity, Iberia still stands, as João de Pina-Cabral was saying, as something which might be profitably considered as a whole – not separate as Spain and Portugal – for further comparative study.'[9]

The important fact here is the consistency of the portrait made of us as a group – one that depicts us as having similar cultural traits – because, if accurate, it may be some consequences in our lives as we become part of a new culture outside Iberia. Indeed, it is perfectly fine to enjoy the sun, spend all one's free time with friends; not be a slave to time (*gozar a vida*, as we say), and so forth, as long as one accepts the consequences of such a style of life. Back home in Portugal, it is easier to do so, since this is a shared ideal; but in a foreign land, an excessive adherence to such alleged cultural habits may hamper us as a whole. It may prevent us from attaining the objectives in life that most of us consider important. If the need to adapt to the new culture (for example, new patterns of work, concepts of time, possibilities for family life in North American contexts) is understood by the Portuguese immigrants immediately on their arrival in the United States or Canada – as represented by the (positive) stereotype of the hard-working Portuguese – other necessary adaptations are not so easily understood.

One example: today's societies, particularly technologically advanced ones such as Canada's, demand that their members, if they want to succeed, attain a high level of education. Personal advancement is accomplished through dedicated study and hard work, activities that are incompatible with the spending of evening after evening chatting with friends or playing cards at the local club. But since education is finally becoming a priority among many Portuguese families,[10] and a route that many young people and even many adults have lately chosen to accept, let me point out one area where our cultural habits have not allowed us to advance very far.

One of the characteristics of modern[11] societies is that individuals join associations according to their specific interests. The interests of such groups are fostered by collective action. Thus objectives that are beyond the powers of the individual are attained through the collective efforts of the group. Unfortunately, this is a weakness of ours if we compare our efforts to those of other cultural groups. We seem to be able to join efforts in causes that strongly shake our emotions: religious events, sports, feasts, and fund-raising for victims of tragedies or diseases that produce outpourings of sympathy. When our emotional side gets activated, we experience intense moments of togetherness.

Yet if the event or the cause lasts too long, we are not able to keep our emotions aroused. When the unifying emotion is gone, the crowd breaks up into smaller and smaller groups, which then work at counter-purposes to one another. Therefore, when a project requires persistent work over a long span of time and results are not immediately visible; or when the cause itself does not continue to inspire strong emotions such as in supporting a local political candidate or working to improve the educational level of a particular group; or when the final objectives are seen as ethereal, then the Portuguese fail to gather enough interested people to carry out the task – that is, if it gets started at all.[12]

During the revolutionary period in Portugal after 1974, someone said that if you have two Portuguese you have three political parties – a line similar to one that I used a few years ago as the title of an article for a new Portuguese newspaper in California, where there already existed a small and rather weak Portuguese newspaper. Instead of joining efforts to make a single, stronger paper, one group had decided to create a new one. The title of my column was: 'Where There Is One Portuguese Newspaper, Let There Be Two.' The seeming clairvoyance of this line became clear a few years later when the 'new' newspaper split in two.

I am sure that this is a familiar phenomenon in Canada. To figure out how telling this example is, just count how many Portuguese newspapers there are in Toronto alone. Or take a look at the program of an exhibit on the 'Portuguese Canadian Press in a Multicultural Society,' which took place at the John P. Robarts Library, University of Toronto, in 1995. Twenty-five newspapers, six magazines, and twenty-two bulletins were appearing regularly in Canada in that year.[13]

We Portuguese are very much affected by our emotions. It is difficult for us to keep cool during the small incidents that always arise in social life. Instead of controlling our reactions and thinking of long-range objectives, we feel that we must react, that we must straighten things out right away and call people by the names they deserve. Then we join with the few who agree with us and proceed to form still another organization, which, once formed, will consume the energies of its members in cold or open war with the other existing groups. And so time goes on. And so energies are wasted. And so we lose opportunities that could benefit us. Once in a while we stop to look at the score and become frustrated. We accuse everybody else of not doing anything and then get together in conferences to talk about how we can and should change things. But usually such conferences are momentary traces. After all the enthusiasm and the earnest celebration of our togetherness, we go right back to our old destructive habits.

Assimilation Ahead?

But none of this has to be. In fact, already many things are changing. The children of the immigrants from the 1950s and 1960s are changing the scenery. Both in the United States and in Canada there are groups working to overcome these pitfalls of our adjustment to urban and modern life. There are organizations that have come a long way and are now gaining significant influence in the larger communities of which they are a part. In the United States, these include Centers of Assistance to the Immigrants (such as the ones in Fall River, New Bedford, and Cambridge), the Luso-American Education Foundation in California, the Portuguese-American Business Association of Southeastern New England, and the Portuguese-American Scholarship Foundation.[14] In Canada, the proliferation of social, civic, and cultural organizations is also encouraging: the Portuguese-Canadian National Congress, the Alliance of Portuguese Clubs and Associations of Ontario, the Federation of Portuguese-Canadian Businessmen and Professionals, and the Chambre du Commerce Portugais du Québec are just a few examples. A visible and growing trend is towards unification of the once parochial organizations. We Portuguese are, in general, a very traditional people, and there is nothing wrong with that. But if we choose to emigrate, for whatever reasons, we must also be willing to change in ways that are going to better our chances and increase our opportunities to fulfill our human needs and desires. The choice is never to change merely for the sake of change. It is not even necessarily a matter of changing aspects of culture that, considered individually and per se, are 'inferior' to those of the new culture.[15]

It is simply a matter of realizing that in a new cultural context some very basic elements of our culture have inevitably changed (and I am not speaking only about snow and incredibly low temperatures). In these new contexts, some of our old ways – as good as they may be in another cultural context – may even have detrimental effects and inhibit attainment of some long-range goals that we, as human beings, consider valuable. We must be rational enough, sometimes, to put our very lively emotions and those little tricks that give us very small victories over our peers into parentheses, so that we may better ourselves in the long run. I hope that we may deepen our understanding of our collective cultural traits, not in order to downgrade our ethnic group but to improve it. Ronald Inglehart (1997: 19) said that 'an awareness of the fact that deep-rooted values are not easily changed is essential to any realistic and effective program for social change.' The advice of Socrates – 'Know thyself' – remains for us a potent admonition.

Conclusion

The anthropologist Esthelie Smith has called the Portuguese-American communities 'the invisible minority,' capturing sharply their discrete presence outside the strong world of their working and family life. A survey of the writings on three Portuguese communities in Canada confirms my long-held impression that the same could be said about the Portuguese-Canadian communities. Recently, *L'Européen* dedicated the main feature of one of its editions to the Portuguese in France, giving it the front-cover title 'Les Portugais de France. Une intégration réussie. Une fierté retrouvée' (*The Portuguese of France. An Achieved Integration. A Recovered Pride*). The opening paragraph quotes an unnamed French minister as having called 'invisible' the 800,000 Portuguese in France.[16] Since it is unlikely that he read Esthelie Smith, the convergence of opinion seems to confirm the main contention of this essay – that there is 'a great coherence' in the world of Portuguese communities outside Portugal. If that is the case, we have now one more reason to hope that the signs of a successful integration and of a recovered pride that are already visible in the Portuguese communities

of Canada and the United States are confirmation that they are following the path of the Portuguese in France.

NOTES

1 24 October 1986.
2 This used to be looked on with suspicion. Things have changed with the
   publication of books such as Geert Hofstede's *Culture's Consequences: Inter-*
   national Differences in Work-Related Values, which argues that 'people carry
   "mental programs" which are developed in the family in early childhood
   and reinforced in schools and organizations, and that these mental programs
   contain a component of national culture. They are most clearly expressed in
   the different values that predominate among people from different countries' (1984: 11). Charles Hampden-Turner and Fons Trompenaars (1993)
   state that in a 'survey of 15,000 executives we found that culture of origin is
   the most important determinant of values. In any culture, a deep structure of
   beliefs is the invisible hand that regulates economic activity. These cultural
   preferences, or values, are the bedrock of national identity and the source of
   economic strengths – and weaknesses' (1993: 4). Obviously these authors
   refer to trends and statistically significant patterns.
      No culture is uniform, and no value is held across the board by every sin-
   gle member of a cultural group. No culture forms a harmonious, cohesive
   whole, nor are its values static. No reference to 'culture' and 'values' in this
   essay should be understood as support for any sort of essentialism. Postmodern discourse tends to emphasize internal diversity, contestation, conflict, negotiation, and so on, sometimes in an extreme form, as if throwing
   the baby out with the bath water. It is precisely against this other extreme
   that I feel that it is still legitimate to refer to the underlying and shared values of a particular culture.
3 Collective names such as 'Portuguese,' 'French,' and 'Italians,' may not be
   rigorous, scientific terms, but we still use them, even though with a grain
   of salt – not just in our daily language, and not only the non-scientists.
   Social scientists, for instance, use them frequently. William Watson, of
   McGill University, author of *Globalization and the Meaning of Canadian Life*
   (Toronto: University of Toronto Press, 1998), wrote recently in an article
   entitled 'Identity in My Own Back Yard': 'It's not very sophisticated, I
   know, to categorize people according to the weather they have to cope
   with. But it's how we southern Canadians categorize the Inuit, Califor-
   nians, Congolese, Jamaicans, Siberians, Arabs and many others' (Mont-

real *Gazette*, 11 January 1999). In regard to the Portuguese, for instance, I have written extensively against attempts to construct an essentialist version of Portuguese culture. See, for instance, my (1985) 'Filosofia Portuguesa – Alguns Equívocos.'

4 From different angles, and different political viewpoints, various studies of the Portuguese in North America seem to agree on the overall characteristics of these communities. See, for instance, Huff 1989; McLaren 1990; and Feldman-Bianco 1992.

5 Jorge Dias, 'Os Elementos Fundamentais da Cultura Portuguesa,' *in Actas do colóquio internacional de estudos luso-brasileiros*, translated by Richard Robinson in his *Contemporary Portugal* (London: George Allen & Unwin, 1979), 24.

I am always hesitant when dealing with generalizations such as this. I take them globally rather than literally, but I cannot reject them outright, for, as impressionistic as they are, just like an impressionistic painting they still capture a portrait. For a theoretical justification of this position, see my study (1997) 'On Distinguishing Cultural Identity from National Character.'

6 Vasconcelos 1958. These findings by the noted Portuguese ethnologist are scattered throughout his voluminous study. I use here the English synopsis made by Richard Robinson in *Contemporary Portugal*, 24–5.

7 In Robinson, *Contemporary Portugal*, 25.

8 For the particular case of the Azoreans, who constitute the largest part of the Portuguese community in Ontario, or for that matter in Canada, I have attempted a detailed analysis of their culture in 'A Profile of the Azorean' (1980).

9 João Pina-Cabral, 'Sociocultural Differentiation and Regional Identity in Portugal,' in Herr and Polt (1989), 230. Rui Feijó, 'Socio-cultural Differentiation and Regional Identity in Portugal and Spain,' ibid., 231.

10 Education became a priority in Portugal soon after the revolution of 1974. Curiously this emphasis occurred much sooner and is more widespread than among the Portuguese communities in the United States or Canada.

11 Some authors prefer to use the adjectives 'industrialized' or 'capitalist.' 'Modern,' however, seems to be a broader, more neutral term.

12 I have expanded on this topic in 'The Portuguese and Politics: A Look at the Cultural Roots of a Distant Relationship,' a paper that I presented at a conference on Portuguese-American communities and political intervention, sponsored by the Portuguese American Leadership Council of the United States (PALCUS), at the University of Massachusetts, Dartmouth, in the autumn of 1996.

13 See the exhibit catalogue *Portuguese Canadian Press in a Multicultural Society* (Marujo, Teixeira, and Marques 1995). For further information on the Portuguese press in Canada, see Teixeira 1999.

14 As if to confirm what I stated above, two of these associations have ceased to exist, and another is struggling to survive. Two promising ones, however, have emerged – PALCUS, in Washington, DC, aimed at uniting the community nation-wide for political intervention, and the Portuguese-American Scholarship Foundation.

15 Even if North America is composed of many cultures, from the point of view of the Portuguese immigrant it is not the indifferences that are striking, but their similarities vis-à-vis the culture in which he or she was brought up.

16 *L'Européen* says that the Portuguese in France 'make France' (font France) in their own way, but without saying a word – so discrete that in 1986 the Commission for the Reform of the Nationality Code did not include them in the public debate: none of their leaders had been invited. *L'Européen*, 13 May 1998, 16 and 18.

REFERENCES

Almeida. O.T. 1980. 'A Profile of the Azorean.' In D. Macedo, ed., *Issues in Portuguese Bilingual Education*, 113–64. Cambridge, Mass.: National Assessment and Dissemination Center.
– 1985. 'Filosofia portuguesa – alguns equívocos.' *Cultura, história e filosofia* 4: 219–55.
– Forthcoming. 'On Distinguishing Cultural Identity from National Character.' In F. Brinkius and S. Talmor, eds., *Memory, History and Critique: European Identity and the Millennium*, CD-ROM. Cambridge, Mass.: MIT Press.
Brown, R. 1958. *Words and Things*. Glencoe, Ill.: Free Press.
Feldman-Bianco, B. 1992. 'Multiple Layers of Time and Space: The Construction of Class, Ethnicity, and Nationalism among Portuguese Immigrants,' *Annals/New York Academy of Sciences*, 145–74.
Hampden-Turner, C., and Trompenaars, F. 1993. *The Seven Cultures of Capitalism. Value Systems for Creating Wealth in the United States, Britain, Japan, Germany, France, Sweden, and the Netherlands*. London: Piatkus.
Herr, R., and J.H.R. Polt. 1989. *Iberian Identity. Essays on the Nature of Identity in Portugal and Spain*. Berkeley, Calif.: Institute of International Studies.
Hofstede, G. 1984. *Culture's Consequences: International Differences in Work-Related Values*. Beverly Hills: Sage Publications.
Huff, T.E. 1989. 'Education and Ethnicity in Southeastern Massachusetts.'

Issues in Planning and Policymaking. Bulletin (New England Board of Higher Education), Aug.: 2–7.

Inglehart, R. 1997 *Modernization and Postmodernization. Cultural, Economic, and Political Change in 43 Societies.* Princeton, NJ: Princeton University Press.

McLaren, P. 1990. 'The Antistructure of Resistance: Culture and Politics in Toronto High School.' In F. Manning and J.M. Philibert, eds., *Customs in Conflict: The Anthropology of a Changing World*, 387–412. Lewiston, NY: Broadview Press.

Malaurie, G., and P.O. François, eds. 1998. 'La fierté retrouvée des Portugais de France.' *L'Européen* (13–19 May): 16, 27.

Marujo, M., Teixeira, C., and Marques, D. 1995. *Portuguese Canadian Press in a Multicultural Society.* Exhibit Catalogue. Toronto: Robarts Library, University of Toronto.

Robinson, R. 1979. *Contemporary Portugal.* London: George Allen & Unwin.

Teixeira, C. 1999. 'Portuguese.' In P.R. Magocsi, ed., *Encyclopedia of Canada's Peoples*, 1075–83. Toronto: University of Toronto Press.

Vasconcelos, J.L. de 1958. *Etnografia portuguesa. Tentame de sistematização.* 3 vols. Lisbon: Imprensa Nacional.

PART THREE

LANGUAGE AND ETHNIC IDENTITY

9

Two Decades of Heritage Language Education

RENA HELMS-PARK

Support and Indifference

This chapter[1] examines instruction in Portuguese as a heritage language within the Canadian public school system at a time when patterns of inter-generational loss of heritage language have become very clear.[2] It looks at, first, the profound ambivalence about such instruction; second, the status of heritage language education in Ontario and Quebec; third, research on the benefits of such instruction; and fourth, the difficult problems that confront it.

A variety of arguments have been put forward in support of the institutionalization of heritage language programs. Language educators, for example, have drawn attention to findings of psycho-educational research which highlight the linguistic, cultural, academic, and cognitive benefits of maintaining or attaining bilingual proficiency in any two languages. Where one of the tongues is a non-official ancestral language such as Portuguese or Italian or Hindi, there are additional psychological benefits to the child of being functional in the language of his or her ethnocultural community (Swain and Lapkin 1982; Cummins and Swain 1986; Danesi 1986; Cummins and Danesi 1990; Harley et al. 1990; Cummins 1994). Some of the most frequently cited studies on 'additive bilingualism' (where one language is added to another without a deleterious effect on either) and 'language shift' (where a second language, generally that of the majority, displaces a first, generally that of a minority) have involved children enrolled in Portuguese programs run by local school boards. In some of these programs the learners' first language – Portuguese – has served as the 'transitional' medium of instruction until adequate proficiency has been attained in the school language (Shapson 1984: 6; Henderson 1977). In other instances, Portuguese has been taught for linguistic and cultural 'enrichment,' as a subject in and of itself (Cummins, Lopes, and King 1987; Cummins 1991; Cummins and Lopes 1994).

Another argument in favour of minority language education has centred on attrition of ethnic language. Some researchers predict that intergenerational loss of ethnic languages in Canada, while not as extensive as in the United States, will culminate in complete or near-complete linguistic assimilation among all but newly arrived immigrant groups. Language attrition in the second and third generations among ethnic groups is undoubtedly a reality in Canada, as is indicated by analyses of census and survey data (O'Bryan, Reitz, and Kuplowska 1976; Herberg 1989; Reitz and Breton 1994). This is true even of a 'newer' language such as Portuguese, revealed by the national retention rates for the language, which can be calculated as a percentage by dividing the number who claim Portuguese as a home language by the number who claim it as a mother tongue. While Portuguese is one of the most frequently reported non-official mother tongues (Teixeira 1995), with approximately 211,000 listing it, the retention rate has been declining over the last few decades – for example from 83 per cent in 1971 to 81 per cent in 1981 (Herberg 1989), and further, to 60.5 per cent in 1991.

In addition, surveys indicate marked differences in the day-to-day use of Portuguese between the Portuguese born outside Canada and those born here – i.e., the second and third generations (O'Bryan, Reitz, and Kuplowska 1976; Reitz and Breton 1994). While language attrition is considerably slower in the Portuguese community than in most ethnic communities (for example, German, Dutch, or Hungarian) (Herberg 1989), generational language loss may be more acute than retention rates indicate. Using the Greek and Portuguese communities in Montreal as samples, Veltman (1986), for example, demonstrated that census questions on home language can fail to reveal the true extent of language loss in an ethnocultural group, since parents tend to identify the language in which their children interact with *them* as the home language, rather than the language used in interaction with siblings and peers. There is no body of research showing that heritage language education can slow large-scale language loss (Cummins 1994), nor is it clear that such a goal can even be considered part of the mandate of a heritage language program. One can argue, however, that neglecting heritage language amounts to relinquishing any hope of maintaining a meaningful level of linguistic diversity in this country, except through new immigration. In communities with lower immigration rates in recent decades, as is the case among the Portuguese, perhaps not even new immigration can substantially compensate for generational language loss.

One complicating factor in public discussion is the ambiguous role of multilingualism in multiculturalism in this country. The existence of Canadian multiculturalism 'within a bilingual framework' makes it abundantly clear that minority languages are 'non-official,' but leaves it uncertain whether their maintenance is integral to multiculuralism (see Cummins and Danesi 1990; Fleras and Elliott 1992). As a result, opinions range from those that uphold multilingualism as indispensable to any true multiculturalism, through those that view multiculturalism as separable from linguistic issues, to those that condemn 'too much' linguistic diversity as being inimical to national unity.[3]

Furthermore, across minority groups themselves there is no clear consensus on the role of ethnic language retention in the retention of ethnic culture (Wardhaugh 1983). For example, while some groups insist that without their own language (let us say, Italian or Portuguese or Ukrainian) their ethnocultural identity would splinter, others feel that they do not need a special language (let us say, Gaelic or Hebrew) to maintain ethnocultural distinctiveness. Variations across ethnic groups in the degree to which language shapes identity have been brought to light by many of the findings of sociological research: 'Language is a vital component of culture, although it is not equally so for all groups. For some, its loss seems to be close to complete acculturation; others can abandon it and yet retain other cultural elements' (Reitz and Breton 1994: 55).

The fragility of meaningful support for multilingualism within the context of Canadian multiculturalism is summed up by Cummins and Danesi (1990: 21): 'The orientation of Canadian educators and policymakers in most provinces towards heritage language education displays a ... disjunction between a surface-level endorsement of heritage language teaching as one aspect of multicultural education and a more deep-rooted rejection of such programs as a potential threat to the societal status quo, specifically the primacy of English and/or French as the languages of power in Canada. Commentators typically have no objection to communities teaching heritage languages quietly in their own homes and schools, but they object strenuously to heritage languages being institutionalized within the public school system and supported by public monies.'

Today, two decades after Ontario's Heritage Languages Program was announced in 1977, the same sort of ambivalence towards heritage language education is reflected in the recent passing of Bill 160 in Ontario. What becomes of heritage language programs as a result of the amalgamation of several local boards of education seems to have received little notice in the political process. It is unclear, for example, how an amalgamated board can foster language programs that were conducted by individual boards, each with its own ethnic composition. According to Alistair Cumming of the Ontario Institute for Studies in Education, 'It's a major concern [to educators] how centralizing the school system can cope with populations that are radically different in the cities [and in] the small towns' (Carey 1997: B5).

Ontario and Quebec

Heritage language programs fall into two broad categories within public school systems. The first consists of bilingual programs, in which the heritage language is used as the medium of instruction for about 50 per cent of the school day, exemplified by the Ukrainian programs in Alberta and Manitoba. Some of these immersion-type approaches can also serve as transitional programs, with the learner's first language as the medium of instruction for school subjects until such time as the child can gain cope with learning content through the school language. In the most common type, a language such as Portuguese is studied as a subject either within the regular school day or outside it, so that students can or maintain proficiency in the language and become well-versed in the culture with which it is associated. In the majority of cases the heritage language is not actually the child's home language and often has to be learned 'from scratch.'

About half of the provinces in Canada – Ontario, Quebec, Manitoba, Saskatchewan, Alberta, and, more recently, British Columbia – have implemented heritage language programs, to varying degrees (Canadian Education Association [CEA] 1991). In student enrolments, Portuguese ranks among the top five in Ontario and Quebec (together with Greek, Italian, Spanish, and Chinese) (CEA 1991), which is unsurprising, given that these two provinces have maintained the highest concentrations of Portuguese Canadians since the pioneer immigrant phase of the 1950s (Anderson and Higgs 1976). The Portuguese programs in the other provinces are, in keeping with their smaller Portuguese populations, much more modest in size. For example, in

Manitoba, of the approximately 6,000 students enrolled in core heritage language programs in 1989, less than 1 per cent were in Portuguese programs (CEA 1991: 10).[4]

Ontario's Heritage Languages Program was legislated in 1977, providing full funding for heritage language instruction outside the regular five-hour school day for up to 2½ hours a week in those cases where a school board agreed to establish such a program in response to a request from a community group. Ontario offers heritage language instruction in a vast array of minority languages, of which Portuguese is one of the most prominent. In a typical downtown school in Toronto such as Palmerston Avenue Public School, a survey is conducted at the beginning of the school year to ascertain which languages are in demand in the community. At other schools, certain heritage language courses have stability within the school curriculum on account of the schools' ethnic composition. For example, St Luke School (within the Toronto Catholic District School Board), has offered Portuguese for several years without interruption, with the majority of Portuguese-background students participating in the program (Lopes and Lopes 1991). At Pope Paul (also within the Toronto Catholic board), the school's consistently large Portuguese population has warranted creation of a stable Portuguese program, as is stated in the literature on the school's curriculum: 'Portuguese heritage language and culture is [sic] taught to all children whose parents request it.'[5]

In Quebec, heritage language instruction has been provided via the Ministry of Education's Programme d'Enseignement de Langues d'Origine (PELO), launched in 1977. Portuguese, one of the first languages to be taught in PELO (together with Italian, Spanish, and Greek), has contributed greatly to the recognition that this program has received over the years. For example, the PELO program in the Commission des écoles catholiques de Montréal, which offers instruction in Portuguese and other European and non-European languages, has received official recognition from the Portuguese government on the basis of favourable reviews (CEA 1991).

Despite these successes, PELO has met with some opposition and scepticism over the years, in particular during its early days, when certain ethnic groups themselves viewed the program as a palliative for Bill 101, which restricted their children's access to English schooling (d'Anglejan and De Koninck 1992). These ethnic communities, however, are now far more favourably disposed to PELO, as is indicated by the ten-fold increase in enrolment between the beginning and the end of the 1980s (CEA 1991). The main opposition has come from certain non-PELO francophone teachers (for example, teachers of French or mathematics), who have viewed the program as being inconsistent with a policy of integrating new immigrants into Quebec society, and they have expressed concern about the adverse effects of heritage language education on students' performance in French and other academic subjects. As d'Anglejan and De Koninck (1992: 101) point out, heritage language issues are even more complicated in Quebec than in English Canada on account of the 'minority' status of French within North America: 'In spite of its privileged legal status, French must compete not only with the minority group child's home language but with the power of the English-language electronic media and the status of English in North America.'

Benefits of Language Retention

Maintenance of Ethnic Identity

Language retention within a community is an important factor in the maintenance of ethnocultural identity (Wardhaugh 1983; Reitz and Breton 1994). In Sapir's words: 'The mere fact of a common speech serves as a peculiarly potent symbol of the social solidarity of those who speak the language' (1933: 159). However, as I showed above, there is great debate on whether or not retention of heritage language is indispensable to cultural vitality, with the likelihood being that it is crucial for some ethnic groups, but not for others (Herberg 1989: 101). There are many indications that the Portuguese consider language a powerful contributor to the community's sense of cohesiveness. For example, noting that the younger generation in Quebec was less fluent in its ancestral language than its elders, Alpalhão and Da Rosa (1980) expressed the view that maintenance of ancestral language had to be given priority in the community, even in the face of criticism that this could further marginalize the community: 'The teaching of Portuguese seems to be justifiable and indispensable, not only as a vehicle of the culture it represents, but also as an essential factor in the identity and survival of this culture' (155). Similarly, Paulston (1990: 194) believes that the success of heritage language programs such as the school-based Portuguese ones in Toronto (see Cummins et al. 1990) lies in their ability to heighten awareness of the value of the language and culture (even if they often fail to help learners gain high proficiency in the language): 'The existence of classes in Portuguese language and culture in the public schools ... recognizes the legitimacy and value of the students' ethnic background in the eyes of the dominant majority. They help contribute to the positive attitudes students display toward *both* their cultures ... Simply by bringing all the children together, the classes contribute to a sense of community cohesion.'

Communication between Generations

The centrality of Portuguese in the lives of first-generation Portuguese Canadians is frequently discussed in the literature on the Portuguese community in Canada. The need for such people to remain in Portuguese-speaking enclaves is often cited as one of the factors responsible for the high residential concentration found among the Portuguese (for example, Teixeira 1995). Likewise, they have usually expected their children to retain Portuguese as their home language, primarily to facilitate easy communication between the generations: 'It is normally the parents who decide what language will be spoken within the family circle. In the case of the first generation, the choice normally falls to the Portuguese language. Generally it is taught to and imposed on children, pretending reasons of a cultural nature. But the truth is that ... [parents choose Portuguese because they] feel ill at ease with the official languages in which their children are most fluent' (Alpalhão and Da Rosa 1980: 153). Today, in numerous Portuguese-background families that have been in Canada since the 1950s and 1960s, grandparents and grandchildren communicate in Portuguese. As well, maintaining Portuguese as the home language has facilitated relocation to the homeland (Anderson and Higgs 1976) – still a common consideration, though probably to a lesser extent (Teixeira 1995).

Ironically, at the time when the majority of Portuguese in Canada were of the first generation, it was common for parents to be asked to speak the school language at home – a measure that not only severely curtailed communication between parents and children but informed children that their home language and culture were somehow less respectable than the majority language and culture. Neither did the rapid attrition of learners' first language that ensued lead to improved performance at school. Recent research actually suggests that communication in the home is more demanding pragmatically and richer linguistically than that in the classroom, irrespective of socio-economic background (for example, Wells 1986).

Benefits of Bilingualism

Perhaps the most compelling reason for maintaining a language such as Portuguese lies its linguistic, cognitive, and academic benefits. A substantial body of research conducted in Canada, as well as the models of bilingual competence associated with it, have helped to dispel the commonly held view in North America that childhood bilingualism invariably creates harmful competition between the two languages. Cummins, for example, in the late 1970s, posited the 'linguistic interdependence model,' which postulates that cognitive/academic and literacy-related skills (i.e., reading and writing) are transferred from one language to another, irrespective of surface distinctions between these languages: 'First and second language academic skills are interdependent, i.e., manifestations of a common underlying proficiency' (Cummins 1985: 44). On the basis of research findings, primarily in French immersion contexts, Cummins and Swain (1986) came to the following conclusion: 'Children instructed through a minority language for all or part of the school day perform over time as well or better in the majority language as students instructed exclusively in the majority language' (xv). Other studies have indicated that literacy in a heritage language greatly facilitates acquisition of additional languages (for example, Swain and Lapkin 1991).

One of the first studies to demonstrate this enhancement of academic performance involved an experimental transitional program in Portuguese for newly arrived Portuguese-speaking students in grades four, five, and six in two Toronto schools (Henderson 1977). After a year, researchers compared their performance with that of a control group (who had received instruction only in English) on the basis of a pre-test in Portuguese and a post-test in English. The students in the experimental group performed better not only in language, math concepts, and problem solving, but also in certain aspects of oral production in English (see Cummins and Danesi 1990 for a review of this study).

Similarly, a longitudinal study that charted the progress of fourteen Portuguese-Canadian children in Toronto from junior kindergarten through grade one found a significant relationship between the students' literate and oral skills in Portuguese (their first language) and their literate and oral skills in English, their second language (Cummins 1991). These children attended an English-language school in the heart of the Portuguese district in Toronto and were also enrolled in a thirty-minute-a-day program in Portuguese as a heritage language in junior and senior kindergarten. This study also revealed a very rapid shift from Portuguese to English among almost all the children, even though the children's parents and grandparents spoke to them primarily in Portuguese at home. On the basis of these findings, which highlight not only the positive transfer of competence in a minority language to the majority language, but also the erosion of the former by the latter, Cummins (1991: 95) proposed: 'Rather than trying to expedite the disappearance of the child's home language, educators should actively explore with parents ways in which the developmental process that underlies growth in both languages can be enhanced.'

In addition, the results of a large-scale study by Cummins, Lopes, and King (1987) involving 191 grade seven Portuguese-background students taking heritage language in inner-city schools in Toronto showed a positive correlation between 'discourse proficiency' in English and in Portuguese (see Cummins et al. 1990; Cummins 1994).[6] A comparison between these young people and grade seven students in the Azores, however, revealed significant deficits in the Toronto group's proficiency in Portuguese – an expected finding, given the marked differences in the two language environments.

None the less, the researchers found a positive relationship in the Toronto-based group between the amount of formal exposure to Portuguese and proficiency. While they could not establish a causal relationship between Portuguese language instruction and overall proficiency in Portuguese, because of confounding factors such as exposure to Portuguese outside the program, they concluded: 'The strong relationship between attendance at Portuguese language classes and the performance of the Toronto students suggests that more intensive exposure to Portuguese in an academic context could have a significant impact on bridging the gap between their Portuguese proficiency and that of native Portuguese-educated students' (Cummins et al. 1990: 126–7).

In sum, the findings of research suggest that retention of a heritage language such as Portuguese not only has no adverse effect on the child's academic and majority language skills but actually seems to contribute to the child's success in these areas. The studies also reveal the inadequacy of a few hours of heritage language instruction in the face of the pervasive influence of a majority language such as English.

Very little is known about curriculum development and teaching practices in these programs, except through accounts of projects undertaken in particular programs (for example, Lopes and Lopes

1991; Cummins and Lopes 1994). It is clear that there is often concern regarding the mandate of heritage language programs and the appropriateness of curricular materials in this regard. For example, there is uncertainty as to whether cultural materials should be based on life in the ethnic homeland (for example, Portugal or the Azores) or the ethnic community in Canada (Bagheera, in Cummins 1983: 73). This problem is exacerbated by lack of appropriate materials of either kind: 'Most materials that are available fail to reflect the Canadian reality of students and are not designed for classes that include students with wide variations in heritage language proficiency' (Lopes and Lopes 1991: 708). Recently, however, there have been attempts to create curricular materials especially for Portuguese language programs. For example, Girol Books in Ottawa, under the auspices of the federal Multiculturalism Program, has put together a variety of Portuguese readers specifically for use in such programs (Yee and Sodhi 1991). Similarly, the Quebec Ministry of Education has created texts for students of Portuguese heritage language – for example, *Os 5 sentidos and As Comunidades culturais do Quebeque* (CEA 1991).

An example of curricular innovation is Lopes and Lopes's (1991) community-based writing project at St Luke School in Toronto. On the basis of interviews with senior citizens from the Portuguese community, students in this program in Portuguese as a heritage language recorded the stories and reminiscences of their elders in a collection entitled *No tempo dos nossos avós* (In Our Grandparents' Time) (Lopes and Lopes 1991). Similarly, with the help of volunteers from the Portuguese community, researchers at Toronto's Ontario Institute for Studies in Education compiled a history of Portuguese immigration for children in grades seven and eight (Cummins and Lopes 1994). These materials were tested in the Portuguese program at St Luke with apparent success, possibly contributing to the highly positive attitudes towards Portuguese language and culture displayed by the students in a language attitude questionnaire at the end of the program (Cummins and Lopes 1994).

Intractable Problems

Despite the reported beneficial effects of even some exposure to an ancestral language in a formal context, it is clear that heritage language programs suffer from a variety of problems. Some of these are remediable through local curricular innovations, teacher education, and the like, as touched on above. Others are more deep-rooted and can ulti-mately be rectified only through major shifts in the policies governing heritage language education.

Most students enrolled in heritage language programs are at an ele-mentary level of proficiency and only rarely achieve high proficiency within such a context. While some generational changes in a language are inevitable under any circumstances, especially when it comes into contact with another tongue (Dias 1994), the complaint in Canada is that the second and third generations may end up speaking a pid-ginized version of their ancestral language, with serious deficits in 'communicative competence,' often despite language classes. Similarly, heritage language programs, at least in their current form, cannot reverse the extensive loss of minority language that takes place in early childhood when the child begins to participate in the majority lan-guage community. This attrition is highlighted, for example, in Cum-mins et al.'s (1990) study of grade seven Portuguese-Canadian children enrolled in Portuguese heritage programs (see above). A comparison between the Portuguese language skills of these students, most of whom had been exposed only to Portuguese before starting school, and their Azorean counterparts found 'significant differences ... on most measures of Portuguese proficiency ... The large differences ... show how formidable is the task of maintaining first language profi-ciency in a minority context' (Cummins et al. 1990, 120).

Similarly, in Cummins's longitudinal study of Portuguese-Canadian children in kindergarten and grade one, most showed rapid language shift coupled with attrition of mother tongue, even though their par-ents spoke to them primarily in Portuguese (Cummins 1991). At the end of grade one, the majority had better conversational fluency in English than in Portuguese and had begun to use mostly English in their interactions with siblings. It was evident that Portuguese as the home language, combined with thirty minutes of heritage language instruction, could not halt the shift to the majority language.

Studies outside a heritage language context also confirm the shift from Portuguese to English among the second and third generations. For example, a survey of young Portuguese Canadians living in Metro-politan Toronto revealed that even though many speak Portuguese with the parental generation, they use English almost exclusively with siblings and peers (Carvalho 1994). Carvalho concluded: 'La plupart des jeunes avouent parler portugais avec leurs parents et autres mem-bres agés de la famille; mais ils communiquent avec leurs frères ou soeurs en anglais. C'est plus facile, disent-ils. Ainsi se crée facilement la dominance d'une langue sur l'autre. L'anglais aura alors tendance à avoir la part du lion dans ce partage inégal. Le portugais risque de devenir une langue affective et de communication minimale' (342).

In the face of this trend towards linguistic assimilation, it is unrealistic to expect students to gain or maintain high proficiency in Portuguese primarily on the basis of 2 to 2½ hours of heritage language instruction per week (the norm in Ontario and Quebec). However, as we saw above, these programs do not seem to be able to stall language loss even among children who speak the minority language as a mother tongue during their pre-school years and whose parents continue to communicate with them primarily in the minority language after they join school. Among various explanations for this failure, two of the most significant will be discussed here – inadequate exposure to the target language and inadequate learner motivation.

It is clear that if there is minimal exposure to the heritage language in the classroom, coupled with little opportunity or need to interact in that language within the community, the student does not hear or produce enough of the language. Moreover, the range of uses to which the language is put within the classroom is limited. In the grade seven study by Cummins et al., for example, 'amount of exposure, both formal exposure in heritage language classes and the informal exposure involved in visits to Portugal, amount of Portuguese television watched, use made of other forms of Portuguese media ... and going to mass in Portuguese, appeared to play a major role in predicting different aspects of proficiency, particularly oral grammatical proficiency' (1990: 125). 'Informal exposure' is jeopardized, however, if children prefer to interact with their siblings and peers in English and if parents communicate with their children in English because their children find English 'easier.' This may be exacerbated if the parents feel a sense of shame regarding their mother tongue.

If we consider the interaction between the learner's psychological characteristics and the socio-cultural environment, we can also attribute students' mediocre attainment to their lack of motivation, either because the heritage language does not seem very 'useful' or because they do not identity closely with their ethnocultural community. (See Gardner 1985 and Kwak 1990 for the positive relationship between learners' motivation and their success in acquiring a second language and a heritage language, respectively.) The kind of 'pidginization' said to result from using language only for communication

(Schumann 1976) is reported by Alpalhão and Da Rosa (1980): 'Sometimes, they [second-generation Portuguese] are conditioned to perpetuate the use of the mother tongue in order to communicate with their parents or grandparents who do not know other languages. These factors in part explain the grammatical mistakes and deformations as well as the tendency to avoid the use of Portuguese once they are aware of their limitations' (154).

Whatever the source of the problem, the only way of getting around it and ensuring that heritage language education can help preserve minority languages is by integrating these languages into the mainstream curriculum in provinces such as Ontario where their curricular status is peripheral or non-existent. In addition, it seems that the only way to implement this integration is by convincing the public and educators alike that multilingualism is 'useful,' not only for self-growth and community well-being, but for the economic and political well-being of the country.

The full integration of a heritage language into the mainstream curriculum involves not just teaching it for credit, which has contributed to the success of programs such as PELO (Cummins and Danesi 1990), but also employing it for instruction in various subject areas for at least part of the school day, as has been done in bilingual Ukrainian schools in Alberta and Manitoba. The majority of heritage language courses in Canada are non-credit, involving little collaboration between mainstream and heritage language instructors. As a result, the heritage language curriculum is not only isolated from the regular curriculum but, more significant, is often identified as peripheral or even suspect because of its non-credit, 'after-hours' status. The schism is poignantly clear in the recollections of a Portuguese-Canadian university student: 'The moment that they bring aspects of Portuguese history into the regular history curriculum then I'll believe it's more for real. In my (community) heritage language classes ... I would learn about the Portuguese presence all over the world (Vasco da Gama, Magellan, etc.) and then I would go to regular English school and there was nothing about that. I used to think (and so did many of my peers) that what I learnt in heritage classes were lies, distortions' (Feuerverger 1991: 673).

In short, for a heritage language to gain full legitimacy within the school system, it needs to be used to teach academic content within the mainstream curriculum. Some have argued, however, that elevating the status of all minority languages in such a fashion would give rise to great linguistic and curricular confusion in the school system and thereby in society at large. While it is obvious that there are not enough resources to incorporate every minority language into the regular curriculum, at least a few such languages could be 'mainstreamed' – for example, if an ethnocultural community with a sizeable membership expressed keen interest in such a move (Herberg, 1989; Cummins and Danesi 1990). In Cummins and Danesi's words, resistance to 'mainstreaming' stems from resistance to the 'valorization of multilingualism' and to the ensuing 'elevation of the status of minority groups whose languages would now be institutionalized within the mainstream curriculum' (1990: 114).

In an age when many politicians and educational administrators seem to have a more utilitarian attitude towards education than their forebears (who, for example, were more open to accepting a liberal arts education purely on the grounds that it 'broadened the mind'), perhaps the only way of 'valorizing' multilingualism is by advertising its potential economic, social, and political benefits to the country – for example, through facilitating trade in a globalizing economy, promoting international relations (without the additional cost of foreign language training for diplomats and bureaucrats), or serving the needs of newly arrived immigrants (Cummins and Danesi 1990).

In 1981, Max Yalden, Canada's commissioner of official languages, predicted: 'I am too much of a realist to think that our heritage languages can long survive purely on the basis of family piety or cultural curiosity. It is their social, commercial and even political usefulness that seems to me more likely to be decisive for their future role in our society' (in Cummins 1983: 16). Two decades later, Yalden's pronouncement continues to make eminent sense. While one could argue that the academic, linguistic, psychological, and cultural advantages of minority language retention for the child are at least as worthy of consideration as the above-mentioned economic, social, and political benefits to the nation, it is perhaps the latter that could help to legitimize heritage language education in the eyes of the Canadian public.

NOTES

1 I would like to thank António Pereira Joel of York University, David Mendelsohn of York University, and the editors of this volume for their generous assistance in the writing of this paper.
2 The term 'heritage language' refers to any minority language other than an

official language and the languages of the First Nations and Inuit people. While certain writers prefer alternative terms such as ancestral, ethnic, minority, third, and non-official (Cummins and Danesi 1990), I use 'heritage' here as a convenient umbrella term for the ethnocultural language of the community to which a learner belongs (excluding the official and Aboriginal languages); it may or may not be the learner's first language.

3 The lack of clarity in Canadians' minds regarding the role of ethnic language retention in multiculturalism and the divergence in public opinion regarding the spending of public money on ethnic language instruction first came to light in a dramatic way in two national surveys commissioned by the federal government in the 1970s. The non-official languages study (O'Bryan, Reitz, and Kuplowska 1976) confirmed that ethnocultural groups strongly favoured public funding for heritage language instruction. The majority attitudes study (Berry, Kalin, and Taylor 1977), however, indicated that anglophones and francophones had somewhat negative views towards funding of heritage language instruction, despite their more-or-less positive attitude towards multiculturalism in general.

4 Note, however, that the findings reported in CEA 1991 are based on questionnaires sent to school boards across the country; since some of the questionnaires remained unanswered, the figures are only approximations.

5 This quotation is from the main page of Pope Paul Catholic School's website, at <http://www.mssb.edu.on.ca/sctr_PopePaul.htm> (11 Dec. 1997).

6 'Discourse proficiency' is the ability to create or follow inter-sentential linguistic connections in discourse and to make connections between thoughts or ideas in discourse.

REFERENCES

Alpalhão, J.A., and Da Rosa, V.M.P. 1980. *A Minority in a Changing Society.* Ottawa: University of Ottawa Press.

Anderson, G.M., and Higgs, D. 1976. *A Future to Inherit: The Portuguese Communities of Canada.* Toronto: McClelland and Stewart.

Berry, J.W., Kalin, R., and Taylor, D.M. 1977. *Multiculturalism and Ethnic Attitudes in Canada.* Ottawa: Ministry of Supply and Services Canada.

Canadian Education Association (CEA). 1991. *Heritage Language Programs in Canadian School Boards.* Toronto: Canadian Education Association.

Carey, E. 1997. 'Immigrant Services Imperiled by New Bill, Educators Warn.' *Toronto Star,* 3 Dec.: B1, B5.

Carvalho, A. de. 1994. 'Images du Portugal, de la langue et la culture portugaises chez les jeunes luso-canadiens de Toronto.' In A. Martins, A.M.

Folco, and A. de Carvalho, eds., *Le portugais: Langue internationale*, 333–45. Montreal: Centre de Langues Patrimoniales.

Cummins, J. 1983. *Heritage Language Education: Issues and Directions*. Ottawa: Ministry of Supply and Services Canada.

– 1985. *Empowering Minority Students*. Sacramento: California Association for Bilingual Education.

– 1991. 'The Development of Bilingual Proficiency from Home to School: A Longitudinal Study of Portuguese-Speaking Children.' *Journal of Education* 173 no. 2: 85–98.

– 1994. 'Heritage Language Learning and Teaching.' In J.W. Berry and J.A. Laponce, eds., *Ethnicity and Culture in Canada: The Research Landscape*, 435–56. Toronto: University of Toronto Press.

Cummins, J., and Danesi, M. 1990. *Heritage Languages: The Development and Denial of Canada's Linguistic Resources*. Toronto: Our Schools Our Selves/Garamond.

Cummins, J., Harley, B., Swain, M., and Allen, P. 1990. 'Social and Individual Factors in the Development of Bilingual Proficiency.' In B. Harley, P. Allen, J. Cummins, and M. Swain, eds., 1986. *The Development of Second Language Proficiency*, 119–33. Cambridge: Cambridge University Press.

Cummins, J., and Lopes, J. 1994. *The Effectiveness of Activity-Based Teaching Strategies in Portuguese Heritage Language Classes*. Toronto: Ontario Institute for Studies in Education.

Cummins, J., Lopes, J., and King, M.L. 1987. 'The Language Use Patterns, Language Attitudes, and Bilingual Proficiency of Portuguese Canadian Children in Toronto.' In B. Harley, P. Allen, J. Cummins, and M. Swain, eds., *The Development of Bilingual Proficiency*, vol. III, *Social Context and Age*, 119–33. Toronto: Modern Language Centre, Ontario Institute for Studies in Education.

Cummins, J., and Swain, M. 1986. *Bilingualism in Education*. London: Longman.

d'Anglejan, A., and De Koninck, Z. 1992. 'Educational Policy for a Culturally Plural Quebec: An Update.' In B. Burnaby and A. Cumming, eds., *Socio-Political Aspects of ESL*, 97–109. Toronto: Ontario Institute for Studies in Education.

Danesi, M. 1986. 'The Heritage Language Classroom as an Academic Support System: A Proposal for Discussion.' *Multiculturalism* 9: 15–18.

Dias, M. 1994. 'Interaction entre le portugais et l'anglais dans la communauté portugaise de Toronto: Sens et implication de cette interaction.' In A. Martins, A.M. Folco, and A. de Carvalho, eds., *Le portugais: Langue internationale*, 324–32. Montreal: Centre de Langues Patrimoniales.

Feuerverger, G. 1991. 'University Students' Perceptions of Heritage Language

Learning and Ethnic Identify Maintenance.' *Canadian Modern Language Review* 47 no. 4: 660–77.

Fleras, A., and Elliott, J.L. 1992. *The Challenge of Diversity: Multiculturalism in Canada*. Scarborough, Ont.: Nelson Canada.

Gardner, R.C. 1985. *Social Psychology and Second Language Learning: The Role of Attitudes and Motivation*. London: Edward Arnold Publishers.

Harley, B., Allen, P., Cummins, J., and Swain, M., eds., 1990. *The Development of Second Language Proficiency*. Cambridge: Cambridge University Press.

Henderson, K. 1977. A Report on Bilingual Transition Programs for Italian and Portuguese Immigrant Students. Unpublished research report, Ontario Institute for Studies in Education, Toronto.

Herberg, E.N. 1989. *Ethnic Groups in Canada: Adaptations and Transitions*. Toronto: Nelson Canada.

Kwak, K. 1990. 'Second Language Learning in a Multicultural Society: A Comparison between the Learning of a Dominant Language and a Heritage Language.' Doctoral dissertation, Queen's University.

Lopes, J.M., and Lopes, M. 1991. 'Bridging the Generation Gap: The Collection of Social Histories in the Portuguese Heritage Language Program.' *Canadian Modern Language Review* 47 no. 4: 708–11.

O'Bryan, K.G., Reitz, J.G., and Kuplowska, O.M. 1976. *Non-Official Languages: A Study of Canadian Multiculturalism*. Ottawa: Supply and Services Canada.

Paulston, C.B. 1990. 'Educational Language Policies in Utopia.' In B. Harley, P. Allen, J. Cummins, and M. Swain, eds., *The Development of Second Language Proficiency*, 187–97. Cambridge: Cambridge University Press.

Reitz, J.G., and Breton, R. 1994. *The Illusion of Difference: Realities and Ethnicity in Canada and the United States*. Toronto: C.D. Howe Institute.

Sapir, E. 1933. 'Language.' *Encyclopedia of the Social Sciences* 9: 155–68.

Schumann, J. 1976. 'Second Language Acquisition: The Pidginization Hypothesis.' *Language Learning* 26 no. 2: 391–408.

Shapson, S.M. 1984. 'Bilingual and Multicultural Education in Canada.' In S.M. Shapson and V. D'Oyley, eds., *Bilingual and Multicultural Education: Canadian Perspectives*, 1–13. Clevedon: Multilingual Matters.

Swain, M., and Lapkin, S. 1982. *Evaluating Bilingual Education: A Canadian Case Study*. Clevedon: Multilingual Matters.

– 1991. 'Heritage Language Children in an English–French Bilingual Program.' *Canadian Modern Language Review* 47 no. 4: 635–41.

Teixeira, C. 1995. 'The Portuguese in Toronto: A Community on the Move.' *Portuguese Studies Review* 4 no. 1: 57–75.

Veltman, C. 1986. 'The Interpretation of Language Questions of the Canadian Census.' *Canadian Review of Sociology and Anthropology* 23 no. 3: 412–22.

Wardhaugh, R. 1983. *Language and Nationhood: The Canadian Experience.* Vancouver: New Star Books.

Wells, G. 1986. *The Meaning Makers: Children Learning Language and Using Language to Learn.* Portsmouth, NH: Heinemann.

Yee, D.S., and Sodhi, S. 1991. 'Resource Guide for Heritage Language Instruction: An Annotated Listing of Projects Supported by Multiculturalism and Citizenship.' *Canadian Modern Language Review* 47 no. 4: 712–85.

10

Influences on Portuguese Spoken in Montreal

MANUELA DIAS-TATILON

This essay examines the extent to which extralinguistic factors, such as the geographical origin of immigrants and the distance between Quebec and Portugal, affect the language spoken by the Luso-Québécois[1] in Montreal as well as the maintenance of their language. I undertook this study during several visits to the Portuguese community of Montreal. These visits put me in contact with Portuguese immigrants and gave me an opportunity to examine the schools and become better acquainted with the way of life of the Luso-Québécois.[2]

The factors that I take into account in this study are the effects on speech of speakers' geographical origin in Portugal; the effect of the distance between country of origin and country of destination (Portugal and Canada) on the maintenance of the Portuguese language and culture for future generations; the involvement of English, which is more socially prestigious than either French or Portuguese; and the role played by age and generation.

A large number of the immigrants who make up the Portuguese community of Montreal came from the Azores and Madeira. They speak several varieties of Portuguese, which represent dialects that differ from the standard language. I first outline some examples of these varying dialects that make up the Luso-Québécois language. Second, I look at the impact of Bill 101 on the Portuguese community. Third, I examine interlingual interferences. Fourth, I consider bilingualism and diglossia in Portuguese Montreal.

Dialectal Characteristics

Madeira and the Azores are Portuguese islands located southwest of

Portugal in the Atlantic. Their inhabitants have emigrated in large numbers either to the United States or to Canada in search of a better life for themselves and their families. As a result, the Portuguese communities in Canada (primarily in Toronto and Montreal) are made up of people from these islands, who maintain the dialectal characteristics outlined below. Residents of the islands of São Miguel and Santa Maria speak a dialect called *micaelense*. It has the following particularities:

- substitution of the palatals [u] (equivalent to [y] in French) and [o] for [ü] or [o], respectively (represented graphically as *u, ou,* and *oi*). For example, *uva* [uvɑ] becomes [üvɑ] (grape); *surdo* [surdu] becomes [sürdu] (deaf); and *pouco* [poku] becomes [pöku] (little).
- substitution of [u] for [o] (represented graphically as *o*). For example, *doze* [doz] becomes [duz] and *amor* [ɑmor] becomes [ɑmur] (love).
- reduction of [ej] and [aj] to [e] and [a]. For example, *ceia* [sej ɑ] becomes [sea] (supper); *baixa* [bajʃɑ] becomes [baʃɑ] (down, downtown); and *caixa* [kajʃɑ] becomes [kaʃɑ] (box).

On the island of Terceira, there are common:

- insertion of the phoneme [w] before [e] and [ɛ]· For example, *perfeito* [pərfejtu] becomes [pərfwejtu] (perfect) and *cuberto* [kubɛrtu] becomes [kubwɛrtu].
- insertion of the phoneme [j] after [u]. For example, *bruto* [brutu] becomes [brujtu] (brute) and *luta* [lutɑ] becomes [lujtɑ].

On the islands that make up Madeira (Madeira and Porto Santo) the following characteristics are noted:

- velarization of the tonal [a], which becomes almost [ɔ]. For example, *casa* [kazɑ] becomes [kɔzɑ] (house).
- replacement of the tonal [i] by a diphthong with the semi-vowel [j] and a vowel pronounced similarly to [ɑ]. For example, *jardim* [jardō] becomes [jardɑj] (garden).
- very common palatization of [l] when it is preceded by [i]. For example, *filetes* [filɛtʃ] becomes [fiʎɛtʃ].

From a lexical point of view, there are many terms used in Madeira and in the Azores that have long since disappeared from the continental Portuguese language (Mateus 1983).

It is not coincidental that certain phonemes used in the Azores and in Madeira – such as the [u] in [üvα] and the [u] in [αmur] – closely resemble French phonemes. They are in fact a superstratum of French that has remained in Portugal. After the French Revolution, a large number of French noble families fled to these islands, and traces of their language still remain.[3]

The Portuguese language spoken by the Luso-Québécois is therefore not standard but based on the varieties of Portuguese spoken in Madeira and in the Azores, which, as noted, share some similar characteristics with French. Thus these immigrants' speech represents a unique combination of *açoreano*[4] and Québécois.

French, English, and Portuguese: Bill 101[5]

In Quebec, there are now two generations of Portuguese. The first immigrants who arrived in the 1950s were quite poor and for the most part illiterate, because schooling in the Azores was generally reserved for the rich. When they arrived in Quebec, they immediately sought work. After long days either as factory workers or as domestics, they had neither the time nor the desire to learn the local language. Furthermore, they realized that they could survive knowing neither French nor English. Ms Rodrigues, director of the Centre Portugais de Référence et Promotion Sociale (CPRPS),[6] explains that a Portuguese immigrant would have no problem living in the St Louis quarter of Montreal, where many of Montreal's Portuguese live (see Alpalhão and Da Rosa 1979), without being able to speak either French or English.

Some of the first-generation immigrants managed to learn a rudimentary level of French, but they still had a very restricted vocabulary, blended with a sort of pidgin. According to a study done in 1984[7] in 255 households, 30 per cent of Portuguese immigrants living in Quebec were unilingual. Most of those who were unilingual were older. This linguistic situation has created serious isolation. Unable to speak either French or English, many immigrants have been living in a 'ghetto' and have not been able to integrate into Quebec society. Furthermore, not having information about that society, they have often been victims of exploitation by those who look to take advantage of immigrants (Marcil 1980).

The government of Quebec has tried to help immigrants – for example, through creation of a permanent committee to study the immigrants' situation and publication of a guide in six languages. The Ministère de l'immigration du Québec also distributes an informational video. The Portuguese community has set up several community centres and information offices to help immigrants, the most influential one being CPRPS, which in 1978 alone rendered services over 10,000 times to 6,000 immigrants, including literacy courses, French courses for adults, and information meetings pertaining to integration into Quebec society.

At the beginning of the wave of immigration, the majority of Portuguese parents sent their children to English schools, since that was the language of the workforce. However, beginning in 1977 (after enactment of Bill 101), the French language took on a larger role among the Portuguese in the Montreal area. Today, French is well on its way to becoming the most widely spoken second language among the Luso-Québécois (see Veltman and Paré 1985).

Age and Generation

Age definitely affects the way in which Portuguese immigrants speak. As we saw above, there are now two generations of Portuguese in Montreal. First-generation immigrants are generally not well educated in the Portuguese language and not at all in French. They have thus created a mix of regional varieties of Portuguese as well as new French words that they have learned in order to cope with life in Montreal.

Members of the new generation have learned this regionally mixed version of Portuguese. However, they are much more conscious of their non-standard way of speaking, since they learned about standard language in they French schools. For the younger students who studied Portuguese in Montreal, this awareness is even more acute. They have developed habits of self-correction in their speech, which may in the long run help sustain the Portuguese language overseas.

It is evident that the language of first-generation immigrants differs from that of the second. Those who were born in Portugal and immigrated to Canada as adults have not been affected much by the interference of the French language, since they had already learned the Portuguese phonemes in their phonetic system. Those born in Montreal have had to deal with unclear boundaries between the two phonetic systems and are thus able to go from one language to another unconsciously.

There is a group of immigrants that speaks a language similar to standard Portuguese, as well as a younger group that has adopted this same system but makes a real effort to speak standard Portuguese. Younger immigrants speak with a 'foreign' accent, while older ones have kept their regional accent from Portugal.

I have done research on this subject to gain an understanding of what language (Portuguese: P; French: F; English: E) the Luso-Québécois speak at home with different members of their families, and what their attitudes are towards the three languages involved. I chose a group of young Luso-Québécois between the ages of nine and sixteen, who were taking Portuguese classes at the Programme d'enseignement des langues d'origine (PELO) and/or in Portuguese schools on Saturday mornings,[8] and interviewed twenty-seven children in this group.

Like Veltman and Paré (1985), I have concluded, first, that Portuguese is, in the majority of cases, the language spoken at home between parents and children; second, that speaking French rather than English is more common for the generation born after the enactment of Bill 101 (affecting those who are under eighteen); and, third, that the attitudes of young Luso-Québécois towards Portuguese is rather positive, but sometimes indifferent (Table 10.1).

Mechanisms and Interferences among French, Portuguese, and English

In this section, I present the results of the study done in Montreal, on the interferences – phonological, grammatical, and lexical – that have changed in the language of the Portuguese living in the St Louis quarter.[9] I take into account not only the Portuguese and French languages (more specifically, Québécois) but also English, since it is also a source of interference, being a part of the daily lives of immigrants.

Once again, I encountered some difficulties in my research, especially in my understanding of the Luso-Québécois language. The mix of the açoreano dialect with Québécois and English has produced a language that only the speakers can really understand.

Phonological Interferences

The consonant /R/. The interference in Luso-Québécois concerning the consonant /R/ is exactly the opposite of what has happened in France. While the Luso-Français tend to pronounce the soft, Portuguese [r] like

TABLE 10.1
Languages used among PELO students (P: Portuguese; F: French; E: English)

Question	Response
Language spoken at home with parents	16 P
	4 F/P
	2 F
	4 P/F/E
	1 P/E
Language spoken with siblings	4 P
	9 F
	9 P/F/E
	2 P/F/E
	1 F/E
Language spoken with friends	2 P
	12 F
	3 P/F
	4 P/F/E
	5 F/E
	1 E
Do you use more than one language in the same conversation?	17 no, 10 yes*
Are you ashamed to speak Portuguese?	19 'No, never, I'm proud to be Portuguese.'
	8 'Yes, sometimes.'
Which language do you prefer to speak?	17 no preference, 3 P, 3 F, 2 PF, 2 PE
Why are you studying Portuguese?	10 'It's my first language.'
	5 'To be able to go back to Portugal.'
	5 'So I don't forget it.'
	5 No specific response.
	3 'To get a good job.'

*It is possible that some students did not understand this question.

a palatal [R] (more fricative, as in the Parisian pronounciation), the Luso-Québécois pronounce the palatal [R] like a rolled [r].[10]

This 'confusion' could well lead to a confusion in meaning, since the phonological difference is a distinctive characteristic in Portuguese. For example, the Luso-Québécois pronounce *ateragem* (landing) [ɑtɜra ɑj] instead of [ɑtɜRaʒɑj]; *bariga* (stomach) [bɑrigɑ], instead of [bɑRigɑ]; and *rapaz* (boy) [rɑpaʃ] instead of [Rɑpaʃ]. I once attended a class where the Portuguese teacher made his students (seven to nine years old) repeat the [r] to make it less hard. This is the opposite exercise of what Portuguese teachers do in France.

It is not only the Québécois /R/ that is more rolled than the Parisian

/R/ that interferes with Portuguese; so also is the English /R/. American songs, radio, and television have surely affected the way in which young Luso-Québécois speak.

The affricated consonants [ts] and [dz]. As foreseen, the Québécois tendency of affricating the consonants [ts] and [dz] has been 'adopted' by Luso-Québécois when they speak Portuguese. For example, I have heard the word *tira* (lift away) pronounced [tsirɑ], instead of [tirɑ]; *tu* (you) pronounced [tsy] instead of [tu];[11] and *duro* (hard) pronounced [dsyru] instead of [duru].[12]

Grammatical Interferences

In this section, I note the three interferences that I observed more frequently in Luso-Québécois than in Luso-Français. These are first, elimination of all forms of the subjunctive; second, exaggerated use of the present participle; and third, use of the form of *tratamento, você,* in place of all the other forms.

In my study of these interferences in France (Dias 1990), I noted that Portuguese immigrants very often 'forget' the subjunctive, especially where it is used in a tense that does not exist in French, such as the future subjunctive, or in tenses that have been for the most part eliminated from oral speech (imperfect and past perfect subjunctive).

In Montreal, I noticed that the Portuguese not only replaced the future, imperfect, and past perfect subjunctive with other tenses or modes, but they also replaced the subjunctive of tenses that existed in French, such as the present and the past. Table 10.2 shows some examples of this type of interference.

The second type of grammatical interference that I noted in Luso-Québécois is exaggerated use of the present participle. For example, there is the use of phrases such as *está nevando* (it is snowing), *eles estão saltando* (they are jumping), and *eles estão jogando* (they are playing), rather than the present tense: *está a nevar, eles estão a saltar,* and *eles estão a jogar.* These types of phrases are not incorrect in Portuguese, but rather a less frequent construct used in the Azores.[13]

The third grammatical interference – replacing other forms such as *senhor, tu,* with the form of *tratamento, você* – is also very practical for the Luso-Québécois. For example, they use *eu vou com você* (I am going with you) instead of *vou consigo,* and *eu tive você* (I am with you) instead of *apanhei-o* or *estou consigo.*

TABLE 10.2
Interferences in the subjunctive

Luso-Québécois	French/English	Standard Portuguese
nas manhãs em que eu iria (f. ind.)	dans les matins où j'irai (f. ind.)	nas manhãs em que for (f. subj.)
bem que eu podia (imp. ind.)	bien que je puisse (pr. subj.)	bem que eu pudesse (imp. subj.)
talvez nós fazemos (p. ind.)	peut-être que nous faisons	talvez nós façamos (p. subj.)
espero que eu tenho (p. ind.)	j'espère que j'aurai (f. ind.)	espero que tenha (pr. subj.)

I believe that these three grammatical interferences in Portuguese are a result of the presence of the English language in Montreal, rather than the contact between Portuguese and French. In fact, English has long since replaced the subjunctive with the indicative mode. Even the Québécois use it less frequently than the French. Luso-Québécois, being in contact with English and Québécois French, have come to 'easily forget' that there are six tenses of the subjunctive that are commonly used in Portuguese, since they prefer to use the indicative.

I would suggest that the exaggerated use of the present participle is most likely the result of translations from the English suffix '-ing' and not the 'progressive form' of Portuguese, rarely used by the Açoreanos. Replacing other forms of address with *você* (*you* in English) also confirms these hypotheses. In fact, the *you* form of addressing someone, which had a significant influence on Québécois French, is now affecting the Portuguese as well.

Lexical Interferences

It is on the lexical level that I observed the most differences between the *imigrês* of France and that of Montreal (see Dias 1990). The formation of such an original vocabulary has surely been influenced by Canadianisms and other English words and expressions.

I have also noticed that the Luso-Québécois employ not only these expressions already used by people in Quebec, but also other original forms such as English calques and adaptations of meaning. Table 10.3 offers some examples of calques from English and Québécois French common in the language of first- and second-generation Portuguese

TABLE 10.3
Calques

Luso-Québécois	Québécois or English	Standard Portuguese
inecessário	unnecessary	desnecessário
majoridade	majorité/majority	maioria
falhasse	failed	perder o ano
destinação	destination/destination	destino
o secundário	le secondaire	o liceu
fazer uma aplicação*	faire une application	fazer um pedido
mesmo se é duro	même si c'est dur	mesmo se é difícil
a aula é plata	la classe est plate	a aula é aborrecida
permita algumas semanas	allow some weeks	espere algumas semanas
esta gente levou vantagem	these people took advantage	esta gente approveitou-se
privacidade	privacy	conservar a sua intimidade
constipações	constipation/constipation	prisão de ventre
dopou-se	s'est dopé(e)	drogou-se
graduações	graduation	obtenção dum diploma
apontamento	rendez-vous	marcar hora

*I noticed that Portuguese immigrants in France tended to say *fazer una demanda*, while the Luso-Québécois adapted the Canadianism *faire une application* as *fazer uma aplicação*.

immigrants. Table 10.4 outlines some examples of borrowing to designate new realities in Quebec. I also noticed some adaptations of English words in the speech of Luso-Québécois (see Table 10.5).

Summary

In summary, the most frequent interferences with the language of the Luso-Québécois for first-generation immigrants seem to be

- elimination of all forms of the subjunctive and their replacement with the indicative
- 'improper' use of the form of tratamento, você;
- a large number of terms borrowed from English and from Québécois French;
- morpho-semantic adaptations of English words

For second-generation immigrants common interferences are

- interference in the pronounciation of the consonant /R/ (Luso-

TABLE 10.4
Terms borrowed to designate new realities

Luso-Québécois	Standard Portuguese
duplex semi-destacado	does not exist
cottages jumelés	casas* geminadas
boeuf à ragoût sem osso	carne de guisar
banho tourbillon	does not exist
cottages em briques	casas de tijolo

*Approximate translation.

TABLE 10.5
Adaptations of English words into Portuguese

Luso-Québécois	English	Standard Portuguese
sinô	snow	neve
alferes	welfare	segurança social
formulas	forms (*formules* in French)	formulários
(filetes de) solo	(filets of) sole	(filetes de) linguado

Québécois tend to pronounce it as a soft /R/ ([r]) as in Portuguese and English)
- tendency to affricate the consonants [t] and [d], pronounced [ts] and [dz], respectively
- elimination of all tenses in the subjunctive
- exaggerated use of the present participle in Portuguese
- exaggerated use of the term você compared to other terms of address
- borrowed terms (especially from English)
- calques from English or from Québécois French words or expressions

There were also other interfering factors that I studied more extensively in the Portuguese communities in France (see Dias 1990). Some examples are

- confusion between nasals
- replacement of Portuguese prepositions by French prepositions
- morphological interferences in words (words with a French root and Portuguese suffix)

- use of words and expressions that belong to the vocabulary of 'international French.'

Bilingualism and Diglossia

The occurrence of bilingualism and diglossia in the Montreal community is very complex. The presence of English in the daily lives of the Luso-Québécois changes their linguistic choices and sets them apart from the Portuguese communities in France.

As I outlined above, Portuguese immigrants often use up to three languages to communicate. Veltman and Paré (1985) state that 30 per cent of immigrants are unilingual (speak only Portuguese); 32.7 per cent are bilingual (Portuguese and French), and 29.8 per cent are trilingual. The number of languages used varies with the age of the speaker. First-generation immigrants generally speak Portuguese at home, with members of their family and in the community; they employ French and English (for those who can speak these languages) only in formal situations such as the workplace.[14]

Almost all second-generation immigrants are trilingual, especially those in the age group seven to twenty-four (those under seven have not usually had enough exposure to Canadian and American culture to gain English skills). Second-generation immigrants generally speak Portuguese at home and French or English (or both) with their friends. The degree of understanding of Portuguese, French, and English varies, however. Those twenty to twenty-four have a better understanding of English, since they were educated in English; younger students have a much better understanding of French, because they go to French schools.

As I stated above, Portuguese is the language most often spoken at home by the first and second generations. In their dealings with the rest of society, they use one of the two official languages, depending on the situation. If individuals work for an anglophone, they speak English, and if for a francophone, French. In stores when shopping, they generally speak Portuguese (or *imigrês*) among themselves.[15]

While Portuguese immigrants are emotionally attached to their language of origin, from a social perspective, English predominates over both French and Portuguese. Ultimately, the purpose of this research has been to understand the adaptation of the Portuguese language to the new milieu and to examine its role in future generations of Portuguese in Quebec. The future of this linguistic pattern, given political uncertainties and Quebec's always-volatile language debate (see Jedwab 1996), remains uncertain.

NOTES

1 Luso-Québécois: Québécois of Portuguese origin.
2 The main portion of the study is based on
   • work written by Portuguese children (grades four to eleven) in the Programme d'enseignement des langues d'origine (PELO) offered in Quebec schools
   • writing and translations done by children (grades four to eleven) who attended Portuguese classes on Saturdays in Portuguese schools
   • studies done on these students in their respective school environments
   • letters written by Portuguese immigrants to the media
   • articles and advertisements published in Portuguese community newspapers
   • casual conversations with immigrants (adults and children) as well as with Portuguese teachers in Montreal.
   For further details concerning method, see Dias (1990).
3 Haudricourt and Juilland (1970: 16) state that this is also the case in the phonetic systems of Greek, Portuguese, and Swedish.
4 *Açoreano*: someone from the Azores, or the variation of Portuguese spoken there; also an adjective to describe a characteristic of the Azores.
5 Bill 101, which was enacted by the Parti Québécois government in 1977, required children of immigrants in Quebec to attend French schools.
6 Centre Portugais de Référence et Promotion Sociale (CPRRS), founded in 1972 to assist Portuguese immigrants integrate into Quebec society. At present the official designation is Centre d'Action Socio-Communautaire de Montréal.
7 The study was conducted by the Institut National de la Recherche Scientifique (INRS – Urbanisation) in 1984.
8 I encountered many difficulties trying to conduct research and gather observations among the Portuguese of Montreal. These people, especially those originating from the Azores, generally like to keep to themselves and do not like to share thoughts about their private lives. Also, many of the adults were too embarrassed to write (either because they cannot write well or are illiterate) and did not like to respond to questions.
9 An interference occurs in a specific language (for instance, Portuguese)

when a speaker uses an element – phonetic, lexical, morphological, or semantic – that belongs to another language (for instance, French).

10 Both versions of /R/ exist in Portuguese, but there is a phonological difference.

11 In this case, there has been a change from the vowel [u] to [y]. This occurs both in Quebec and in France.

12 This could also be a dialectal characteristic of the Azores.

13 The use of the present participle with the auxiliary *estar* (to be) or *andar* (to walk) is very common in southern Portugal (Alentejo and Algarve), as well as in Brazil. These structures correspond to the progressive form in English and the French structure of (conjugated verb) + *en train de* + (verb in the infinitive). For example, 'I am studying' would be translated as 'Je suis en train d'étudier' in French and 'Estou a estudar' in Portuguese.

14 Those who make up the 30 per cent of immigrants who are unilingual conduct their lives only in Portuguese and live in a ghetto-like environment.

15 I had the opportunity to go shopping several times in the St Louis quarter. While I always spoke Portuguese, people responded to me in Luso-Québécois.

REFERENCES

Alpalhão, J.A., and Da Rosa, V.M.P. 1979. *Les Portugais du Québec: Éléments d'analyse socio-culturelle*. Ottawa: Éditions de l'Université d'Ottawa.

Dias, M. 1990. 'Deux langues en contact: Le français et le portugais dans les communautés de Paris et de Montréal.' Doctoral dissertation, University of Toronto.

Haudricourt, A., and Juilland, A. 1970. *Essai pour une histoire structurale du phonétisme français*. Paris: Mouton.

Jedwab, J. 1996. *English in Montreal: A Layman's Look at the Current Situation*. Montreal: Images.

Marcil, C. 1980. 'Les Portugais au Québec.' *Éducation Québec* 11 no. 2: 18–23.

Mateus, M.H. 1983. *Gramática da língua portuguesa*. Coimbra: Livraria Almedina.

Veltman, C., and Paré, O. 1985. *L'insertion sociolinguistique des Québécois d'origine portugaise*. Montreal: Institut National de la Recherche Scientifique – Urbanisation.

11

Diasporic Identities at Century's End

EDITE NOIVO

In a world of global transnational migrations and diasporas, where self-identities have become reflexively organized endeavours, how are Portuguese Canadians forming and reforming their ethnic identity? How have recent cultural, social, and political transformations in Portugal and Europe influenced the identity politics of the hundreds of thousands of *lusitanus* settled in Canada? To what extent is the racial demography of incoming immigrants and the cohabitation of diverse ethnic cultures affecting the identities of established, white immigrants? Ultimately, how are expanded heterogeneities in class and generational membership shaping the ethnocultural consciousness of Portuguese Canadians?

This essay deals with the diasporic identities of three generations of Portuguese Canadians at the end of the millennium. It first examines current definitions of ethnic identities and, second, locates diaspora groups in transition in the context of contemporary pluralist societies. It argues that we must place the Portuguese in Canada within a diaspora of nearly five million dispersed across the planet and analyse their sense of 'we-ness' in terms of their generation, gender, and class memberships. Third, and since diasporas are about roots and routes (Gilroy 1993), this essay looks at how three generations of Portuguese Canadians appear to be chartering their identity journeys into the next century.

Deconstructing Ethnic Identities

Instead of 'unpacking' the debate over the theoretically saturated notion of ethnicity, I trace some of the propositions more likely to help us understand the equally complex notion of ethnic identity. First and foremost, we should recall that ethnicities, like identities, are two-way processes that occur in the course of social transactions. Whether identity emerges via ethnic ascription or subscription, by outsiders or by self-identification, is a purely analytical distinction. In reality, all individual and collective identifications are the outcome of largely consensual definitions and categorizations by in- and out-group members.

In fact, a problem with common claims that ethnic groups are formed by self-identification with real or imagined cultural communities is that they overlook the need of all social identities for external recognition. On the other side, contentions that ethnic identifications, are politically engineered by the state, institutions, and elites – all of which are said to designate, stigmatize, and impose categories of identity so as to maintain social stratification and ethnic hierarchies – generally misrepresent identities as compulsory. Such misconceptions, which disregard the fact that groups and actors may contest and resist 'mandatory' identities, also neglect the historical struggles of minority groups to appropriate and instrumentalize their ethnic identities in fighting ethnic inequality.

On this issue, it is useful to recall Barth's classical work (1969), in which he theorizes that ethnicity is really about the processes of defining identities and ethnic boundaries. Barth emphasized the internal and external definitions of ethnicity and that its production or reproduction is a two-way process, which takes place across the boundary between 'us' and 'them.' The politics of collective boundaries and ethnic identification are not always intended to oppress others; they often seek to mobilize resources, to compete and/or further the interests of the ethnic group (Rex 1986). Although most people undergoing 'ethnicization' and 'minoritization' are immigrants, ethnicity is not synonymous with economic subordination.[1]

In most contemporary pluri-ethnic contexts, the politics of identity are actually about cultural locations and contested belongingness. The most effective explanations of ethnic phenomena describe them as reactions to globalization, ultra-individualism, alienation, and the rootlessness and impersonal relations of modern societies. For many, they represent collective attempts to hold on to, or even forge, primordialist ties and communal identities in a standardized, alienated world (Allahar 1994). Many authors believe that modernization does not so much create melting pots as it promotes tribalism and turns ethnic groups into interest groups. They maintain that recent ethnic and religious fundamentalisms are a reaction to the process of de-traditionalization and the emergence of global society (Giddens 1991).

In recent years, new approaches to ethnic identity place it at the heart of the ongoing struggles among minorities as well as those between majority and minority groups. It has now been established that in defining strategies and mobilizing resources to pursue their ends, ethnic collectivities – much like dominant groups – develop or reinforce ethnocultural identities around selected salient features, such as language, religion, cultural traits, and skin colour. Other propositions, which focus on the individual in modernity, add to our understanding of identities by claiming that 'the self is no longer centred, unified and in place, but is multiple, shifting and decentred' (Westwood 1994: 258).

A central claim is that in the new 'planetary society,' in which a shift has taken place from national collectivities to particularistic identities, 'the self' is permeable and fluid (Melluci 1997).[2] The argument made by Melluci and others, and which concerns us here, is that at this century's end it is not classes, genders, or ethnic groups, but really everyone, who has to face the questions of who they are, where they belong, what their place in society is, and why. Identities have become essential tools that many people call upon almost constantly.

This proposition is reasonable on several grounds. First, ethnic identities are not represented in the usual monolithic terms, but rather conceived as interwoven into multiple other social identifications. Second, myriad situations now compel us to define, affirm, and reshape our identities. As Melluci suggests, as one moves across disparate settings, one affirms one's multiple identities according to the environments and the strategies that one develops. Thus when a person moves across international borders and cultures, he or she must keep his or her roots in national society and yet respond to the question 'who am I?' in global terms. Of course, Melluci's remark – that technologically advanced societies, which enable individuals to compare and differentiate themselves and their cultural particularities from others across the planet, corrode national cultures and a sense of roots and homeland – is not new.[3] But ethnic identities are embedded in similarity and differentiation. In real life, individuals construct or refashion their identities in relation to real or imagined differences with surrounding dominant and/or other minority cultures, and also according to their similarities with the ancestral group(s) with which they identify. This is why the idea that ethnic identities are always defined situationally – and thus liable to shift – connects personal experiences to external events.

Individual identities are of course not the only ones located between sameness and continuity. In describing 'identity,' Erikson (in Jenkins 1994) speaks of the 'unity of personal and cultural identity,' although he regards it as something never really established or achieved. If the view that individual identities usually proceed from family and group identity is taken a step forward, one might then see that families and ethnic groups – in mediating the identities between an individual and society – do more than just affect the degree of positive or negative self-identity. Families usually hold the decisive power to transmit or not ancestral cultures; it is they that select the symbols and traditions which eventually shape their members' ethnocultural identities. But 'families' here is a misnomer. The transmitters of ethnic identities across generations are not so much families as women.

As Taboada-Leonetti (1983) and others have argued, ethnic women reproduce ethnocultures. As depositories of cultural traditions, immigrant/ethnic mothers commonly transmit their minority cultures to their offspring, including a 'mother language.' This viewpoint also holds that women's individual decisions to assimilate to a dominant culture end up jeopardizing, if not halting, ethnocultural reproduction. Taboada-Leonetti rightly denounces both the pressures and responsibilities placed on women to transmit their cultural traits to their children and women's lack of freedom to assimilate to the dominant culture. But she overlooks an important feature. Although cultural identity is transmitted by mothers and other close kin, the acceptance or rejection of ethnic cultures greatly depends on the relationships between transmitter and receiver. There is an old cliché that 'what the son wants to forget ... [about the ethnic culture and practices] the grandson wishes to remember' (Hansen 1938: 9–10). Youths tend to contest or reject ethnic identities, however, mostly because those identities are transmitted by those with greater (generational) power and also amid psychopolitical struggles and emotional confrontations. The apparent difficulty of disassociating one's family experiences and parental impositions from one's ethnic background is evidenced whenever individuals reclaim or reappropriate their cultural identities (with invigorated strength) when their parents are no longer around or have lost authority over them.

Diasporic Identities in Transition

Diasporas can be described as 'expatriate communities, dispersed from an original "centre," that maintain a memory, vision or myth about their homeland, or hold a collective identity defined by that relationship' (Clifford 1994: 305). Although they are not immigrant communities or ethnic neighbourhoods, in this age of cyberspace,'a diaspora can, to some degree, be held together or re-created through the mind, through cultural artefacts and through a shared imagination' (Cohen 1997: 26). Some diasporas invoke imagined geographies, but most draw on the relationships of populations displaced from their native territories. In either case, a diaspora always entails the notion of 'homeland,' whether as a mythical place existing in one's imagination or as the geographical location where one actually originated.

The Portuguese diaspora discussed here is obviously not that of colonialism, but refers to the diasporization following the Second World War. As Perlmutter suggests (in Cohen 1997), the term is tied up with 'the territorialization and deterritorialization of identities.' In the Portuguese case, members regard Portugal as their 'home.' However, it does seem somewhat ironic that diasporization, which refers to 'homelessness,' should involve a sense of 'homeland.' In these, as in other massive labour migrations, the phenomenon entails what Clifford (1994) calls 'travelling cultures,' which means a decentring of the home. But unlike cultures that have lost their territorial mooring, the millions of Portuguese migrants who 'displaced themselves' to advanced economies resettled their ethnocultures in their new geophysical contexts. Yet diasporas are not just about deterritorializing or large groups being denied social citizenship. Diasporic identities are generally embedded in the cultural politics of the receiving countries. As such, they reflect the status accorded to the ethnic group in question, which in most cases is not fully accepted by the dominant society.

As in most cases, the ethnicization of the Portuguese in Canada occurred through immigration, particularly in the first generation. But at the century's end, this ethnic group is made up of 'the canonical three generations,' and a fourth is emerging. At the moment, of the nearly quarter-million Portuguese Canadians, 160,000 were born in Portugal. While most share both the journey and the struggles to forge a 'new home' in Canada, 90,000 were born in diasporic spaces. For both groups, however, 'home' seems to be where they live and where they cannot live – a sort of multiplaced locality that some people recall as pre-migratory experiences and where others forge meanings and a sense of belonging built on storytelling and transmitted affections.

In *Inside Ethnic Families: Three Generations of Portuguese-Canadians* (Noivo 1997), I remarked that some Portuguese report 'feeling at home' only during their periodic sojourns in their native land. Others refer to 'home' as their membership and social networks in their new communities. A few equate 'home' with *pátria* and invoke Fernando Pessoa's adage: *A minha pátria é a língua portuguesa* (My homeland is the Portuguese language). In fact, these different responses made me question whether for them 'home' is actually decentred or rather metamorphosed into a mother tongue, which seems to act as a sort of psychic home and uniting force with their homeland. Therefore the notable decrease in Portuguese fluency among younger generations deserves greater attention. Yet my extensive, ongoing observations of Canadian-born 'Portuguese' tell me that most are strongly socialized into a diasporic consciousness. In other words, the vast majority develop affective, 'symbolic ethnic identities' (Gans 1979), which means that their 'Portuguese-ness' is anchored not by their linguistic practices but rather in their sense of belonging to that diaspora.[4]

Moreover, I have remarked that for the three generations of Portuguese Canadians I have studied (Noivo 1997), 'Portuguese-ness' seems to be a sort of internal space to which they regress in their fantasies, vivid memories, or wishful dreams. Regardless of their birthplace, the diasporic identities of grandparents, parents, and children seem constituted by both positive and negative sentiments towards their original or imaginary 'homeland,' in addition to both positive and negative experiences of exclusion and minoratization within Canadian society. On this issue, I would add three brief comments. First, diasporic membership or having polyethnic identities does not mean lesser participation in mainstream society. Second, Portuguese diasporic identities are not faint, diluted versions of territorialized Portuguese identities. Third, despite the self-representation of diasporic groups as safeguarding presumably threatened traditions, cultural survival in reality does not depend on deterritorialization or patridalgia.

This statement takes me to my earlier claim that the diasporic identities of Portuguese Canadians cannot be apprehended outside the global Portuguese diaspora or apart from the identities articulated inside Portugal. I also believe that the contested meanings of 'we-ness' and 'otherness' observable between resident and diasporic Portuguese have to be brought into its analysis. The constituted, contested, and re-created signifiers of Portuguese identity are, like others, based on processes of differentiation and commonality. By this I mean that territorialized and deterritorialized Portuguese share a common culture and identity. Yet the personal, family, and collective experiences of diasporic members are radically different from those of non-migrants. Each group's identity has obviously evolved in quite different geocultural contexts and sociopolitical locations.[5] Given this, territorialized and deterritorialized Portuguese speak to different perceptions of 'otherness' and to contested notions of identity, and they have undergone historical conditions that ultimately mean the sociocultural inclusion of some and the exclusion of others.

Years before Portugal joined the European Community in 1986, Eduardo Lourenço (1982) delivered a brilliant analysis of Portugal's national identity in *O labirinto da saudade*. Portugal, despite being one of Europe's oldest nation-states, has an identity that is no longer viable and urgently needs reconfiguring. Lourenço calls for a recasting of the Portuguese identity, by arguing that it ought to be recontextualized in light of Portugal's current size, politics, and economic standing. Surely the author of *The Labyrinth* is not referring to Portuguese transnational or diasporic identities. Portugal's existentialist questions – '*Quem somos? O que somos?*' (Who, what are we?) (in Lourenço 1982: 98), though striking (for a nation founded in 1143), are really not so surprising if we relate them to our earlier discussion of globalization. In other words, this line of questioning is intrinsic to the current context of global restructuring and unprecedented societal reflexivity (Giddens 1991), and it only reflects the type of uncertainty that old and new nation-states seem to be feeling. Thus, at century's end, it is not merely individuals but even 'old' states that must come to terms with their identities.

Having Portuguese Canadians question and reformulate their ethnocultural identities at a time when Portugal itself is rebuilding its self-image is non-coincidental and historically significant. But before looking at how Portugal's task of re-creating its identity affects its diaspora, I want to bring Lourenço's claims into the late 1990s. His suggestion that Portugal's uneasiness with its historical identity, and its urgent task of remapping itself on the world's cartography, derives from its recent territorial reduction following decolonization is undoubtedly true. However, that malaise has also been exacerbated by Portugal's location in the new world order, not least within the 'new Europe.' Portugal's integration in the European Union now means that its destiny and identity lie within a reconfigurated European-ness.[6]

Having said that this century ends with the entire Portuguese ethnos questioning its self-identity,[7] I want to turn to the role that diasporic groups play in redefining 'Portuguese-ness.' To begin with, Portugal could not exclude its diaspora (for example, Portuguese Canadians) from the remaking of its identity without undermining its legitimation. A reformulated sense of 'Portuguese-ness' has to include and represent territorialized and deterritorialized collectivities alike. For the reconstruction of cultural symbols and meanings has to reflect the cultural commonalities and the distinctiveness of Portuguese residing inside and outside Portugal. Therefore diasporic groups must create new forms of dialogue among and across Portuguese collectivities, develop new forums of communication, establish new transnational connections, and so on. All of these efforts will probably strengthen and revitalize their identities – in this case, those of Portuguese Canadians.

Until recently, interaction across diasporic communities was difficult and somewhat limited. However, technological innovations in communication and transportation now enable these groups to create links with transnational Portuguese organizations. In fact, a significant part of the Portuguese diaspora's artistic production (literature, music, theatre) already moves across several continents.[8] Family and social networks dispersed across diasporic spaces are also being established or revived. Eventually, diasporic members may develop multi-locale attachments. For example, Portuguese Canadians visiting relatives in Germany may take part in local community celebrations, which, besides creating links across communities, help reinforce their diasporic identity. In Portugal, a considerable number of summer festivities are being organized by emigrants, and events cater to diasporic members on holidays. Luistanus in the Americas already have daily chat-group discussions in cyberspace. I have remarked that such occasions bring emigrants together, to the point that some, overwhelmed by the number of experiences they share with fellow minorities in other countries, show a strong interest in pursuing further inter-diasporic communication and action.

It is unquestionable that such contacts and networks influence the community consciousness of diasporic members, who may develop what Edward Said (1984: 171–2) has called 'contrapuntal' awareness. Whereas 'most people are principally aware of one culture, one setting, one home ... exiles are aware of at least two,' and their habits and actions tend to 'occur against the memory' of two settings, which renders them more vivid and actual. If we relate this to my earlier statement that diasporas are always embedded in multiple localities (through memory and affective attachments), it then becomes clearer that members of the Portuguese diaspora – with enriching experiences as migrants and minorities – add enormously to the multiple ways of being Portuguese. Also, many immigrants are acquainted with and relate to more than one diasporic community.[9]

Furthermore, for a reconfigurated Portuguese identity to include and represent its ethnos, it needs to incorporate further differences – namely, those based on class, gender, and generation. In so far as diasporic identities also intersect with sexual and occupational identifications (on this, see Brah 1996), the former have to encompass the multiple practices and meanings of men and women, workers and professionals. Let us look more closely at the evolving identities of the following groups.

Three Generations in the New Millennium

The ethnic identities of Portuguese Canadians remain largely unanalysed. The limited literature available – most of which adopts a binary, linear, culturalist perspective of ethnicity – has focused on the formation, persistence, and reproduction of their presumed bicultural identities.[10] Still, stimulating theorizations of ethnic identities and the multiplicity and fragmentation of subjectivities – namely, the works of Gilroy (1993), Rattansi (1994), Brah (1996), and others – may inspire more valuable analyses in the near future. For now, I merely want to supplement my earlier suggestions regarding the arising 'multiplicity of Portuguese ethnic identities' with some of the challenges confronting Portuguese Canadians. To identify those issues, I propose three levels of analyses.

At a first, macro level, inasmuch as a 'Portuguese identity' is embedded in current meanings of 'Western Europeanness,' it will alter according to shifting meanings of the latter. But while redefinitions of 'Western-ess' and 'European-ness' affect the identities of all Portuguese, those in Canada report other reasons for representing themselves as western Europeans. Following the massive immigration of non-Europeans to Canada, white 'older' immigrant groups seem to be distancing themselves from the immigrant category and stressing their Europeanness.[11]

At a second, mezzo level, the ethnic identities of Portuguese Canadians are inextricably tied to their minority status. As I mentioned above, those identities are also intersected by gender and generational differences, in addition to being further divided according to class and occupation. Their analyses must therefore take all these distinctions into account. Also, changes in the ethnic and gender consciousness of members (on this, see Hein 1991 and Brah 1996), or new understandings of how their ethnic and class memberships converge (see Rex 1986), are likely to affect the cultural identifications of these groups. For example, women for whom self-identification as Portuguese prompts images of female subordination or traditional norms may seek to distance themselves from their ethnocultural group.

At the third, individual level, ethnic identifications involve both personal experiences and ideologies. While (diasporic) culture and kinship generally intersect, neither is chosen. I am not endorsing the sense of fatality that Lourenço (1982) claims as inherent to a presumed Portuguese character. Rather, family ties and relational dynamics strongly affect, if not determine, the trajectories, external and internal journeys, and continuities and discontinuities in the identity of the third generation. Contested identities are often reactions to parent–child relational dynamics. Accordingly, changes in those relationships tend to alter the ethnic identifications of younger members significantly. For example, I have witnessed youths disdaining what they conceive as 'Portuguese traits' displayed by their parents. However, some of those young people, after visiting Portugal, become quite enthralled with the characteristics that they formerly censured and then speak proudly of their cultural background.[12]

This point takes me to the presumed 'cultural clashes' among Portuguese- and Canadian-born generations. Popular depictions of ethnic youths as 'torn between two cultures' have vastly misrepresented the situation.[13] As shown in *Inside Ethnic Families*, clashes between parents and youths are extensive, but usually related to age. Most conflicts are actually based on family dynamics and power struggles, not on ethnocultural differences.

Conclusion

Because ethnocultures are 'dynamic multitextured productions subject to constant change and revisions' (Westwood 1994: 260), Portuguese Canadians will probably chart their diasporic identities into the next millennium, by celebrating 'hybridity,' reconciling 'old' and 'new' cultural symbols, reinventing old meanings, and forging new practices. Yet as creative as they may be in re-creating their ethnic identity, their ethnicity is also shaped by external forces beyond their control. They will undoubtedly be carrying their minority status for generations to come. Meanwhile, many of those born into these diasporic communities will have to rely on the recollections and migration stories of their ancestors. Others may activate their diasporic consciousness by establishing personal contacts with Portugal, or perhaps with fellow members of the diaspora. Also, new communication technologies – which currently render interaction across transnational groups strikingly easy – may presumably offset the noticeable decline in ethnic community involvement.

As I discussed above, in the next millennium, ethnic identities will become ever more permeable, instrumental, and plural. An overwhelming number of choices and options in terms of identities and in most areas of our lives will proliferate and confront us almost daily. But if, as Jenkins (1994) and others contend, ethnicity becomes largely 'voluntary,' and communities continue to create series of 'identity options' (Rex, Joly, and Wilpert 1987; Waters 1990) for their members, then multiple, novel forms and manifestations of 'Portugueseness' will arise. Throughout their lives, Portuguese Canadians may stress one identity, then another, at times questioning and at other times invigorating their ethnicity. At the collective level, some communities may cling to symbols and practices long defunct in other localities, including Portugal. What seems certain is that in this age of diasporic consciousness, with Portuguese culture gaining broad international recognition, Portuguese Canadians will not be lacking in identity capital or cultural resources with which to remap themselves into the next century.

NOTES

1 On the argument that ethnicity is voluntary while 'race' is not, see Rex 1986 and Lieberson 1985. For a discussion of the processes of ethnicization and minoritization, see Hein 1991. As much as I consider the term 'minority group' (advanced by Wirth in 1945) to have become sociologically meaningless, it conventionally means groups that occupy subordinate positions of wealth, power, and prestige.
2 He suggests that rather than juxtaposing the particular with the universal, or associating patterns of social exclusion–inclusion with ethnic identifications, we do better to observe how all these conditions coexist.

3 See Stone (in Rex 1986).

4 Gans uses 'symbolic ethnicity' to explain that when individuals no longer speak minority languages or display distinct cultural practices, they may nevertheless maintain symbolic attachments and a sense of belonging to the ethnic culture(s) of their ancestors.

5 The occasional friction and resentment between emigrants and non-emigrants to which I am referring is widely known and is documented in the Portuguese-Canadian press. My comments are also based on 'insider' observations in Portugal, where state-funded programs have been developed to promote more congenial relations between visiting emigrants (regarded by many non-migrants as second-class citizens) and permanent residents (who have stayed and transformed the country). Concerns about social, cultural, and political citizenship of non-resident Portuguese, along with the demands that diasporic collectivities make on the Portuguese state to develop protective policies towards citizens abroad, are also documented (see, for example, Hily and Poinard 1987).

6 The extent to which the EU superstructure directly affects Portugal's political and economic life as well as its cultural production and national identity is wide-ranging. For an overall analysis of the impact of the European Union (EU) on Portugal, see José Magone (1997: 176), who believes that the Portuguese will go from considering themselves as European Portuguese to describing themselves as Portuguese Europeans. On the structural relations between the EC/EU and Portugal, see also José S. Lopes 1993, particularly Mário Bacalhau's (1993) chapter on EC/EU integration and Portuguese national identity.

7 For an analysis of identity and modernity, see Giddens 1991.

8 Most cultural production of the diaspora is consumed by it and never reaches Portugal's markets.

9 Some have migrated to France before settling in Canada; others visit their relatives in other countries.

10 In Canada its proponents include Anderson and Frideres (1981) and Breton, Isajiw, Kalbach, and Reitz (1990).

11 Elsewhere I explore how changes in the racial backgrounds of new immigrants affect on the identifications and alliances among white, European groups already settled in Canada (Noivo 1998). The self-reporting of the Portuguese in Canada has changed from just 'Portuguese' in the 1960s and 1970s, to 'Portuguese Canadians' in the 1980s. In the 1990s, an increasing number are 'dropping the hyphen' and claiming to be Europeans, Euroethnics, or Canadians/Québécois of Portuguese origin. For a theorization of hyphenated ethnics, see Lieberson 1985 and Waters 1990.

12 In some cases, those who refused to learn Portuguese from their parents now read Fernando Pessoa or José Saramago in English or French. This type of appreciation for Portuguese art, cuisine, music, history, and more is well portrayed by contributing authors of *Silva Magazine* (a trilingual cultural magazine published in Toronto).
13 For criticism of such accounts, see Noivo 1997.

REFERENCES

Allahar, A. 1994. 'More Than an Oxymoron: Ethnicity and the Social Construction of Primordial Attachment.' *Canadian Ethnic Studies* 26 no. 3: 18–33.
Anderson, A., and Frideres, J. 1981. *Ethnicity in Canada: Theoretical Perspectives*. Toronto: Butterworths.
Bacalhau, M. 1993. 'EC Integration and Identity.' In Lopes 1993, 182–92.
Barth, F. 1969. *Ethnic Groups and Boundaries: The Social Organization of Culture Difference*. Oslo: Universitetsforlaget.
Brah, A. 1996. *Cartographies of Diaspora: Contesting Identities*. London: Routledge.
Breton, R., Isajiw, W., Kalbach, W., and Reitz, J. 1990. *Ethnic Identity and Equality: Varieties of Experience in a Canadian City*. Toronto: University of Toronto Press.
Clifford, J. 1994. 'Diasporas.' *Cultural Anthropology* 9 no. 3: 302–38.
Cohen, R. 1997. *Global Diasporas: An Introduction*. London: UCL Press.
Gans, H. 1979. 'Symbolic Ethnicity: The Future of Ethnic Groups and Cultures in America.' *Ethnic and Racial Studies* 2 no. 1: 1–20.
Giddens, A. 1991. *Modernity and Self-identity: Self and Society in Late Modern Age*. Stanford, Calif.: Stanford University Press.
Gilroy, P. 1993. *The Black Atlantic: Modernity and Double Consciousness*. London: Verso.
Hansen, M. 1938. *The Problem of the Third Generation Immigrant*. Rock Island, Ill.: Augustana Historical Society.
Hein, J. 1991. 'Do "New Immigrants" Become "New Minorities?"' *Sociological Perspectives* 34: 61–78.
Hily, M.A., and M. Poinard. 1987. 'Portuguese Associations in France.' In J. Rex et al., eds., *Immigrant Associations in Europe*. Aldershot, England: Gower Publishing.
Jenkins, R. 1994. 'Rethinking Ethnicity: Identity, Categorization and Power.' *Ethnic and Racial Studies* 17 no. 2: 197–223.
Lieberson, S. 1985. 'Unhyphenated Whites in the United States.' *Ethnic and Racial Studies* 8: 159–80.

Lopes, J.S., ed. 1993. *Portugal and EC Membership Evaluated*. London: Pinter Publishers.

Lourenço, E. 1982. *O labirinto da saudade*. Lisbon: Dom Quixote.

Magone, J. 1997. *European Portugal: The Difficult Road to Sustainable Democracy*. London: Macmillan.

Melluci, A. 1997. 'Becoming a Person: New Frontiers for Identity and Citizenship in a Planetary Society.' Paper presented at the European Sociological Conference, University of Essex, England.

Noivo, E. 1997. *Inside Ethnic Families: Three Generations of Portuguese-Canadians*. Montreal: McGill-Queen's University Press.

– 1998. 'Neither "Ethnic Heroes" nor "Racial Villains": Inter-Minority Group Racism.' In V. Satzewich, ed., *Racism and Social Inequality in Canada: Concepts, Controversies and Strategies of Resistance*, 223–41. Toronto: Thompson Educational Publishing.

Rattansi, A. 1994. '"Western" Racisms, Ethnicities and Identities in a Postmodern Frame.' In A. Rattansi and S. Westwood, eds., *Racism, Modernity and Identity on the Western Front*, 15–86. Cambridge: Polity Press.

Rex, J. 1986. *Race and Ethnicity*. Milton Keynes: Open University Press.

Rex, J., Joly, D., and Wilpert, C. 1987. *Immigrant Associations in Europe*. Aldershot, England: Gower Publishing.

Said, E. 1984. 'Reflections of Exile.' *Granta* 13: 159–72.

Taboada-Leonetti, I. 1983. 'Le role des femmes migrantes dans le maintien ou la destructuration des cultures nationales du groupe migrant.' *Etudes migration* 20: 214–21.

Waters, M. 1990. *Ethnic Options: Choosing Identities in America*. Berkeley: University of California Press.

Westwood, S. 1994. 'Racism, Mental Illness and the Politics of Identity.' In A. Rattansi and S. Westwood, eds., *Racism, Modernity and Identity*, 247–65. Cambridge: Polity Press.

Wirth, L. 1945. 'The Problem of Minority Groups.' In R. Linton, ed., *The Science of Man in the World Crisis*, 347–72. New York: Columbia University Press.

PART FOUR

'LITTLE PORTUGALS'

12

Building a Neighbourhood in Montreal

GILLES LAVIGNE and CARLOS TEIXEIRA

Geographers' and sociologists' understanding of the settlement and mobility patterns of ethnic groups and of segregation and integration remains limited.[1] The mobility of individuals and groups that one finds in North America, and the various constraints that are also prevalent in Europe, suggest the complex social forces at work. The Portuguese in Montreal represent a significant example of these processes extending as far back as the 1960s.

Canada has been an immigrant country since the first Europeans stepped foot on the shores of Newfoundland. Until the late 1960s most of Canada's immigrant population came from Britain and other European countries, with subsequent migrations coming mostly from the 'Third World.' Like other big Canadian cities, such as Toronto and Vancouver, Montreal is made up of many ethnic neighbourhoods. This may appear to be an ordinary occurrence, given that it seems natural for immigrants of the same cultural background to settle together when far from home. However, this question of segregation versus integration is complex and controversial. Does the spatial polarization of ethnic groups inhibit immigrants' integration in the indigenous society?

The Portuguese in Montreal

Arriving in the 1950s, the Portuguese made up the last wave of immigrants of European origin to settle in Canada. Almost all the Portuguese immigrants arriving in Quebec in the last five decades have settled in Montreal. Underestimated as a result of illegal immigration, the number of Portuguese living in Quebec by the mid-1990s numbered between fifty thousand and sixty thousand, and they proved to be very dynamic. In less than twenty years, they settled one part of the city, developed a significant business district, set up institutions, and built a very business-minded middle class (Lavigne 1979). This 'institutionally complete' community offers an excellent opportunity for us to analyse the settlement patterns of the first immigrants and their subsequent mobility. A comparative examination of maps based on various census data from the years 1941–81 shows an immigrant corridor running along rue St-Laurent from the downtown core up to the northeastern suburbs. The ethnic make-up of this corridor varies (McNicoll 1993), with neighbourhoods ranging from Jewish, Italian, and Greek to Portuguese, most of whose residents eventually move to the suburbs.

There is still some mystery surrounding the first Portuguese immigrant settlements (Lavigne 1979). Agreement on landing and transit locations, as defined first by Burgess (1967) and later by Rex (1968), does not fully explain how the first immigrants settled. The Portuguese followed the classic and theoretical settlement model (Lavigne 1979, 1987; Teixeira 1986; Teixeira and Lavigne 1991). None the less, whether they immigrated before 1960, between 1961 and 1970, or after 1971, 75 per cent of those who moved directly to Montreal settled in the so-called Portuguese neighbourhood (Figure 12.1). Moreover, 71.7 per cent of the Portuguese in question admit to having been helped on arrival by relatives who either allowed them to stay in their homes or apartments or helped them find homes (Teixeira 1986).

Our study of the formation of the Portuguese neighbourhood in Montreal links a variety of factors that contributed to its make-up since the 1950s. Montreal is much like any other North American city except for its claim to a basic biculturalism, in which two majority groups live together: one is francophone and Québécois, the other anglophone and 'Canadian.' This duality, which is specific to Canada, occurs in Montreal amid the presence of Jews, Germans, Poles, Ukrainians, Italians, Greeks, Portuguese, Asians, and Africans from the Caribbean. Of these immigrants, some have formed ethnic neighbourhoods, and others have not.

As we noted above, the Portuguese were the last European group to migrate to Canada, mainly to Toronto and Montreal.[2] Their transplantation began in the 1950s, peaked in 1974, and then dropped. In Montreal, the new arrivals settled along the immigrant corridor, in the St-Louis neighbourhood (Figure 12.1). By 1971 the Portuguese neighbourhood was clearly visible and statistically important. By 1981 the

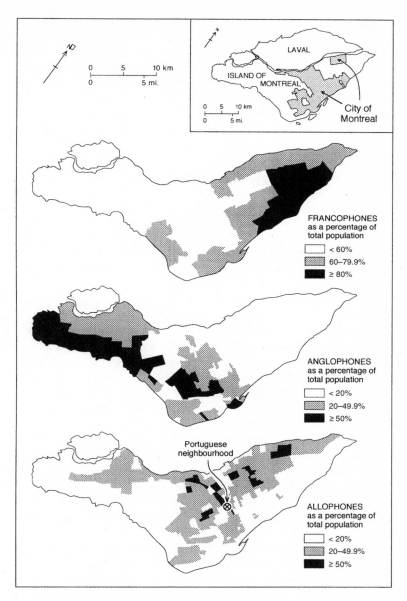

Figure 12.1. Geographical distribution of ethnic communities on the island of Montreal. *Source*: Adapted from Monière and Côté 1995, 162–3

Portuguese seemed to have begun moving to the north of the city (Teixeira 1986), without really relinquishing the St-Louis area, where in 1986 they built a church and set up a community centre. The Portuguese have left their cultural mark on the physical landscape of Montreal and indeed feel very much at home there (Lavigne 1980; Lavigne and Richot 1991).

We attempt in this essay to explain, first, the emergence of a Portuguese neighbourhood in Montreal and, second, its very distinctive characteristics.

Emergence of the Portuguese Neighbourhood

Spatial Change and Ethnic Differentiation

Not all immigrants comprise ethnic groups, and not all ethnic communities occupy a neighbourhood.[3] Thus the creation of an ethnicized geographical location calls to mind a number of factors, with immigration status as the first and foremost. Most host countries generally recognize two types of immigration: dependent and independent. From 1896, free as it was, Canadian immigration became selective. The revised immigration act of 1952, which remained in effect up to 1977, was especially designed for two types of immigrants – those who came to Canada to look for a job and who had to meet certain conditions, and those who came through some sort of sponsorship and selection. The first group would be educated and professionally qualified; the second group, less educated and unskilled. Successive changes to the legislation have not altered this basic distinction.

Groups are organized differently from one ethnic cluster to the other. In Montreal, Germans, Poles, and Russians have a dispersed, unorganized community structure. Chinese, Greeks, Italians, and Jews, in contrast, appear to have a higher level of institutional completeness. These groups have generally stood out in the Montreal landscape, even though over time the situation has somewhat changed (Bailly, Hamel, and Polèse 1976; Constantinides 1983; McNicoll 1993).

It seems as if these variations are closely tied to immigration status. Communities created from independent immigration have a somewhat loose organization, as opposed to communities resulting from sponsorship. Sponsored immigration is based on family ties. It reunites relatives, often poorly educated individuals with no professional qualifications, and imposes a dependent relationship between these individuals. A 1962 study characterizes it as a chain and as institution-alized migration (MacDonald and MacDonald 1962). An ethnic com-munity is said to be a structured community in which individuals help one another and that shuts out extra-group relationships and repro-duces itself, while maintaining its ethnic specificity. The term 'colony' would best describe this type of community.

Dependent Immigration and Ethnic Neighbourhoods

In Canada, most immigration became dependent from 1976 (Statistics Canada 1982, 1984). Factor analysis of Canadian agglomerations (Bailly, Hamel, and Polèse 1976; Carlos and Polèse 1978) shows that the most segregated groups in Montreal, as well as Toronto, are, in ascend-ing order, Jews, Greeks, Portuguese, Chinese, Italians, and West Indi-ans (Kalbach 1980; Bourne et al. 1986). Except for Jews, most of these groups were landed through sponsorship.

As for the Portuguese, 60 per cent come from the Azores, and nearly 90 per cent of them were landed through sponsorship or selection (Teixeira 1986, 1995). As early as 1971, the calculation of dissimilarity coefficients showed a concentration of Portuguese in certain census areas on the island of Montreal: thirteen census tracts out of 566 con-tained 52.2 per cent of the Portuguese population (Lavigne 1979).

Were there at that time any differences between conglomerating and dispersing Portuguese? As their immigration is recent, their dispersion could not be a sign of greater assimilation. Moreover, the comparison made from several socio-economic and demographic variables does not reveal any significant difference.[4] Dispersion was more synony-mous with 'captive' mobility (Teixeira and Lavigne 1991; Teixeira 1995) – mobility constrained by members of one's own community (friends, family members, and ethnic real estate agents).

Ethnicized immigrants often stake out neighbourhoods or territories to call their own. For Portuguese this normally presupposes individu-als' buying a plot or a house, for the dream of owning a house is part of their 'Canadian dream' (Anderson and Higgs 1976; Alpalhão and Da Rosa 1979; Teixeira 1993). However, as Mercier (1986, 1992) argues, (small) private property is desirable in so far as a potential owner is ready to work to acquire it. Since hard labour is not enough for that purpose, credit too is necessary. Therefore, work becomes worthwhile only as it creates access to credit and then to property.

The Portuguese immigrant of the 1950s arrived in this context but was cut off from credit. Thanks to hard work, thrifty and stringent household savings, and family cooperation, most Portuguese acquired old real estate in the St-Louis neighbourhood, which was inexpensive. Land rent entered the picture (Lavigne 1985, 1988) as a means of accumulating capital, of opening the ethnic corner store, all of which explains the importance of analysing how the Portuguese came to own land (property) and of studying the type of mortgage financing used, as well as the ethnic-based relationship between owners and tenants. Integral to this analysis is understanding what kind of information Portuguese relied on in choosing a house and a neighbourhood.

Access to Real Estate

The first question we asked ourselves was simple. As of 1971, had the Portuguese bought the land on which they had a perceivable statistical presence? From the city of Montreal's evaluation list for 1976, Lavigne (1979) found that in 1976 the Portuguese owned about 20 per cent of the real estate in the study area – eight hectares bearing census tracts 133–9 and 163, bounded to the north by St-Joseph/Mont-Royal, to the east by Parc, to the west by St-Denis, and to the south by Sherbrooke (Figure 12.2).

We later examined fifty-two purchase contracts of real estate located in the mostly Portuguese-settled section (census tract 136) in the registration office of the Montreal judicial district. In more than half of the transactions (57.7 per cent), the vendor was not of Canadian origin (not French or English), and in 25 per cent of the cases it was a Portuguese. 'Ethnic' (Portuguese) property ownership seems to have begun around 1961. In 1966, the first Portuguese-to-Portuguese transactions (seller–buyer) took place. From 1972, the number of transactions began increasing.

Some observations regarding financing need to be made here. Cash payments – 17 per cent of the transactions – were made on the cheapest real estate. In the case of loan purchases, realtors financed 60 per cent of the sales themselves. The financing problem was thus solved between immigrants without the involvement of mortgage lending institutions.

We later selected forty-seven buildings from census tract 136 to analyse the rapport between tenants and owners based on ethnicity. From the city's evaluation sheet for rental property, and using a dis-

Figure 12.2. First (A) and last (1984) (B) residence, Montreal, by immigration period

similarity coefficient calculation, we checked to see if landlords selected a tenant from their own ethnic group. The results showed that this was the case for all groups, especially for the Portuguese. Portuguese, however, seemed to be turned down as tenants by non-Portuguese landlords, particularly by those of Québécois or British ancestry. This part of the analysis brought to light an invasion strategy – not one of filtration – by the Portuguese, as well as a defensive reaction from residents affiliated with other ethnic groups.[5]

The social and spatial organization of the Portuguese in Montreal was thus defined by the acquisition of real estate property. If only about 20 per cent of a given neighbourhood is settled by immigrants of the same origin, and if small businesses are added, the occupation appears ethnicized. Today, in the St-Louis ('Portuguese') area, twenty years after its appropriation by the Portuguese, there remain only an increasingly few die-hard Portuguese residents (first generation) and some Portuguese institutions and businesses. We know that many Portuguese are moving to the north of the city as well as to Laval and the South Shore.

Who stays in the district? Who moves out? Will another neighbourhood be set up elsewhere? Based on the Portuguese experience in Toronto and Montreal, Teixeira (1993, 1995) believes that satellite communities are being created through this inter-urban migration.

Moving: How and Why?

Second, we asked: why do Portuguese move and on what kind of information do they rely when they are choosing a house and a neighbourhood? To answer these questions, we carried out a study of Portuguese households on the island of Montreal. We selected two areas – first, the eighteen census tracts of Montreal's Portuguese neighbourhood in which 41 per cent of the Portuguese population settled (St-Louis and Mile-End; see Figure 12A) and, second, the rest of the island of Montreal (Figure 12B). We aimed at separating the Portuguese living within the neighbourhood from those living outside, in order to determine whether geographical mobility was associated with subsequent social mobility.

We set up two groups of thirty respondents each. We selected only first-generation immigrant family heads (born in Portugal). We used the *Guia Comercial Português Quebec – 1984* as our basic source for identifying respondents whom we chose with simple random selection.[6]

We then asked each respondent to complete a questionnaire of thirty-seven questions, grouped under five themes: socio-demographic data, settlement patterns, residential mobility, housing aspirations, the search for a new dwelling, and future moves.[7]

Results from the survey show that all respondents moved at least once. They generally left their first place of settlement but did not abandon the Portuguese neighbourhood. The sixty households had a total of 143 moves (an average of 2.38 per household) in fifteen years of residence in Canada – that is, one move every six years. Fifty-one per cent of these moves occurred within the same urban area or the same neighbourhood (Figures 12.2a and 12.2b). The majority (59.4 per cent) took place within very short distances (less than one kilometre). Moreover, whereas the first immigrants settled south of Pine (cf. Figures 12.2a and 12.2b), after 1960 they conglomerated around Duluth. As more people went north, the Portuguese neighbourhood moved in the same direction.

The main reason put forward for these moves was the desire to become a homeowner (51.9 per cent). This was followed by the condition of the home – too small (44.4 per cent) and repairs (20.4 per cent). The major reasons for choosing their present residence were the size of the house (40 per cent), presence of a basement (30 per cent), and quality of the dwelling (30 per cent). Also, 20 per cent of respondents mentioned the 'backyard' as a notable attraction. Classic factors such as proximity to transportation, schools, shopping centres, and services and a quiet neighbourhood seemed to play only a small role. Finally, 41.7 per cent of respondents found their present residence through Portuguese friends, relatives, and real estate agents (31.7 per cent). Most of the real estate agents used (94.8 per cent) were Portuguese.

A few more observations need to be made. All respondents rented their first homes, and 60 per cent of them moved because they had acquired property. All bought houses with at least two apartments, which means that they could get revenue from renting. One-third of those who still rent expect to buy a house in the near future; most of the others, who intend to remain tenants, plan to return to Portugal. All tenants live in the Portuguese area; owners reside in both study areas. In 90 per cent of the cases, people moved voluntarily. In fact, even if the respondents were satisfied with their homes (between 80 per cent and 90 per cent), a majority still planned to move – some to acquire property or return to their motherland, others to buy a bungalow.

A Distinctive Case

How Different Is the Portuguese Urbanite?

Findings in this research show that the theories used to explain inner-city residential mobility paint only part of the picture (see Teixeira and Murdie 1997). Certainly the dream of owning a bigger house is related to changes in way of life – these factors are highly interrelated. However, access to work, services, transportation, and so on seemed to play little or no role in residential mobility, which suggests that theories explain the behaviour of certain groups selectively or may have simply lost their effectiveness.

The weight of the ethnic component stands out in this study. Reasons such as looking for a home with a basement or a kitchen garden are consistent with the Portuguese cultural way of life in Montreal and Toronto. The family kitchen would be set up in the basement, whereas the first-floor kitchen serves as a showcase. The kitchen garden grows cabbage, tomatoes, and saffron, even though they are available in grocery stores. These needs indicate a way of life that can not be measured in simple social trends.

As for becoming homeowners, the Portuguese were not the only ethnic group that possessed this dream. In Montreal many Greeks, Italians, and Jews also bought houses. Indeed, the desire for homeownership is not even particularly ethnic, for the 'dream' of a home is something that entices most of us (Lavigne 1988). However, what is specifically ethnic are the types of information networks used. Given that co-ethnic family, friends, and contacts are the main sources of data about tenants and/or residents of the neighbourhood, the Portuguese can be said to actively participate in resegregation. Such internal ethnic relations are no longer simply a reaction to discrimination from without or protection vis-à-vis a foreign environment.

The same reliance on a co-ethnic network of information applies vis-à-vis real estate agents. According to respondents, the agents with whom they did business were also Portuguese. Within the same period when only a fraction of the immigrants were acquiring property, a pool of Portuguese real estate agents was gradually emerging – an indication of an ethnically specialized market. During this study, one question remained unanswered: did the agents bring about the resegregation of ethnic groups via an urban exodus to the suburbs that these agents had worked towards creating? And if so, why?

Since then, there has been an answer to this question. In Toronto, Teixeira found that 'Portuguese real estate agents seem to be important "ethnic" filters and "key" actors in determining the Portuguese home-buyers' search strategies, and final choice of a residence ... [They can] be a key factor in creating and/or maintaining ethnic residential concentration' (1993: 239, 244).

Portuguese mobility in Montreal only very partially met previous theoretical criteria. If this mobility matched the so-called succession process model, it did so only in appearance. The observed mobility seems to be directly subject to significant factors of ethnic control. The end result seems to be the setting up of an ethnic real estate market, defined and promoted by an ethnic middle class.

This finding updates a hidden dimension of the spatial (and social) integration of immigrants. It also forces us to reconsider the phenomenon of segregation in its contemporary form. Segregation can no longer be considered solely the product of a 'dominant–dominated' relationship. As the situation in Montreal reveals, the forces involved are sometimes more complex and varied than earlier theories allow.

An Internal Dynamic

The ethnic organization based on urban space examined above, in the example of the settlement of Portuguese in Montreal, is a known social phenomenon. In Montreal, and elsewhere in North America, the transplantation of Chinese, Greeks, Italians, and so on has been well described but rarely analysed from the angle of homeownership and inter-ethnic relations.

The making of an ethnic neighbourhood requires an attendant cycle of migratory influx and of neighbourhood appropriation, just as it needs a certain amount of inter-ethnic complicity. Moreover, the acquisition of real property is possible only when there is strong motivation on the part of the new arrival. The latter must be able to surmount the reality of disqualification and exploitation. Access to property is the route to success in the new social environment (Marques and Medeiros 1978; Teixeira 1986).

The Portuguese example in Montreal suggests that this self-segregation of immigrants occurs in four phases: migration, first settlement, second settlement, and movement towards a third settlement.

Migration is exo-regulated, or controlled by outside social forces (Ritchot 1985, 1991, 1992). Living in a rural society without any possibility of upward mobility – continental Portugal having nothing to offer – the Azoreans listen to the Canadian recruiter. They then begin their emigration to Canada.

First settlement is risky but endo-regulated, controlled by internal social forces. It begins with arrival in Canada. Once they have honoured their initial contract, the first immigrants come together. They move to the city and to the 'freedom' that cities symbolize.

Second settlement, in the St-Louis neighbourhood/'reception area,' takes shape in the sedentary, nineteenth-century suburban life-style and is possible because of the urban landscape in which the immigrants live but is created by dependent immigration and the institutional organization of the community. It is a phase of consolidation, during which the lower middle class capitalizes and organizes.

Movement towards a third settlement begins when, with a little money and the help of friends and family, they move into a home of their own. Some remain in the Portuguese district, while others leave for other parts of the city designated by Portuguese friends, relatives, or realtors. An immigrant 'colony' is born. It now provides all the cultural signs that characterize it as being ethnic, as being Portuguese. The lower middle class prospers because of its ethnic quality, even if this quality sometimes engenders prejudice and discrimination from parts of the host society.

Conclusion

Urban sociology, especially American, has always conflated the issues of mobility and settlement as being one and the same, with settlement only a particular moment, an instance of immobility, in a global and perpetual movement. This view, in keeping with the theoretical construct which states that geographical mobility is tributary to social mobility, presents mobility as constant and upward. For ethnics, geographical mobility and social mobility are supposed to influence one another under the combined effect of segregation and discrimination.

This explanation may be seen to have loopholes. Whereas some researchers see segregation decreasing along with assimilation – assimilation that in theory would facilitate social (and geographical) mobility by reducing discrimination – for others segregation remains, reinforcing and reproducing itself (see Teixeira and Murdie 1997).[8] In fact, the creation and resettlement of an ethnic neighbourhood, under favourable conditions such as the ones that the Portuguese in Montreal experienced, may be first and foremost an ethnic matter, not a natural or a socio-politically induced phenomenon. The Portuguese seized the opportunity to be the architects of an urban space of their own.

NOTES

1 The concept of 'segregation' has been a basic one in American sociology since the late nineteenth century, when the concept of 'integration,' as applied to ethnic relations, was developed by T. Parsons (1965). The entire theoretical corpus can be found in numerous books that one could group as the Chicago school (see Lavigne 1987). One may also consult, in the special issue of *Urban Studies*, 35 no. 10 (1998), dedicated to ethnic segregation in cities, the paper by van Kempen and Ozuekren (1998).
2 The emergence of a new ethnic neighbourhood, mid-twentieth century, inhabited by immigrants of European stock, is almost unique to North America.
3 'Community' refers to a small group or sub-group of individuals sharing common interests. It could be a shared ethnic or racial reality enhanced by organizations formed to undertake collective social action (establishing group associations, exchange of information/services, and so on). An ethnic neighbourhood is a geographical location occupied by immigrants of the same stock who make up at least about 20 per cent of the total population living in that location.
4 The criteria used to determine the qualities of spatial occupation in this case are numerous and include family income, education, profession, and activity rate.
5 'Invasion' and 'filtration' are part of the urban dynamics model put forward by sociologists of the Chicago school – mainly E.W. Burgess – in the first quarter of the twentieth century and is still in use (Burgess 1967).
6 In 1984, this directory listed 6,658 Portuguese family names.
7 The investigation took place from September to November 1984. In all, eighty respondents were selected, seventy-five were contacted, sixty responded. For further details concerning the method and the socio-demographic characteristics of the Portuguese sample, see Teixeira 1986.
8 The debate on the dynamics of segregation is dealt with by two major American researchers: Lieberson (1963, 1980) and Kantrowitz (1973, 1981); Guest and Weed (1976) offer an excellent review of these works. But some criticisms have emerged. First, equivalence distribution does not have the same impact as random distribution. Second, the value of the coefficient fluctuates

with the size of the measured groups. Third, the value of the coefficient fluctuates with the size of the census figures. Fourth, the interpretation requiring movement to account for equivalent distributions is false (Cortese, Falk, and Cohen 1976: 631).

REFERENCES

Alpalhão, J.A., and Da Rosa, V.M.P. 1979. *Les Portugais du Québec: Éléments d'analyse socio-culturelle*. Ottawa: Éditions de l'Université d'Ottawa.
Anderson, M.G., and Higgs, D. 1976. *A Future to Inherit: The Portuguese Communities of Canada*. Toronto: McClelland and Stewart.
Bailly, A., Hamel, C., and Polèse, M. 1976. *La géographie résidentielle des immigrants et des groupes ethniques à Montréal*. Études et documents 12. Montreal: Université du Québec, Institut National de la Recherche Scientifique – Urbanisation.
Bourne, L.S., Baker, A.M., Kalbach, W., Cressman, R., and Green, D. 1986. *Canada's Ethnic Mosaic: Characteristics and Patterns of Ethnic Origin Groups in Urban Areas*. Toronto: Centre for Urban and Community Studies.
Burgess, E.W. 1967. 'The Growth of the City: An Introduction to a Research Project.' In R.E. Park and E.W. Burgess, eds., *The City*, 47–62. Chicago: University of Chicago Press.
Carlos, S., and Polèse, M. 1978 *L'écologie factorielle d'un système urbain: Une analyse globale de facteurs de différenciation en milieu urbain pour les principales villes du Canada*. Études et documents 13. Montreal: Institut National de la Recherche Scientifique, Université du Québec.
Constantinides, S. 1983. *Les Grecs du Québec*. Montreal: Éditions O Metoikos – Le Métèque.
Cortese, C.F., Falk, F.R., and Cohen, J.K. 1976. 'Further Considerations on the Methodological Analysis of Segregation Indices.' *American Sociological Review* 41: 630–7.
Guest, A.M., and Weed, J.A. 1976. 'Ethnic Residential Segregation: Patterns of Change.' *American Journal of Sociology* 81: 1088–1111.
Kalbach, W.E. 1980. *Historical and Generational Perspectives of Ethnic Residential Segregation in Toronto, Canada: 1851–1971*. Research Paper No. 118. Toronto: Centre for Urban and Community Studies, University of Toronto.
Kantrowitz, N. 1973. *Ethnic and Racial Segregation in the New York Metropolis*. New York: Praeger Publishers.
– 1981. 'Ethnic Segregation: Social Reality and Academic Myth.' In C. Peach, V. Robinson, and S. Smith, eds., *Ethnic Segregation in Cities*, 43–57. London: Crom Helm.

Lavigne, G. 1979. 'La formation d'un quartier ethnique: Les Portugais à Montréal.' Doctoral dissertation, Université de Montréal.
- 1980. 'Le pouvoir ethnique: Ses assises et ses objets.' In N. Assimopoulos, J. Godbout, P. Hamel, and G. Houde, eds., *La transformation du pouvoir au Québec*, 171–82. Montreal: Albert Saint-Martin.
- 1985. 'La rente urbaine.' In G. Ritchot and C. Feltz, eds., *Forme urbaine et pratique sociale*, 101–35. Montreal: Le Préambule et CIACO.
- 1987. *Les ethniques et la ville*. Montreal: Le Préambule.
- 1988. 'Land Rent: Questions and Answers.' In C. Yadav, ed., *Urban Economics*, vol. 13, 107–92. New Delhi: Concept Publishing.
Lavigne, G., and Ritchot, G. 1991. 'De la typologie architecturale à la morphologie urbaine.' In J.C. Croizé, J.P. Frey, and P. Pinon, eds., *Recherches sur les typologies et les types architecturaux*, 218–34. Paris: L'Harmattan.
Lieberson, S. 1963. *Ethnic Patterns in American Cities*. New York: Free Press.
- 1980. *An Asymetrical Approach to Measuring Residential Segregation*. Research Paper No. 115. Toronto: Centre for Urban and Community Studies, University of Toronto.
MacDonald, J.S., and MacDonald, B.D. 1962. 'Urbanization, Ethnic Groups and Social Segmentation.' *Social Research* 29: 433–48.
McNicoll, C. 1993. *Montréal: Une société multiculturelle*. Paris: Belin.
Marques, D., and Medeiros, J. 1978. *Imigrantes portugueses: 25 anos no Canadá*. Toronto: Movimento Comunitário Português.
Mercier, G. 1986. 'Prémisses d'une théorie de la propriété.' *Cahiers de géographie du Québec* 30: 319–41.
- 1992. 'La théorie géographique de la propriété et l'héritage ratzélien.' *Cahiers de géographie du Québec*, 36: 235–50.
Monière, D., and Côte, R. 1995. *Québec 1996*. Montréal: Fidès.
Parsons, T. 1967. 'The Nature of American Pluralism.' In E. Sizer, ed., *Religion & Public Education*, 249–61. Boston: Houghton.
Rex, J.A. 1968. 'The Sociology of a Zone of Transition.' In R. Pholh, ed., *Readings in Urban Sociology*, 211–31. London: Pergamon.
Ritchot, G. 1985. 'Prémisses d'une théorie de la forme urbaine.' In G. Ritchot and C. Feltz, eds., *Forme urbaine et pratique sociale*, 23–65. Montreal: Le Préambule et CIACO.
- 1991. *Études de géographie structurale*. Cahier spécial no. 15. Quebec: Université Laval, CRAD.
- 1992. 'La valorisation économique de l'espace urbain.' *Cahiers de géographie du Québec* 36: 175–214.
Statistics Canada. 1982. *Immigration – statisques*. Ottawa: Emploi et immigration.

– 1984. *Recensement de 1981*. Ottawa: Statistiques-Canada.

Teixeira, C. 1986. 'La mobilité résidentielle intra-urbaine des Portugais de première génération à Montréal.' Thèse de maîtrise, Université du Québec à Montréal.

– 1993. 'The Role of 'Ethnic' Sources of Information in the Relocation Decision-Making Process: A Case Study of the Portuguese in Mississauga.' Doctoral dissertation. North York: York University.

– 1995. 'The Suburbanization of Portuguese Communities in Toronto and Montreal: From Isolation to Residential Integration?' In A. Laperrière, V. Lindstrom, and T.P. Seiler, eds., *Immigration and Ethnicity in Canada*, 181–201. Montreal: Association for Canadian Studies.

Teixeira, C., and Lavigne, G. 1991. 'Mobilidade e etnicidade.' *Boletim de geografia teorética* 21: 81–92.

Teixeira, C., and Murdie, R.A. 1997. 'The Role of Ethnic Real Estate Agents in the Relocation Process: A Case Study of Portuguese Homebuyers in Suburban Toronto.' *Urban Geography* 18: 497–520.

van Kempen, R. and Ozuekren, A.S. 1998. 'Ethnic Segregation in Cities: New Forms and Explanations in a Dynamic World.' *Urban Studies* 35 no. 10: 1631–56.

13

The Portuguese Community in Quebec

VICTOR M.P. DA ROSA and CARLOS TEIXEIRA

Next to Ontario, Quebec is the Canadian province with the highest concentration of Portuguese. This can be explained by the Portuguese perception of common cultural and socio-economic conditions between Quebec and Portugal. Indeed, when one moves from Portugal to Canada, Quebec is a particularly suitable milieu for settlement, as cultural and geographical similarities ease the immigrants' adaptation. Moreover, the presence of members of the same ethnic group becomes a 'pull' factor, facilitating emigration of more Portuguese to Quebec. Similar to what was found by Anderson (1974) for the Portuguese of Toronto, immigrants living in Quebec usually made the decision to emigrate as a result of networks created by friends or family members.

Once in Canada, Portuguese immigrants sought to reconstitute their families here. As we observed above (see chapter 1), in the early 1950s Canada promoted an immigration policy based on sponsorship and family reunification, which helped launch 'chain migration.' This process reunited entire Portuguese families in Canada. This type of immigration also strongly influenced the occupational opportunities available for the new immigrants, as well as their areas of settlement (cf. Anderson 1974, 1978; Lavigne 1987; Teixeira 1986, 1993).

In this essay we examine the community life of the Portuguese in Quebec: first, social characteristics, including occupations; second, areas and types of residence; and third, community life. The conclusion speculates on the future of the community.

Social Characteristics

The form of Portuguese immigration to Canada has affected the social characteristics of the group in general. For example, Portuguese families tend to have large households – an average of 3.85 persons, with 1.9 children (Teixeira 1986). In addition, Portuguese offspring tend to live with their parents longer than do those of other groups.

According to Statistics Canada, in 1991, 54.3 per cent of Portuguese in the Montreal census metropolitan area (CMA) were married, with very few being divorced (2.1 per cent). The low proportion of divorces is not a surprise, since for many Portuguese women, particularly of the first generation, divorce (or separation) is not a viable alternative to marital problems. The fear of being criticized by members of the family, as well as of ostracism by the community, if they leave their husbands still inhibits many Portuguese women (cf. Coutinho 1986; Noivo 1997). Their lack of knowledge – of French and/or English, of their own legal rights, and about agencies to look to for help, both within and outside the community – can leave them stuck in a difficult and/or abusive relationship.

The value accorded by Portuguese to the family unit, the existence of strong kinship networks, and ethnic solidarity are cultural traits brought from the homeland. However, the new generations (second and third) often see too much contact and proximity to fellow Portuguese as a problem. According to Anderson and Higgs (1976: 131): 'while the first generation is a centripetal force trying to draw the scattered extended family together again in Canada, the second generation is a centrifugal force attempting to place some living space between older members of the kin group and themselves.'[1]

Parents' attitudes towards children about dating, marriage, and socializing seem to be changing. According to our observations, the large majority of Portuguese parents approve of their children's mixing with, socializing with, even marrying non-Portuguese. However, the same is not true with respect to religious background; Portuguese parents still expect their children to marry a Roman Catholic.

Current changes in the Portuguese family may soon lead to new types of relations between husbands and wives and between parents and children. As Alpalhão and Da Rosa (1980: 148, 149) noted: 'Any adaptation implies a certain evolution. In the case of Portuguese families ... the changes and contrasts which they experience may act as a positive stimulus, but may also force them into a violent transition.'

Occupations

On arrival, Portuguese immigrants often took jobs very different from the ones they had at home. Immigrants to Quebec in the early 1950s came to meet needs in agriculture and railway construction. Those who followed them came to join families or friends and on arrival found work in construction, services, and industry-related occupations (Anderson 1974).

When Portuguese women immigrated to Quebec, they generally did not work outside the home, either because they had large families to look after or because their husbands, often for cultural reasons, did not want them to work. Most of these women were sponsored by their husbands, had little education (less than four years, on average), and had few skills other than housework. Consequently, those who took jobs tended to become garment workers, cleaners, or domestics. Because of their unfamiliarity with French and English languages and their lack of special skills, many took on repetitive piece work for low wages, often under demeaning conditions (Alpalhão and Da Rosa 1980; Labelle et al. 1987; Januário 1988).

Although unfamiliarity with Canadian labour legislation and lack of strong representation in unions (Alpalhão and Da Rosa 1980; Aguiar 1991) left Portuguese workers (whether male or female) unhireable, they have made significant gains in the last decade in their struggle for equality and rights in the workplace (Nunes 1986; Giles 1992; Teixeira 1999).

Figures from Statistics Canada for 1991 indicate that the majority of the Portuguese in Quebec had less than nine years of schooling, as reflected in their employment picture. For instance, Teixeira (1986) found in Montreal that approximately half of the Portuguese active population was in manufacturing and construction; 35 per cent worked either in offices or in sales and services, and 5 per cent in administration, health, and the social sciences.

The majority of first-generation Portuguese have remained in unskilled and semi-skilled occupations, and Portuguese manual labourers have acquired the reputation of being hard-working, reliable, and thrifty (Anderson 1974). Most of these immigrants simply have not experienced upward mobility from their low initial 'entrance status' (Goldlust and Richmond 1973; Reitz 1981). However, more recent Portuguese immigrants, particularly since 1975, and the Canadian born, appear less segregated occupationally. The new generations have greater opportunities in education (Marques 1992). In general, the second generation seems to experience upward mobility, with higher job status and better pay (Richmond 1986). However, the general picture is not rosy. As Noivo states: 'Unfortunately, findings suggest that the hopes and desires of the second generation will not be satisfied; the overall educational, social, and economic lives of the third generation are alarming' (1997: 134).

Despite low job status and income, pioneer Portuguese households attained a certain economic stability and often their ultimate 'dream' – owning a home. Often several members of the household contributed to the family income. The wife and the children (some of whom left school early to help the family finances) worked hard and sacrificed to improve their family's life. As a result, Portuguese households have high levels of homeownership (Alpalhão and Da Rosa 1980; Teixeira 1986; Lavigne 1987; Lavigne and Teixeira 1990). Portuguese have considerably improved their housing conditions, from boarding or renting when they arrived to owning homes in Montreal and its suburbs.

Residence

The 1991 census enumerates people of Portuguese ethnic origin (single origins) for Quebec's major CMAS as follows: Montreal, 32,330; Hull (with Ottawa), 6,580; Quebec City, 710; Sherbrooke, 135; and Chicoutimi-Jonquière 70. We estimate that almost 60 per cent of them come from the Azores. In this section we look at Montreal, neighbouring Laval, and Hull.

Montreal

The metropolitan region of Montreal has been the main pole of attraction for immigrants settling in Quebec since the early 1950s. Today, even though there are Portuguese in all the districts of greater Montreal, the majority are settled in an area bounded by Sherbrooke to the south, St-Denis to the east, avenue du Parc to the west, and the CN/CP railway lines to the north (see 'core of the Portuguese community' in Figure 13.1). These neighbourhoods, known as quartier St-Louis and quartier Mile-End, have served as the reception area for several other ethnic groups, including Jews, Poles, Greeks, and Italians.

Straddling the border of the city's two main communities (English and French), these neighbourhoods have affordable housing, employment close by, and accessible transportation. In the 1970s, the area north of Sherbrooke was clearly the heart, and is now the core, of the community. Within this area, and particularly in St-Louis, Portuguese

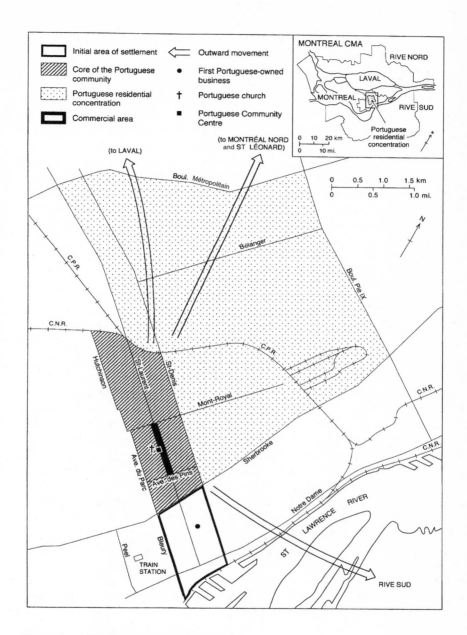

Figure 13.1. The Portuguese in Montreal

residents have done a remarkable job of renovating their houses and improving the neighbourhood's quality of life (for example, the Park of Portugal) (Alpalhão and Da Rosa 1980; Teixeira 1986).[2] One observer has stated: 'Les Portugais semblent monopoliser un espace assez précis. Ils l'occupent et ils l'aménagent. Commerces. Logements. Institutions. Ils signifient leur présence. Façades multicolores. Affiches en langue portugaise. Ils investissent. Restauration. Reféction ... ils sont là' (Lavigne 1987: 20).

Within the core of the community ethnic visibility becomes important, and a Portuguese ethnic atmosphere exists. The Portuguese, being a sociable people, have tried to re-create through their institutions their rich culture and traditions. Their institutions are not only meeting places but also a means of promoting the language and culture of origin, of sponsoring educational, social, and recreational activities, and of assisting immigrants who face language or other social problems.[3] From this perspective, they help to bridge generational and cultural differences among Portuguese Canadians as they assist them in adapting to their new home.

Da Rosa and Laczko (1984–7) identified four major types of organizations – mutual, or benefit; recreational; religious; and educational. Benefit societies include the Centro Português de Referência e Promoção Social and the Caixa de Economia dos Portugueses de Montréal; recreational associations, the Associação Portuguesa do Canadá and the Club Portugal de Montréal; religious associations, the Missão Portuguesa de Santa Cruz and the Igreja Evangélica Baptista; and educational associations, the Escola Primária Elementar Português do Atlântico.[4] The 'institutional completeness' is evident in the numerous social and religious institutions and ethnic businesses. In 1993, Portuguese in Quebec had approximately 750 businesses, twenty-one clubs and associations, five community schools, and five churches (see Teixeira 1996). As Alpalhão and Da Rosa (1980) noted, ethnic community institutions are necessary and must be preserved and encouraged. However: 'It seems nevertheless advisable to promote exchanges and relations among different ethnic groups, because this is essential to mutual adaptation and is also a means of combating ethnocentrism' (26).

In the 1990s the heart of the Portuguese community remains at the crossroad of St-Laurent and Rachel, where the main church and community centre have been built. Some new arrivals settled further west or north, with some families going as far as Villeray, far to the north, bounded by boulevard Métropolitain. The availability of better housing was often a major factor in this move. However, for sponsored immigrants, the choice was often made for them; they often lived with their sponsors or in housing belonging to them. Some Portuguese have moved to other neighbourhoods or to Laval and the South Shore. The majority of these households are homeowners.

In the last two decades, the settlement patterns and distribution of the Portuguese population of Montreal have clearly changed (see Teixeira 1986, 1996). Several factors have contributed to these changes. For instance, some of the new immigrants, particularly those who arrived after 1975, had better education, skills, and experience and so did not need to settle in the core of the community. Also, with 'chain migration,' many selected residences where their sponsors and relatives already lived. As well, some first-generation families became better off, and could acquire a home, preferably in the suburbs (such as Laval and the South Shore). Thus the central city, particularly the core of the community, gradually became less attractive to the new immigrants.

These forces were largely responsible for the emergence of new Portuguese settlements further from the core, in areas such as Anjou, Laval, Longueuil, Montréal Nord, and St Léonard. This exodus shows up clearly in the 1976, 1981, and 1991 censuses (see Figures 13.2A and 13.2B). This movement, however, has not yet noticeably lessened the vitality of the core's ethnic institutions, businesses, and services.

Laval

Laval has become the most important relocation area for Montreal's Portuguese. The movement out to Laval is a recent phenomenon (see Figure 13.2). The Portuguese community in this suburb expanded from 635 people in 1971 to 2,780 in 1991 (data from Statistics Canada 1971 and 1991), and community leaders estimate numbers today at 8,000 to 10,000.

In 1991, the Portuguese were not evenly distributed in Laval. A questionnaire survey (Teixeira 1996), informal interviews, and census data indicate resegregation in Laval, with some families, particularly from the Azores, living in or near existing pockets of Portuguese concentration. For instance, nearness to friends, relatives, and the Portuguese church affected choice of location. Almost every socio-cultural

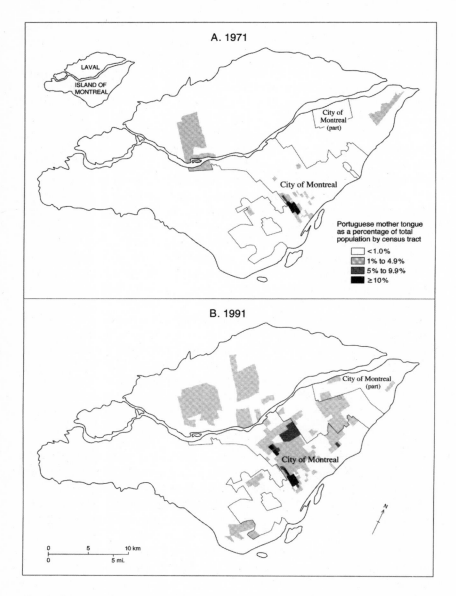

Figure 13.2. Portuguese mother tongue, as percentage of population, island of Montreal and Laval: (A) 1971 and (B) 1991. *Sources*: Data from Statistics Canada, 1971 and 1991

event centres around Our Lady of Fátima Church, which contains both the community centre and the Portuguese language school. For other families, relocation led to geographical dispersion. Thus two distinct and separate Portuguese communities seem to be forming in Laval (see Teixeira 1996).

Hull

Another large Portuguese concentration in Quebec is situated in Hull, the twin city of Ottawa, the federal capital. Some of the first Portuguese to settle there did so in the early 1950s, following their departure from the La Tuque region of Quebec, where they had worked in the lumber industry. Today, the Portuguese population of the Hull region (not including Ottawa) is estimated at close to 3,500, the majority of whom come from the Azores and, more specifically, from the parish of Maia on São Miguel Island.

Community Life

Leadership and Politics

Portuguese communities are differentiated on the basis of social class, politics, and regionalism (Anderson and Higgs 1976; Alpalhão and Da Rosa 1980). Class distinctions – a strongly established tradition in Portuguese society – are still pronounced today among the Portuguese in Canada. The community may be divided into two major social groups: 'The one to which the majority of the people belong is made of tens of thousands of members of the working class. They struggle everyday facing a vast complexity of preoccupations in the fight for a position of survival and well-being which they culturally identify with factors of economic and financial nature. The other to which the minority belongs is made up of people who, because of the status they hold in the social, economic, educational and religious structure, fill positions of leadership and representation in the community ... [While] the Portuguese working class is not divided ... [the leadership is divided] since the attempts to unify our community may have been until now, of a merely individualistic and selfish nature' (Couto 1982: 8). It is not surprising that the Portuguese have been described as a class-conscious community.

Portuguese Canadians have also been criticized, particularly by other Portuguese, for their lack of political unity and participation in the political and social life of their host society. However, opinions about Portuguese communities' unity or lack thereof are often contradictory and inconclusive. Some critics express concern, arguing that the lack of unity is a serious problem. Others see the lack of success in creating large-scale projects, such as 'umbrella' organizations to represent the communities' interests, as being manifestations of the Portuguese 'personality.' For example, there has been some concern about the proliferation of small Portuguese clubs and associations in the last two decades, given the absence of clear leadership and the financial means necessary to support them; indeed some never develop beyond the stage of good intentions (Anderson and Higgs 1976; Alpalhão and Da Rosa 1980; Teixeira 1999).

The failure of certain projects and the divisiveness within the communities are, according to Alpalhão and Da Rosa (1980), a result of individualistic temperaments of the personal ambitions of certain 'pseudo-leaders,' and of regional differences among the Portuguese immigrants. But as the community comes of age, and the new generations mature, some of these problems may vanish.

Portuguese participation in Quebec's political life, even in terms just of voting, has always been minimal. The Portuguese community in Quebec, as well as in Canada in general, has been described as not being sufficiently cohesive and politically aware to defend and promote its own interests and rights within the political institutions of the host society (Alpalhão and Da Rosa 1980). Only in the 1990s was the first Portuguese school trustee (Commission des Écoles Catholiques de Montréal), Clara Pires, elected in Montreal. At about the same time António de Sousa was elected councillor in Hull. In 1997, for the first time, a Portuguese-Canadian, Luís Miranda, was elected mayor of Anjou.

First-generation immigrants have shown in the past what Alpalhão and Da Rosa (1980) termed a certain 'political backwardness,' even an aversion, for things political. First-generation Portuguese – the majority of the population in Montreal – lived under the Salazar regime, which denied them experience and education in the political process. This translated into a low level of political participation in Canada. Until quite recently, for first-generation Portuguese, politics and community involvement have been minor concerns. Distrust or fear of authority of all forms was and is quite common among them. However, as Alpalhão and Da Rosa (1980: 220) wrote: 'On the one hand, the

Portuguese ethnic group is still first generation and thus is a population still in the process of adapting. On the other hand ... the majority
of immigrants ... have been victims of the obscurantism of a dictatorial
political regime which never encouraged them to participate in the
social and political life of the community.'

Therefore, despite the many Portuguese living in Quebec, and their
concentration in particular urban neighbourhoods, few registered to
vote. The resulting absence of Portuguese representation at the provin-
cial or federal level weakens the group's position vis-à-vis mainstream
institutions. Nevertheless, in the last ten years Portuguese women
have become more actively involved in Canadian political life.

Culture, Language, and Religion

To separate the Portuguese ethnic group from its culture and language
of origin would be to dispossess it of its identity. In a recent survey
done in Toronto, of all the ethnic groups polled, the Portuguese felt the
strongest about retaining their language and culture and passing them
on to their children.[5] According to our observations, this phenomenon
also occurs in other Canadian cities, including Montreal (Da Rosa and
Poulin 1986).

From many formal and informal contacts with members of Montreal's Portuguese community, we conclude that the Portuguese culture
in Quebec is in transition, still adapting to a new milieu. The Portuguese language is also in a transitional phase, with the new generation
using their mother tongue mainly at home to communicate with their
parents and grandparents, while preferring French and/or English
when in public. According to the 1991 census, after Ontario the largest
number of people whose mother tongue is Portuguese is in Quebec
(33,890), particularly in metropolitan Montreal.

Already there is some evidence of a 'mother tongue shift' within
Portuguese communities. For example, Veltman and Paré (1985) provide relevant data concerning the linguistic evolution (*l'évolution
linguistique*) of the Portuguese in Montreal. They found that while Portuguese immigrants frequently use their own mother tongue, they do
so most often in their contacts with family members and friends. Generally unilingual on arrival, they frequently acquire a second language
– French and/or English – and most of this learning process occurs in
the workplace.

Veltman and Paré (1985) also looked at the linguistic integration of

Portuguese youths (from four to twenty-four years old) in Montreal. They concluded that these young people employ their mother tongue only with their parents and grandparents, and French and English mainly with siblings or outside the home. Similarly, Dias (1990) has also found that the first generation is unilingual, while youths are bilingual or trilingual. However, most Portuguese of Azorean descent feel little need to maintain their language, especially because they do not intend to return to their home islands. Mainlanders, in contrast, many of whom intend one day to return to Portugal, are keen to preserve their language and culture.[6]

In general, Portuguese communities strive to maintain their language and culture. This is particularly evident in their creation of social, cultural, political, and religious institutions that use their language and transmit their culture and traditions to the new generations. These institutions dominate their socio-cultural life and not only preserve and promote their language and culture but also promote friendship and solidarity through a range of social, cultural, and recreational activities.

For those wishing to prepare typical Portuguese meals, the community cores have commercial suppliers of suitable products, many of them imported from Portugal. Groceries, bakeries, fish shops, and restaurants with 'ethnic products' and a distinctly Portuguese atmosphere help maintain a distinctive cuisine in Quebec. As most of these businesses are in the major urban cores of Portuguese concentration, they have provided not only familiar products but also services in Portuguese, thus easing immigrants' adjustment to their new country.

The Portuguese media in Quebec, particularly the newspapers, are crucial in the transmission and preservation of the language and culture of origin, with both the spoken and written media well established today. But, like the community that they serve, the media are also in transition.[7] None the less, this major source of information should continue as a cultural bridge between 'new' and 'old' immigrants, while adapting to the needs of the younger generations, whose knowledge and use of the Portuguese language will certainly decline, but who still take pride in their heritage.

Portuguese immigrants have developed a remarkable network of community schools throughout Canada. For first-generation Portuguese, whose knowledge of both official languages is minimal and who still use Portuguese at home, the teaching of Portuguese to their children was important.[8] And throughout the years, the Portuguese churches in Quebec have functioned not only as a cornerstone for the community, but also as a key element for cultural and language maintenance.

Conclusion: Ethnic Commitment and Survival

In conclusion, given the above socio-cultural analysis of the Portuguese in Quebec, the question of ethnic commitment and survival remains open. This ethnic group has been in Canada less than a half century, but the majority of its members have come to stay. With varying degrees of loyalty to their cultural heritage, they seem to be adapting relatively well into the host society. However, if Quebec is to achieve an optimal degree of accommodation of ethnic minority groups, it must undertake urgent efforts to make this a reality.

The existence of high geographical concentrations of Portuguese slowed assimilation. Instead, these ethnic neighbourhoods favoured socio-economic isolation. While Portuguese attachment to traditions can offer a valuable contribution to Quebec's ethnic mosaic, it has sometimes inhibited upward mobility. Is this the fault of the Portuguese? Perhaps. Already there is a feeling among community leaders that the Portuguese should become more actively involved in social and political life.

In most Portuguese communities in Quebec there are numerous signs that suggest the host society's acceptance of the newcomers, but not full assimilation. The move to the suburbs has been not a radical step towards assimilation, but rather a movement towards gradual blending into Québécois society. Many families move in search of 'privacy' and are fluent in French and/or English. However, despite suburbanization, they tend to have frequent contacts with the core of the Portuguese community, visiting relatives and friends, shopping on weekends, and attending social events.

Other structural factors include the constant decline of the number of Portuguese settling in Quebec, the gradual but apparently inexorable, long-term assimilation of the group into Quebec society; and the remarkable improvement of living standards in Portugal with its full membership in the European Union. All these factors together make us feel uncertain about the survival and the ethnic commitment of the Portuguese in Quebec.

It is impossible to predict the future of Quebec. Many scenarios exist, and it is within an ongoing variety of political and economic frameworks that the Portuguese must envisage the next decades. At this stage it is difficult to delineate the exact patterns of change that the Portuguese communities of Quebec will undergo during the lifetime of the present generations. For future generations, the process of cultural identification may become the most problematic challenge. For many of them, whether to be 'Canadian,' English Quebecer, Portuguese Canadian, and/or Portuguese, or to be *Québécois tout court*, will remain a continuing dilemma.

NOTES

1 See also Noivo 1997, who studied the inter-generational kin relations of Portuguese Canadians in Montreal.
2 In 1975, Montreal's Order of Architects awarded its annual prize to the residents of the Portuguese community, in recognition of their architectural innovations in the St-Louis district. In 1993, the Association des Architectes Paysagistes du Québec honoured them for their work at the Park of Portugal, in the heart of the community.
3 A good example of this is the Portuguese Association of Canada, founded on 7 January 1956 and the first major Portuguese organization in Canada. It was set up to give immigrants the chance to meet one another. Its chief aim now is to bring Portuguese nationals together through cultural, artistic, recreational, and sports activities. Its achievements include formation of a philharmonic orchestra and sports, folklore, and theatre groups.
4 Obviously this list is not exhaustive but merely provides a few examples of the diversity of Portuguese organizations.
5 See *Toronto Star*, 14 June 1992.
6 According to the *Voz de Portugal*, 12 March 1981, 5, only between 10 per cent and 15 per cent of Azorean children attended Portuguese language schools.
7 In 1958, the first Portuguese newspaper in Canada was founded (*Luso-Canadiano*). Until 1995, as many as twenty newspapers, magazines, and bulletins appeared regularly in Quebec. Today ten are still being produced, mostly in Montreal, plus two programs on radio and one on television
8 There are three Portuguese community schools in Montreal (Escola Portuguesa de Santa Cruz, Escola Português do Atlântico, and Escola Secundária Lusitana), one in Laval (Escola Portuguesa de Laval), and one in Hull (Escola Portuguesa Amigos Unidos de Hull).

REFERENCES

Aguiar, L. 1991. 'Struggling on So Many Fronts: Attempting to Unionize a Textile and Garment Factory in Montreal.' MA thesis, McMaster University.

Alpalhão, J.A., and Da Rosa, V.M.P. 1980. *A Minority in a Changing Society: The Portuguese Communities of Quebec*. Ottawa: University of Ottawa Press.

Anderson, G.M. 1974. *Networks of Contact: The Portuguese and Toronto*. Waterloo, Ont.: Wilfrid Laurier University Publications.

– 1978. 'Spearhead Anchorages and Initiation of Networks with Special Reference to the Portuguese Case.' In M.L. Kovacs, ed., *Ethnic Canadians: Culture and Education*, 381–7. Regina: Canadian Plains Research Center, University of Regina.

Anderson, G.M., and Higgs, D. 1976. *A Future to Inherit: The Portuguese Communities of Canada*. Toronto: McClelland and Stewart.

Brazão, E. 1964. *La découverte de Terre-Neuve*. Montreal: Les Presses de l'Université de Montréal.

Coutinho, T. 1986. *Report on Services to Battered Women in the Portuguese Community with an Overview of Services to Battered Women in Other Ethnic Communities*. Prepared by the Portuguese Interagency Network for the Ministry of Community and Social Services, Toronto.

Couto, E. 1982. 'Keynote Speech.' In *The Portuguese Community of Toronto: Needs and Services*, 5–12. Prepared by the Portuguese Interagency Network, Toronto.

Da Rosa, V.M.P., and Laczko, L.S. 1984–7. 'Ethnic Organizational Completeness: A Discussion of Trends in Montreal's Portuguese Community.' *Gávea-Brown* 5–8 nos. 1–2: 17–27.

Da Rosa, V.M.P., and Poulin, R., 1986. 'Espaces ethniques et question linguistique au Québec: À propos des communautés italienne et portugaise.' *Canadian Ethnic Studies* 18 no. 2: 143–50.

Dias, M. 1990. 'Deux langues en contact: Le français et le portugais dans les communautés de Paris et de Montréal.' Doctoral dissertation. Toronto: University of Toronto.

Giles, W. 1992. 'The Battling Women Who Fought for Dignity.' *Toronto Star*, 10 Sept.: G7.

Goldust, J., and Richmond, A.H. 1973. *A Multivariate Analysis of the Economic Adaptation of Immigrants in Toronto*. North York, Ont.: Institute of Behavioural Research, York University.

Januário, I. 1988. 'Les activités économiques des immigrantes portugaises au

Portugal et à Montréal à travers les récits de vie.' MSc thesis, Université de Montréal.

Labelle, M., Turcotte, G., Kempeneers, M., and Meintel, D. 1987. *Histoires d'immigrées: Itinéraires d'ouvrières colombiennes, grecques, haitiennes et portugaises de Montreal*. Montréal: Boréal.

Lavigne, G. 1987. *Les ethniques et la ville: L'aventure urbaine des immigrants portugais à Montréal*. Montreal: Le Préambule.

Lavigne, G., and Teixeira, C. 1990. 'Mobilité et Ethnicité.' *Revue européenne des migrations internationales* 6 no. 2: 123–32; and see Erratum, 6 no. 3 (1990), 187.

Marques, D. 1992. 'Here to Stay.' *Toronto Star*, 12 Sept.: G1–G3.

Marques, D., and Medeiros, J. 1980. *Portuguese Immigrants: 25 Years in Canada*. Toronto: West End YMCA.

Noivo, E. 1997. *Inside Ethnic Families: Three Generations of Portuguese-Canadians*. Montreal: McGill-Queen's University Press.

Nunes, F. 1986. 'Portuguese-Canadian Women: Problems and Prospects.' *Polyphony* 8 nos. 1–2: 61–6.

Reitz, J.G. 1981. *Ethnic Inequality and Segregation in Jobs*. Toronto: Centre for Urban and Community Studies.

Richmond, A.H. 1986. 'Ethnogenerational Variation in Educational Achievements.' *Canadian Ethnic Studies* 18 no. 3: 75–89.

Teixeira, C. 1986. 'La mobilité résidendelle intra-urbaine des Portugais de première génération à Montréal.' MSc thesis, Université du Québec à Montréal.

– 'The Role of "Ethnic" Sources of Information in the Relocation Decision-Making Process: A Case Study of the Portuguese in Mississauga.' Doctoral dissertation, York University.

– 1996. 'The Suburbanization of Portuguese Communities in Toronto and Montreal: From Isolation to Residential Integration?' In A. Laperrièrre, V. Lindstrom, and T.P. Seiler, eds., *Immigration and Ethnicity in Canada*, 181–201. Montreal: Association for Canadian Studies.

– 1999. 'Portuguese.' In P.R. Magocsi, ed., *An Encyclopedia of Canadian People*, 1075–83. Toronto: University of Toronto Press.

– *Toronto Star*. 1992. 'The Portuguese: Sticking Together Through Bad Times.' 14 June: Al, A6–7.

Veltman, C., and Paré, O. 1985. *L'insertion sociolinguistique des Ouébécois d'origine portugaise*. Montreal: INRS – Urbanisadon.

A Voz de Portugal. 1981. 'O Ensino da Língua Portuguesa no Quebeque: Apenas 10 a 15 por cento de crianças açorianas vao à escola de sábado.' 12 March: 5.

14

On the Move: Portuguese in Toronto

CARLOS TEIXEIRA

It is a commonplace today to observe that Canada, particularly its large metropolitan areas such as Montreal, Vancouver, and Toronto, have become increasingly cosmopolitan (Hiebert 1994; Trovato and Grindstaff 1994).[1] A multitude of cultures, races, and religions have transformed the urban landscape of our cities – first in the immigrant reception areas (such as Kensington in Toronto) and today in the suburbs.

The Portuguese have helped reshape Canada's urban geography to reflect the dreams and aspirations of its multicultural population. The purpose of this essay is to show how and where Portuguese settled in Ontario; with particular reference to Toronto, Canada's largest Portuguese community. I look mainly at their settlement patterns, geographical distribution, residential mobility, and housing choices. I collected information for this study from interviews with leaders of the Portuguese communities in Toronto and Mississauga and from a questionnaire administered to a sample of 110 Portuguese recent home buyers in Mississauga, a western suburb of Toronto. Other sources included statistical data from the Canadian census, written documents, the Portuguese ethnic press, and participant observation.[2]

This essay looks at, first, early settlement in the Kensington area in the 1950s and 1960s; second, expansion, particularly into Portugal Village, from the mid-1960s on; and third, the dispersed community today.

Early Settlement

'Port of Entry'

Since the early 1950s the number of Portuguese immigrants choosing

Ontario has grown considerably. The 1991 census indicates approximately 176,300 people of Portuguese ethnic origin (single origin) in Ontario. By far the majority of these resided in the Toronto census metropolitan area, or CMA (Figure 14.1). Other centres include Hamilton, Kitchener, and London CMAs.

Since 1945 Toronto's ethnic character has changed dramatically, from a predominantly homogeneous city to one characterized by ethnic diversity. According to the 1991 census, 59 per cent of Toronto's population reported non-British or non-French ethnic origins, up from 45 per cent in 1986. Among about 3.7 million people living in the Toronto CMA, about one million declared mother tongues other than English or French. Portuguese (95,305) was one of the most frequently reported non-official languages, ranking third, after Italian (189,265) and Chinese (175,035). The number of people citing Portuguese increased by about 22 per cent between 1986 and 1991. Within the former Metropolitan Toronto,[3] the largest number of Portuguese (mother tongue) lived in the city of Toronto (44,955), where theirs was the most reported non-official language. Outside the Metro area, as we see below, Mississauga is one of the most important cities in Ontario for the Portuguese (see Teixeira 1993).

Initial Settlement

The initial settlement took place within the heart of the city of Toronto in two well-defined neighbourhoods – Kensington Market and Alexandra Park (initial area of settlement in Figure 14.2). These were poor working-class districts, with run-down housing, and were already ports of entry to other immigrant groups such as Hungarians, Italians, Jews, Poles, and Ukrainians (Murdie 1969; Lemon 1985).

Kensington: Immigrant Reception Area

The Kensington area (bounded to the north by College, to the east by Spadina, to the west by Bathurst, and to the south by Dundas) became a reception area for Portuguese in Toronto during the 1950s and 1960s. It was there that the first Portuguese-owned business in Toronto (and probably in Canada) opened during the 1950s (Figure 14.2).[4] A restaurant on Nassau Street was one of the city's first meeting places for the Portuguese. On the same street the First Portuguese Canadian Club

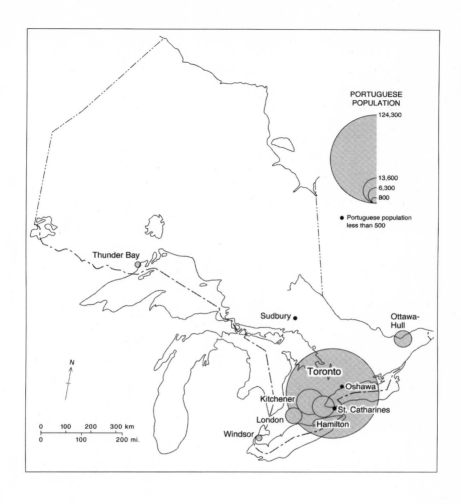

Figure 14.1. Population of Portuguese ethnic origin, census metropolitan areas, Ontario, 1991. *Source*: Data from Statistics Canada

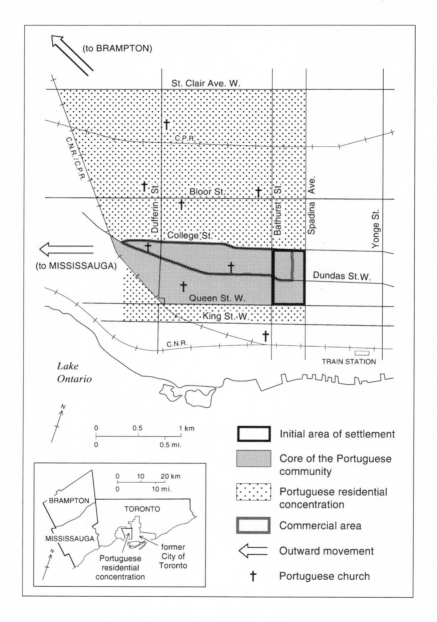

Figure 14.2. The Portuguese in Toronto

was born – one of the oldest and most important Portuguese cultural institutions in Canada (Ribeiro 1990).

Other Portuguese businesses started up during the 1950s and 1960s on Augusta Avenue and surrounding streets. Gradually the Portuguese transformed what was known as a 'Jewish market' into a 'Portuguese market' (Brettell 1977). Augusta became a very popular commercial artery for Portuguese immigrants and soon became known as the 'street of the Portuguese' (*A rua dos Portugueses*).

From the late 1950s to the early 1970s, Kensington was the city's major commercial area for the Portuguese and housed a notable concentration of Portuguese families. It had affordable housing for sale or rent and was close to job sites and transportation – determining factors in residential choice. Moreover, for sponsored immigrants during the 1960s and 1970s the choice was often made for them; newly arrived Portuguese often lived with their sponsors or in housing belonging to them (Anderson 1974; Anderson and Higgs 1976).

Most Portuguese started out as renters and roomers, and apartments were often overcrowded, with two or three families sharing the same house or apartment/flat (Marques and Medeiros 1980). The majority of these immigrants came from rural areas of Portugal and arrived with little money, no English, and no skills. These disadvantages – together with the Portuguese propensity to settle near friends and relatives and the availability of inexpensive housing/flats, jobs, and transportation – decided settlement location.

Boarding-houses became a transitional phase for these boarders (who aspired to become homeowners at a later stage through rent savings), as well as for the Portuguese families who owned the houses and wanted to pay their mortgages as soon as they could. As a result, Portuguese homeownership increased considerably during the 1960s and 1970s in the Kensington area, as well as in the surrounding neighbourhoods.

The Portuguese left their imprint on Kensington. Marking their presence were their businesses and colourful painted houses, with their front yards filled with flowers, vegetables, and grape vines. The Toronto *Star* observed: 'The Portuguese, like the equally charming Newfoundlanders, like to paint their houses bright colours, scarlet being the favourite. They will even occasionally paint the mortar between the bricks white. They often grow cabbages and other vegetables in their front yards unless the yard contains a shrine to Our Lady of Fátima, in which case flowers are preferred' (Turner 1973: A3).

Saints and religious figures were also depicted on *azulejo* (Portuguese glazed tiles)[5] and placed beside the main door of the house. Immigrants brought the azulejos representing religious figures (such as Our Lady of Fátima, St Anthony, Christ of Miracles, and popular saints from regions or islands of Portugal), as well as seeds for flowers and vegetables, directly from Portugal on their frequent trips back home. In the few private spaces available, in both their back and front yards, first-generation immigrants recreated the rural atmosphere of the homeland. For some, this type of 'urban farming' was a way to put into practice some of their old agricultural skills. Even today, their businesses and 'Portuguese houses' still remain.

Expansion

Portugal Village

During the mid-1960s and early 1970s, the Portuguese in Toronto began to move westward from the Kensington area, creating 'Portugal Village' (see Figure 14.2). Overcrowding in the old area, the increase in Portuguese immigration to Toronto, and the desire to purchase a better house in a better neighbourhood contributed to this movement into adjacent neighbourhoods west of Bathurst Street. The area bounded mainly by College Street to the north, Bathurst to the east, King Street West to the south, and Ossington Street to the west was the principal destination, with College and Dundas in the northern part gradually becoming Portuguese commercial strips.

Other 'Colonies'

Other Portuguese 'colonies' in Toronto began taking shape across the metropolitan area during the 1960s (see Figures 14.3A and B). The constant arrival of entire families through chain migration led to their establishment – a significant stage in the life cycle of the ethnic community.

Attitudes to Housing

Results from our questionnaire survey of Portuguese who bought homes in 1989 and 1990 revealed that the majority of respondents (72 per cent) were sponsored by a member of the nuclear or the extended

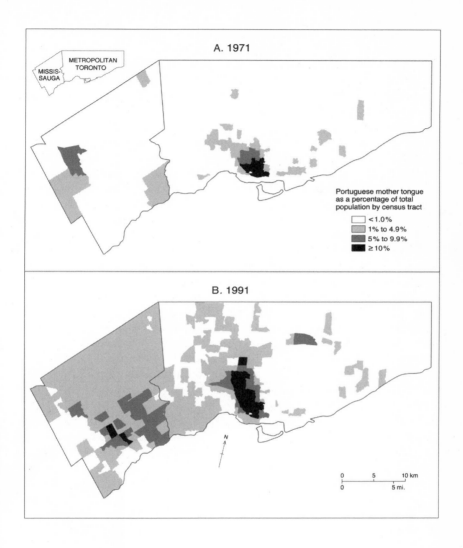

A. 1971

METROPOLITAN
TORONTO

MISSIS-
SAUGA

Portuguese mother tongue
as a percentage of total
population by census tract

☐ <1.0%
▢ 1% to 4.9%
▦ 5% to 9.9%
■ ≥10%

B. 1991

N

0   5   10 km
0   5 mi.

Figure 14.3. Portuguese mother tongue, as percentage of population, Metropolitan Toronto and Mississauga: (A) 1971 and (B) 1991. *Source*: Data from Statistics Canada

family when they immigrated to Canada. Information provided by friends and relatives in Ontario helped them become established. More than 70 per cent of respondents indicated that friends and relatives were 'very important' or 'important' in helping them find a job and housing, as well as in selecting city and neighbourhood. Through chain migration, Portuguese quickly reconstituted their families (nuclear as well as extended) in Canada (see Anderson 1974).

Among the cultural traits that they transplanted from Portugal was their marked propensity for owing a home (Anderson and Higgs 1976; Alpalhão and Da Rosa 1980; Lavigne 1987). Many bought houses in and near Kensington (west of Spadina), particularly in Portugal Village, at low prices. Their own extensive renovations included new plumbing, new wiring, finishing of the basement, building of a wine cellar, construction of an additional kitchen and/or bathroom, painting of exterior façades with bright colours, and subdivision of the house into one or two more apartments/flats to accommodate one or two more families and thereby provide extra income.

Some of the new homeowners worked in construction, often with Italian immigrants, and acquired skills and knowledge about house building. Most renovated their houses with the help of family members and friends. Indeed, mutual help and support were very common among Portuguese immigrants (see Khron, Fleming, and Manzer 1977). The Portuguese rejuvenated neighbourhoods in Toronto with little or no financial assistance from the government and set a precedent that was much imitated.

The majority of Portuguese immigrants still see homeownership and housing as a steady and secure economic investment and a realization of a dream. Our questionnaire revealed that for first-time Portuguese home buyers, the two concepts are synonymous with symbolic security in the New World. More than 90 per cent of respondents indicated 'very important' or 'important' to the following motivations: 'To have something of my "own"'; 'As a symbol of security to the family'; 'Homeownership as an investment'; 'It brings greater privacy to the family'; 'Brings a feeling of having succeeded in this country (Canada)'; and 'Accomplishment of a "dream."'

For these Portuguese immigrants, a house is therefore more than a commodity, a physical structure, or an investment. The importance that they attach to homeownership reflects the immigrants' dream of settling down in one place and acquiring security, privacy, and a home of their own.

The Dispersed Community Today

The distribution of the Portuguese in the Toronto area in 1991 (Figure 14.3B) confirms the gradual dispersion of members of the group. Still, their major concentration continues to be in the west and central part of the former city of Toronto. The proportion living there, however, declined from 78 per cent (49,360) in 1981 to 69 per cent (44,955) by 1991. The area bounded by Spadina, King West, Landsdowne/Canadian National Railways (CNR), and St Clair West formed their major area of concentration (see Figure 14.2). There were about 38,000 Portuguese in this area in 1991, accounting for approximately 86 per cent of the Portuguese living in the city of Toronto and 60 per cent of the Portuguese in the Metro area. Within this larger area there is a 'core' settlement, bounded by Spadina, Queen West, CNR, and College, which includes most of the community's social, cultural, and religious institutions, as well as the two major Portuguese commercial strips – Dundas and College (see Figure 14.2).

The community has expanded since its original settlement in the immigrant reception area in the 1960s and 1970s. Two patterns emerged – first, a northwest movement in the traditional immigrant corridor, where the Portuguese are replacing Italians, and second, a shift to the suburbs, especially Mississauga (Figure 14.3B), discussed below. Yet while the 1991 census shows a community dispersing, the core in Toronto remains.

Those families who remain in the city of Toronto, particularly within Portugal Village, are largely of the first generation, to whom the move to the suburbs is not a priority. The neighbourhood is the place where they feel comfortable, where they can live a Canadian life in a 'Portuguese way,' among those who share culture, way of life, and language. Portugal Village and its environs are a re-creation of their homeland – an area where they can keep some of their cultural traditions alive in the New World. Now we look at their institutions, their propensity for residential concentration, and their growing shift to the suburbs.

Institutions

The Portuguese community in Toronto is self-contained and self-sufficient. In the last four decades they have constructed a thriving, complex community, setting up organizations, businesses, and communication-information services in their own language. The high

degree of institutional completeness (Breton 1964) is well demonstrated by the appreciable number of ethnic businesses – from grocery
stores, through bakeries, travel agencies, and real estate agencies, to
furniture stores and restaurants.

A major support in the growth and evolution of Portuguese communities in Canada has been their institutional structures, particularly
their churches and parishes. The Catholic church still plays a significant role in the lives of many Portuguese families. As shown in Figure
14.2, most of the Catholic churches in Toronto are located in and
around the core of the Portuguese community. Clusters of Portuguese
immigrants (mainly of the first generation) live near the churches,
which provide religious services daily in their mother tongue. The
church, as a 'pole of attraction,' was a major force in shaping Portuguese settlement patterns in the city.[6]

Residential Concentration

The Portuguese show high levels of residential concentration. In 1981,
the Portuguese in the Toronto CMA had the second-highest indices of
dissimilarity in residential patterns (68.7), after the Jews (74.1) (Bourne
et al., 1986). These indices measure the unevenness in the spatial distribution of each ethnic group, as compared to the distribution of the balance of the CMA's population. The high index of dissimilarity for the
Portuguese is not a surprise, because the majority of them are relatively recent immigrants (first generation). Many factors – such as language barriers, socio-economic status, cultural values, way of life, and
heavy reliance on internal sources of information in looking for and
locating a new dwelling – may explain their concentration in particular
neighbourhoods of Toronto.

The variety of cultural, social, and religious institutions and businesses within the core area, while providing a focus for the community,
also partially explains the high level of residential concentration. The
presence of these businesses and institutions marks the presence of this
dynamic ethnic group. At the same time, it assures the group's survival by promoting Portuguese culture, customs, and traditions.

Suburbanization

The slow dispersion of the Portuguese from the city of Toronto is a
fairly recent phenomenon. The movement out of the core, especially to

suburban Mississauga, took place mainly in the last two decades (see Figures 14.3a and 14.3b for comparison of movement patterns). With a population of approximately 463,000, Mississauga is a major 'bedroom' suburb of Toronto. For the Portuguese in Toronto, it has become one of the most notable destinations outside the city, and their community there expanded from about 1,500 in 1971 to approximately 14,000 in 1991.[7]

Most of the Portuguese living in Mississauga came from Toronto. In our survey of recent Portuguese home buyers in Mississauga, 35.1 per cent of respondents mentioned the size of the house/lot as the most important reason for choosing their present residence; 19.3 per cent, area/neighbourhood; 15.8 per cent price of house/good investment; 14 per cent, type of housing; and 6.1 per cent mentioned 'proximity to relatives and/or friends.' The wish to acquire the modern 'dream' house – preferably a single-family dwelling with certain amenities such as a basement, backyard, garden in front, garage, modern kitchen, and location in a quiet place with pleasant surroundings and good schools – represents the ultimate goal for Portuguese families relocating to Mississauga.

Even if we verify a continuous and gradual move out of the core of the Portuguese community in Toronto, this movement has not yet affected noticeably the vitality of the core neighbourhood's institutions and services. Many Portuguese suburbanites return regularly to the core to go to church, to shop, and to participate in cultural events. How much will these areas retain their 'Portuguese identity'?

Conclusion

What about the new generations of Portuguese Canadians? Levels of education are rising, and assimilation is expected to increase. At this stage in the life of the Portuguese community, it is not clear whether these new generations will follow the same path as their parents and grandparents. Nor is it clear whether they will be able to preserve any of their ancestral culture and traditions. The long-term survival and integrity of Portuguese neighbourhoods and communities in Canada may thus be problematic.[8]

Many forces contribute to this uncertainty – the apparent decrease in the in-migration of Portuguese to Canada; the departure of the first-generation Portuguese from the core to the suburbs; existing internal and external threats to the community, such as the arrival of other ethnic groups (such as the Chinese in Toronto); inner-city revitalization/ gentrification/redevelopment; and rising housing prices in the inner city. To these forces we should add the wish of some families (mainly first generation) to return to Portugal's islands or to its mainland to retire.[9] The changes that the Portuguese communities will experience within the next decades will be critical for their survival and integrity, cohesion, culture, and traditions. However, one fact is certain: the Portuguese, as a group, control their own mobility. Therefore whatever happens will reflect Portuguese needs and aspirations within the general context of Canada's future.

NOTES

1 This is a revised version of an earlier paper: *Portuguese Studies Review* 4 (1995), 57–75. I would like to thank Douglas L. Wheeler, editor of the journal, for authorizing reproduction of the paper in this volume. I would also like to express my gratitude to Robert A. Murdie of the Department of Geography, York University, for his support and encouragement in the last few years and for his comments on an earlier draft of this essay.

2 For further details on the method and the socio-demographic characteristics of the Portuguese sample, see Teixeira 1993. Of the 110 Portuguese who participated in the questionnaire survey, almost all 97.3 per cent were born in Portugal, and 70 per cent spoke Portuguese most of the time at home. Of 'first generation' respondents born in Portugal, (60.7 per cent) were born in the Azores. Most respondents (67.3 per cent) arrived in Canada during the period 1966–75 and emigrated mainly for economic reasons (43.0 per cent) and to join members of the family already living in Canada (40.2 per cent). Of the respondents, the majority (79.1 per cent) were already homeowners, and sixty-five (59.1 per cent) lived in the city of Toronto before moving to Mississauga. Almost all of these (former) Torontonians lived in the core of the Portuguese community.

3 On 1 January 1998 East York, Etobicoke, North York, Scarborough, Toronto, and York amalgamated into the new city of Toronto.

4 Interview with A. Sousa, owner of the first Portuguese restaurant in Toronto, Toronto, 3 July 1989.

5 Concerning the Portuguese glazed tile, or *Azulejo*, see Wheeler 1993.

6 Interviews with Father A. de Melo, Toronto, 21 June 1989; Father E. Rezendes, Mississauga, 16 June 1989; and Father A. Cunha, Toronto, 28 Aug. 1989.

7 According to leaders in the Portuguese community whom I interviewed in Mississauga and Toronto, there are about 40,000 Portuguese living in Mississauga.

8 On the future of the Portuguese core in Toronto, see Carey 1999.

9 Although the majority of Portuguese Canadians are satisfied with Canada as a place to live (see *A Minority Report* 1985), returning to Portugal for retirement still is a priority for some. In our Mississauga survey, 10.9 per cent of respondents had plans to return to Portugal, and 18.1 per cent were undecided ('I want to but my wife doesn't,' or 'We [husband and wife] want to go to Portugal but our kids don't'). Some of these families (including the 'undecided') had already purchased homes and land in Portugal.

REFERENCES

Alpalhão, J.A., and Da Rosa, V.M.P. 1980. *A Minority in a Changing Society: The Portuguese Communities of Quebec*. Ottawa: University of Ottawa Press.

Anderson, G.M. 1974. *Networks of Contact: The Portuguese and Toronto*. Waterloo, Ont.: Wilfrid Laurier University Press.

Anderson, G.M., and Higgs, D. 1976. *Future to Inherit: The Portuguese Communities of Canada*. Toronto: McClelland and Stewart.

Bourne, L.S., Baker, A.M., Kalbach, W., Cressman, R., and Green, D. 1986. *Canada's Ethnic Mosaic: Characteristics and Patterns of Ethnic Origin Groups in Urban Areas*. Toronto: University of Toronto, Centre for Urban and Community Studies.

Breton, R. 1964. 'Institutional Completeness of Ethnic Communities and the Personal Relations of Immigrants.' *American Journal of Sociology* 70: 193–205.

Brettell, C.B. 1977. 'Ethnicity and Entrepreneurs: Portuguese Immigrants in a Canadian City.' In G.L. Hicks and P.E. Leis, eds., *Ethnic Encounters: Identities and Contexts*, 169–80. North Scituate, Mass.: Duxbury Press.

Carey, E. 1999. 'Close-knit Portuguese Community Starts to Spread Its Wings.' *Toronto Star*, 13 June, A1, A60.

Hiebert, D. 1994. 'Canadian Immigration: Policy, Politics, Geography.' *Canadian Geographer* 38: 254–8.

Krohn, R.G., Fleming, B., and Munzer, M. 1977. *The Other Economy: The Internal Logic of Local Rental Housing*. Toronto: Peter Martin Associates.

Lavigne, G. 1987. *Les ethniques et la ville*. Montreal: Le Préambule.

Lemon, J. 1985. *Toronto since 1918*. Toronto: Lorimer.

Marques, D., and Medeiros, J. 1989. *Portuguese Immigrants: 25 Years in Canada*. Toronto: West End YMCA.

A Minority Report. 1995. Toronto: *Toronto Star*.

Murdie, R.A. 1969. *Factorial Ecology of Metropolitan Toronto, 1951–1961: An Essay on the Social Geography of the City.* Research Paper No. 116, Department of Geography, University of Chicago.

Ribeiro, M.A. 1990. *O Canadá e a presença portuguesa.* Toronto: Correio Português.

Teixeira, C. 1993. 'The Role of "Ethnic" Sources of Information in the Relocation Decision-Making Process: A Case Study of the Portuguese in Mississauga.' Doctoral dissertation, York University.

Trovato, F., and Grindstaff, C.F. 1994. *Perspectives on Canada's Population: An Introduction to Concepts and Issues.* Toronto: Oxford University Press.

Turner, D. 1973. 'The Portuguese Find "Making It" Has a New Twist.' *Toronto Daily Star* 8 Dec.: 1, A3.

Wheeler, D.L. 1993. *Historical Dictionary of Portugal.* Metuchen, NJ: Scarecrow Press.

PART FIVE

'A FUTURE TO INHERIT':
HISTORY AND LITERATURE

15

Literature of Portuguese Background in Canada

ANTÓNIO AUGUSTO JOEL

The literature of Portuguese background in Canada faces a problem that also affects other writing in this country – it fails to achieve the status of mainstream literature.[1] In fact, the use of expressions such as 'ethnic fiction' and 'immigrant fiction' (Simone 1995: xvii) or 'multicultural fictions' (Hutcheon and Richmond 1990: 2) implies the existence of American or Canadian literature as a reality opposed to these other literatures.

Such a perception cannot be considered just a matter of prejudice. In the Portuguese case, multiple factors contribute to the marginal status of this literature: some of the writing relates exclusively to homeland ways of life, emerging as ethnographic exercises of memory and nostalgia rather than literature (for example, Vincente 1995). Other texts do achieve an acceptable literary form but suffer from the same content-related problems (for example, Melo 1996, 1994). Yet others assume the form of chronicles, being published primarily within so-called ethnic newspapers either in Canada or elsewhere (for example, Carvalho 1997; Joel 1995). A feature that most of these works share is that they appear in the Portuguese language, without the involvement of any Canadian publisher.

Such characteristics undoubtedly help to segregate these works of fiction. But it is a conscious and self-imposed segregation, sometimes cast within the tradition of a single writer who epitomizes the homeland's literature. As D'Alfonso points out: 'The challenge for ethnic writers is to derail this tradition, by forcing the past to really go off on a tangent and into another dimension, where tradition, if this is what we are after, will endow them with a true collective significance. Without this voluntary act of reanalysis ethnic writers can never find their place in any country. They will always remain the outsider, at the margins of literature' (1996: 61). It is clear, however, that D'Alfonso defends the idea of ethnic writers, but not that of a compartmentalized literature, turning and closing itself around a centripetal and narrow movement, which may be more self-destructive than constructive.

The tendency to label literature of ethnic backgrounds has given rise to a variety of studies devoted to identifying and defining such literature (Baden 1979; Simone 1995, among others), as well as bibliographies that systematically catalogue these works (Miska 1990; Simone 1995). Although Teixeira and Lavigne (1992, 1998) list literature of Portuguese background in Canada dating from the 1970s, Miska (1990) ignores these works for methodological reasons. These bibliographies do not highlight recent authors, whose works have made a significant contribution to the literature of Portuguese background either in the United States or in Canada.

One of the two notable omissions is Katherine Vaz, the author of several recent novels, inspired by her Azorean heritage and life in Portuguese-Californian communities, which transcend this reality through her sense of the fantastic.[2] In Canada, Erika de Vasconcelos wrote *My Darling Dead Ones* (1997). Both authors are already case studies within the literature of Portuguese background – not just because they write in English, but primarily because they reject the self-imposed segregation. Their work is clearly and consciously intended to be mainstream literature. However, since Vaz's novels do not relate directly to Canadian realities, this essay focuses on the work of Vasconcelos and others writing within a Canadian context.

For purposes of analysis, I narrowed the existing corpus of literary works of Portuguese background down to a few examples, representing its diversity. My first decision was to consider just prose texts. Of these, I considered only those that relate to or describe Canadian experiences (i.e., those illustrating first-, second-, or even third-generation Portuguese experiences in Canada). For this reason, I set aside several of the forty titles compiled by Teixeira and Lavigne (1998). Unfortunately, none of the existing titles in French fit these criteria.

The structure of the essay takes a diachronic pattern, starting with fictional spaces situated in the mid-1950s and illustrating the arrival and settling of first-generation immigrants. The second part relates to post-settlement experience, and the third, to the second generation. Although I take more of a socio-literary approach than an exclusively literary one, I refer to interviews related to *My Darling Dead Ones* in order to offer an exegesis of Vasconcelos's work.

Pioneers: Anxiety of Departure, Arrival, and Settlement

The only known works that relate to first-generation Portuguese-Canadian experience might be considered unorthodox, but for the intrinsic unorthodoxy of this literature in itself. Both texts were written more than two decades after the first official arrival of Portuguese immigrants in Canada (1953), and both are presented in literary forms that may be considered peripheral – one is a journal, and the other is a novel that combines fiction and non-fiction.

'Dollar Fever: The Diary of a Portuguese Pioneer' has an additional singularity – it was written by an author of Italian background, C.D. Minni (1993), as a supposed translation of a diary in Portuguese.[3] This short story takes place in 1954–5 and describes the journey of three Azorean immigrants from São Miguel to Halifax via Lisbon, as well as their settlement in Canada. The narrator describes himself and his need to start a diary by declaring: 'For me the pen is heavier than a shovel; I left school at the age of ten to work on the farm. But I have a need to record my feelings; I do not know why. Perhaps it is not knowing what we will find in this mysterious country of Canada' (1993: 49).

Healthy, strong, working-class men – such were the pioneers required. But this story presents a certain fear of the unknown, as embodied above all by solitude. Most of the immigrants were leaving behind, if not family, at least a community with a strong sense of cohesiveness and a tradition that did not favour enterprises which led to displacement and solitude, far away in space and memory. That was the immigrants' first struggle: 'I've been reading the little green book our government has prepared for emigrants. The quote in the cover was: *Imigrar e travar uma grande luta*, to emigrate is to put up a big fight. But ... on Sao Miguel many have no other choice. Farms are small; jobs are scarce. Most can hope to better their conditions only by leaving. No, it was not the idea of emigrating which the elders thought foolish, but the choice of place. If we had chosen Brazil, where many families have relatives, or even France perhaps ... but Canada? Who did we know there?' (Minni 1993: 50).

The big fight of emigration was to survive distance and loneliness. It was also to survive 'solitudes,' to use Hutcheon and Richmond's (1990) extension of a famous expression coined by Hugh MacLennan.[4] The world was newly dimensioned, the climate and the landscape were strange, and a different mindset was needed to cope with this transformation: 'March, 18. On the CPR train, going to a place called Leamington. Outside, the landscape is bleak – farms, telephone wires, bare trees, a distant church steeple; the snow has not yet melted. On Sao Miguel, when I left, the trees were in bloom. We have been traveling for two days already. I did not realize before the extent of this country and, as the official who met us in Halifax explained, there is much more to the West' (Minni 1993: 51).

It is the human factor, however, that conveys the sense of difference or strangeness – above all, the lack of human feelings towards immigrants, who were treated like numbered or tagged objects: 'We, instead, have been divided into groups, at random like so much baggage, and have been tagged with lapel colours; orange for Quebec, red for Ontario, and blue for British Columbia. Estevan received orange. Peero and I are red. So we are not to remain together after all' (51).

The consciousness of not being in command of their lives, and the denial of their innermost sense of freedom and humanity, create feelings of revolt and indignation, of shame and dishonour. Honour, pride, and dignity are sometimes the only possessions that immigrants can rely on to survive in a strange or even hostile environment. The deprivation of these basic rights provokes bitter remarks from the narrator: 'Arriving, we stayed at the YMCA, which I understand is a Christian place, until our owners came to collect their baggage – us. I am bitter about that day; never was I so humiliated. Still with our red tags, we gathered in the gymnasium and stood in a line along the wall while the farmers inspected us. Like slaves at a market, I thought' (51–2).

It is a thought that is going to remain deep inside him for a long time; as he later remarks: 'It is different for me. My resentment, which began at the slave market, has grown steadily, and now I do not think I will last the year of my contract' (53). However, mixed feelings follow these thoughts, reflecting one of the immigrants' myths – the need to succeed in the host country, not just as catharsis but also as a matter of pride and dignity. Such pride and dignity are often related not to the new country but to the homeland: 'Can I be deported for not fulfilling my contract? I have mixed feelings about this. If my father were here now, I'd kiss his feet and beg forgiveness, but I can not go back to Sao Miguel a failure and face the derision of the village elders. Even now I can still hear their scorn, "Young fools. Young fools." When I go back, it will be as a success and that means I must find a job' (55).

This excerpt, reminiscent of the biblical parable of the prodigal son, also introduces another concern common to a large number of newcomers – a firm decision to return home after some years of hard work and saving. This feeling, however, is often based on fantasies, since immigrants can not clearly estimate in advance the influence that their new country will exercise over their lives and worldview. Similarly, many immigrants imagine that they will never be able to readapt to the homeland left behind, as indicated in this anecdote by one of the characters in the story: '"I have a friend," Nikos said, "who worked twelve hours a day and saved every penny to return to Greece. Five years it took him, and when he went back to his native village, he realized that Canada had become the dream. Now, here he is again, working in Sudbury"' (58).

Such decisions do not imply any lack of critical vision regarding the new country, as we can see when the narrator himself reflects over the meaning of Christmas for Canadians. Being used to regarding it as essentially a season of joy, family gatherings, and spiritual values, he notes that 'Christmas here begins in November. It is a worship of Mammon ... Everywhere cash registers ring up. The dollar is God ... I know now that dollar fever is a virus people in this country carry in their blood' (59).

Negative as some of these remarks may be, they do not exceed the bitterness in some passages of *Os bastardos das pátrias*, by Lourenço Rodrigues (1976). The narrative, spanning almost two decades (1956–74), ends with the suicide of a maddened immigrant and is introduced by this epigraph (9):

> Canadians receive us but they don't accept us
> They need us but they don't want us
> They recognize our value but they don't respect it
> Our sweat made them prosperous and the rich, richer
> But they hate the smell of our perspiration.

As in 'Dollar Fever,' the writer refers (78) to the viewing of immigrants as products to be tagged and catalogued: 'Ao achá-lo, carimbou-o com "Land Emigrant," data de entrada e escreveu um número. A partir daquele momento, as suas "características" seriam: (After finding it, the person stamped it with a "Land Emigrant," date of entry, and wrote a number. From that moment on, his "characteristics" would be:) (Product: "New Canadian." – Classification: "Land Emigrant." – Type: "Portuguese Male." – Manufactured: "Airport of Montreal." – Production date: "May 13, 1957." – Category: "Latin Inferior." – Serial number: 14.783).'

The same idea of solitude and family loss arises (90), but Rodrigues offers severe judgments about Catholics' lack of access to certain jobs (97), along with some comments (139–40) about what is demanded and expected from immigrants if they are to obtain full social integration:

> Quando aqui cheguei deram-me o número 415-743-368 para usar com o meu nome. Mas não foi em troca do meu nome! Ou foi! É certo na maioria dos departamentos perguntam-me pelo número e não pelo nome. Mas terei eu, também, de perder o meu nome, a minha personalidade, a minha religião, a minha alma, a minha cultura, a minha educação? Em troca de quê? De retalhos de dólar? Oh! Isso não!!! Já perdi a fala. Ja perdi um nome. Já perdi ...
>
> (When I arrived here they gave me the number 415-743-368 to use with my name. But it was not a true substitute for my name! Or was it! It is true that in most of the departments I am asked for my number, not my name. But should I also lose my name, my personality, my religion, my soul, my culture, my education? In exchange for what? Dollar's crumbs? Oh no, not that!!! I have lost my language, I have lost my name, I have lost ...)

This sense of loss recalls the ideas of honour and dignity pointed out in the earlier story. But the most interesting concept arises from the speech (367) of one of the characters, the son of the protagonist, that relates to the novel's title. Talking to his father, he declares: 'Como vês, nem cá, nem lá: não passo, como vocês, de um bastardo de duas pátrias! (As you see, neither here nor there: as you, I am no more than a bastard of two fatherlands!)'

The idea underlying this expression and the feeling that it conveys is familiar in immigrant literature, although it is not often related to second-generation immigrants. Its recurrent appearance as a central issue in fiction motivated my coinage of the expression 'Paradox of Nowhere' (Joel 1997a) to refer to the fact that some immigrants and immigrant characters exist, *here* and *now*, but in fact happen to be *nowhere*; they are simultaneously strangers in their country of origin and in their adopted country. It is as if immigrants lived in neither space nor time but only in that ambiguous reality called memory.

It is a concept well illustrated in the work of José Rodrigues Miguéis, a Portuguese writer who lived in the United States from 1935 to 1980 and who wrote, among other notes of fiction, short stories dealing with Portuguese immigrant realities on the east coast.[5] He does not write just about pining for the other side and nostalgia. He also writes about the immigrants' social concerns, as well as about their role and status in the new homeland. As well, he gives the reader detailed portraits and analysis of the United States in the 1930s and 1940s, thus making his work an inevitable reference point for the literature of Portuguese background in North America.

Struggling for Life, Integration, and Identity

In 1986, Laura Bulger published *Vaivém*, later translated into English as *Paradise on Hold* (Bulger 1987).[6] The book is a compilation of short stories that mostly reflect the day-to-day life of Portuguese immigrants in Canada. The focus in these stories, however, is not the social confrontation or the cultural clash central to the works mentioned above. Rather, these stories deal much more with the anxieties, hopes, and dilemmas of integrated immigrants, as opposed to the bitterness of unlucky or socially unintegrated immigrants (17–18). Some unilateral disappointment even arises from cultural changes motivated by female integration. A male character in 'The Letter' questions his wife's new attitudes and the impact that these changes have had on their lives: 'She stopped ironing his shirts and instead sends them to the cleaners. She answers him in English and complains about the children, her job, her migraines. What the hell does she want? She's got everything; a house in the suburbs, a car, a real fur rotting in the closet' (3).

The comments, however, do nothing other than acknowledge change, an irreversible change in relationships between husband and wife, parents and children. This change is, above all, vis-à-vis memory and feelings generated by the concept of homeland: 'And really he has no idea if he'll ever go back. One of these days he has to talk to the kids. The grandparents are getting older. The old country seems farther away. We, here, are even becoming indifferent' (7).

The permanently postponed return implies not just integration but also erasure of ties to the past, homeland, and family. The change in the character's identity is based not necessarily on adoption of the values and culture of the host culture but in some ways simply on a negation of the old self, as indicated by the words: 'We, here, are even becoming indifferent.' The indifference lies sometimes in vague reasons or in a lack of assertiveness or self-determination, as illustrated by a character in 'At the Doctor's' who claims that he would have left Canada were it not for his children: 'If it weren't for him, if it weren't for the two of them [his children], I don't know what I would have done. I would have probably left, gone back ... I know, there's no future for them there. Here, they have more opportunities' (57).

His decision not to return is not individually motivated but is instead allegedly based on the individual's ties with the new generation and its interests. Such a decision, however, is not always final, highlighting once again the 'Paradox of Nowhere.' In *Vaivém*, an old character ends up summing his life in these terms: 'My children like it here and she ... she doesn't want to go back. She is used to it ... I like to go there for holidays. The place I come from is beautiful but ... its difficult now, with my grandson. What a hellava life! Always coming and going, from here to there, there to here, *um vaivém*' (98).

These family-based excuses are not always echoed in the second generation, as witnessed in *Os bastardos das pátrias* (Rodrigues 1976) when a son replies to his father (367): 'Eu sei, eu sei, que eles não dão trabalho aos filhos dos emigrantes, por não terem feito a tropa ... – atira com a cabeça para trás. – Eu vou para lá porque foi onde nasci e, porque gosto muito mais daquele povo do que deste. – E recostando-se no sofá. – E vocês sabem bem, que eu não tenho necessidade de vos mentir! (I know, I know they don't offer jobs to the children of emigrants, because they didn't join the military service ... – he threw his head backwards. – I am going to return because it was there where I was born, and because I love these people much more than these   ones – reclining in the sofa – And you know very well that I have no need to lie to you!)'

This character left Portugal when a child. His sense of identity relies much more on memory and a sense of loss than is the case in Bulger's short stories. He expresses not a longing for a heritage, as it is seen below in Erika de Vasconcelos's novel, but a desire to become an integral part of that heritage. The idea of integration is not consciously assumed or prepared in most of this fiction. Instead, integration emerges from the struggle for survival in a new society. It is something that occurs inevitably, growing inside characters and within family simultaneously with that anxious pursuit of 'the other side.'

When characters cannot assume a new identity or evolve into patterns flowing towards a change of personality and adaptation, individual catharsis can be achieved only through a drastic measure – a rite of passage that often requires a 'death,' be it symbolic or real, such as the suicide at the end of *Os bastardos das pátrias*. However, adaptation in matters of cultural identity and citizenship eases integration, as exemplified in *Um poeta no paraíso*, by Manuel Carvalho (1994: 115):

Sabiam que antes da vossa mãe viajar, falámos na eventualidade de regressar a Portugal? – Talvez lá a vida seja menos complicada – disse Jorge, com um olhar intenso carregado de subentendidos. E logo Miguel acrescentou: – Também já estou farto de tanta neve. E já me disseram que agora aquilo está cheio de Mcdonalds e de Pizza Huts. Tanto me faz estar aqui como lá desde que tenha uma boa pizza para comer. Desataram os três às gargalhadas. (Did you know that before your mother travelled, we spoke about the possibility of returning to Portugal? – Maybe there life is less complicated, said Jorge, with an intense look full of subtleties. And Miguel added soon afterwards: – I am also tired of so much snow. And I have also been told that now the place is full of McDonald's and Pizza Huts. I don't mind being here or there, having a nice pizza to eat. All three of them started laughing.)

These easy-going attitudes contrast starkly with those expressed in a bitter mood by another character, which resemble much more closely the resentful feelings of *Os bastardos das pátrias*. When bitterness and resentment against Canadian society and culture arise, they do so generally in first-generation characters. Costa, a first-generation immigrant, is told the following (Carvalho 1994: 31): 'É por causa de gajos como tu que a comunidade portuguesa não passa da cerpa torta. Há gente que não faz o mínimo esforço para evoluir e integrar-se. – Integrar-me?! – saltara o Costa. – Integrar-me nesta merda de sociedade? E, ao redor, acenos de cabeça concordantes davam-lhe força. – Se não gostas disto, o que fazes aqui? – Os dólares. Só por causa dos malditos dólares.' (It is because of guys like you that the Portuguese community doesn't progress. There are people who do not make the slightest effort to evolve and to integrate themselves. – Me, to integrate myself?, Costa jumped. – To integrate myself in this shit of a society? And around him, agreeing nodding heads gave him support. – If you don't like this, what are you doing here? – Dollars. Just because of the damned dollars.')

This pragmatic approach to life, focusing on the value of financial security, is also shared by a female character (4–5): 'Já lá vai o tempo em que o Canadá era o Canadá ... Quando eu vim para o Canadá, há dez anos, enchia-se a frisa, de carne, com trinta dolas. Agora nem com trezentas.' (The time when Canada was Canada is gone ... When I arrived in Canada, ten years ago, one could fill the frisa (freezer), with meat, for thirty dolas (dollars). Nowadays, not even with three hundred.)

Nevertheless, this novel is not a simple reflection of the life of Portuguese immigrants in Montreal. Above all, it is the sense of a fantastic
and magical reality that pervades the novel, establishing it as mainstream literature. The 'conceit' could not be more literary – Luís Vaz de
Camões, the sixteenth-century Portuguese writer, survives a shipwreck
and reaches twentieth-century Montreal by swimming. When he
arrives, the reader is faced with three different characters named Luís,
Vaz, and Camões, whose lives form the fictional structure. of the work.
The novel moves towards mainstream literture, although it has been
published only in Portuguese. It also clears the path to *My Darling Dead
Ones* as a contribution to literature of Portuguese background heading
towards the mainstream.

Longing for a Heritage

Marcus Hansen's thesis 'What the son wishes to forget, the grandson
wishes to remember,' quoted by T. Kanoza (Simone 1995: x), applies
entirely to the experience related by Erika de Vasconcelos (1997) in *My
Darling Dead Ones*. Leninha – daughter of Helena, niece of Magdalena,
and mother of Fiona – declares: 'Portugal is in the past ... I could never
live there again' (170). Leninha is a first-generation immigrant. Fiona,
in contrast, will return often to Portugal, where she will completely
understand and acknowledge traditional feminine values, accepting
them as an act of conscious and personal reassurance.

At the very end of the novel, in Portugal, Fiona stretches out her
hands (9) to receive her grandmother's bones, recently washed and
white, as white as the photograph that she took at the beginning of the
story: 'I climb up to the highest turret. On a clear day I could see the
ocean from here, trace with my finger as on an ancient map the line
that edges a continent, where the *earth ends and the sea begins*, as
Camões wrote. But I am completely in mist. I take a picture of the
whiteness.'

Symbolically, whiteness may be something waiting to be filled, or
inscribed, or covered. The initial whiteness of the photo that Fiona took
ends up being filled and inscribed with stories from Fiona's ancestors
and from her own past. The whiteness of the bones will be covered by
Fiona's future, since she, at last awake, has meanwhile decided to give
up her dead-end marriage. Memory and affection, thus, are the key
concepts for cultural (re)integration in Vasconcelos's novel. Language
is a settled question, for even though the memories and culture are of
Portuguese background, the language is English. The question here is

not one of integration in the host country's culture, but of reintegration in the ancestral country and culture. Memory in fact seems to have been one of the main concerns of the author when she conceived the novel: 'I was interested in memory and how memory works and I wanted the structure of the book to reflect the way we actually experience memory, and how we experience the past and stories from the past. You don't experience memory in one big linear lump. You don't come to know your ancestors or your country or who you are in one linear sweep' (Alfano 1998: 3).[7]

This very same interview also gave us information about Vasconcelos's social and literary concerns (Alfano 1998: 8): 'This is not an immigrant book. It's not about the immigrant experience. It's about a Canadian woman discovering who she is by understanding the lives of her ancestors.' Authors' views of their own works are not necessarily definitive. As the eminent Canadian literary critic Northrop Frye (1990) observed: 'The poet speaking as a critic produces not criticism, but documents to be examined by critics. They may also be valuable documents: it is only when they are accepted as directives for criticism that they are in any danger of becoming misleading' (6).

Undoubtedly, Vasconcelos intends to go beyond a mere exercise of style in the labyrinths of memory and cultural heritage. Above all, her novel assumes itself as an exercise of style towards mainstream literature. As the author herself implicitly admits in the interview: 'I haven't read anything Canadian that was written about Portugal. I mean I'm sure there are articles and stuff like that, but certainly not in mainstream fiction, so it's kind of nice to be the first to do it.'[8]

Conclusion

Given this overview of contemporary literature of Portuguese background in Canada, we can infer that most of this fiction tends to enclose itself within a centripetal movement, almost crystallized in models that do not reflect either Portuguese or Canadian literary reality. But it is not just this fact that contributes to these fictions' outsider status. It is also a certain obsession with reflecting immigrant experience as an experience exclusive and valuable *per se*. Instead of reflecting fictional spaces, experiences, and characters – according to an open view of society, a macrocosm full of literary potential and an open field for literary experiences – the tendency is to create contained microcosms, reflecting memories of a long lost individual past or social reality related to the country of origin or the contained reality of community.

Such exclusive use of these factors in literary production will maintain literature of Portuguese background at an inevitable level: immigrant literature, ethnic literature, multicultural literature ... everything but mainstream literature.

NOTES

1 I am grateful to Rena Helms-Park, vice-president of the *Wire* and my colleague at York University, for the use of computer facilities and her assistance regarding the syntatic editing of my original text in English. I am also grateful to Vamberto de Freitas, at the University of Azores; to Onésimo T. de Almeida, at Brown University, in Providence, RI; and to the editors, for their insights regarding a previous and different version of this essay.
2 Katherine Vaz is author of *Saudade* (New York: St Martin's Press 1997), *Mariana* (1997) and *Fado and Other Stories* (Pittsburgh: University of Pittsburgh Press, 1997), a compilation that received the Drue Heinz Literature Prize in 1997.
3 Some details, however, may give the impression of a totally fictional production – for example, the erudite references to Mammon (fifty-nine), Ulysses (sixty-one), and cornucopia land (sixty-two), as well as the unexpected sight of an immigrant generously tipping a steward (forty-nine).
4 MacLennan's expression 'two solitudes' refers to the (in)difference between anglophone and francophone Canada.
5 See, for example, the short stories 'Dr. Crosby's Christmas' and 'White Christmas,' in *Steerage and Ten Other Stories* (Providence, RI: Gávea-Brown, 1983).
6 *Vaivém* (Lisbon: Vega, 1986).
7 Cf. a similar declaration in Marchand 1997.
8 Actually, mainstream Canadian literature contains at least two texts related to Portugal – 'Electrico Utensilio,' by W.P. Kinsella, in *The Alligator Report* (Minneapolis: Coffee House Press, 1985), and 'An Orange from Portugal,' by Hugh MacLennan, in *Cross-Country* (Toronto: Collins, 1949). Recently, Sarah Dearing (1998) published her first novel, *The Bull Is Not Killed*, presenting a plot set entirely in Portugal.

REFERENCES

Alfano, M. 1998. 'Interview: By the Force of Their Own Will: The Women of *My Darling Dead Ones*.' Paragraph: The Canadian Fiction Review 23: 3–9.

Baden, N.T. 1979. 'Portuguese-American Literature: Does It Exist?' *MELUS* 15–31.

Bulger, L. 1987. *Paradise on Hold: Short Stories.* Toronto: Bramble House Inc.

Carvalho, M. 1994. *Um poeta no paraíso.* Laval: Éditions Luso.

– 1997. *Parc du Portugal.* Laval: Éditions Luso.

D'Alfonso, A. 1996. In Italics: *In Defence of Ethnicity.* Toronto: Guernica Editions Inc.

Dearing, S. 1998. *The Bull Is Not Killed.* Toronto: Stoddart.

Fanning, P., and Goh, M., eds. 1993. *Home and Homeland: The Canadian Immigrant Experience.* Toronto: Addison-Wesley and Rubicon Publishing.

Frye, N. 1990. *Anatomy of Criticism: Four Essays.* Princeton, NJ: Princeton University Press.

Hutcheon, L., and Richmond, M., eds. 1990. *Other Solitudes: Canadian Multicultural Fictions.* Toronto: Oxford University Press.

Joel, A. 1995. 'Impressões do Outro Lado: Chronicles.' *A Voz de Chaves* (1995–8).

– 1997a. 'Impressões do Outro Lado.' *A Voz de Chaves,* 26 Dec.: 5.

– 1997b. 'Miguéis, E. de Vasconcelos, and Their Characters in North America: Strangers in a Strange Land?' Paper presented at the Fourteenth Biennial Conference, Canadian Ethnic Studies Association, Montreal.

Marchand, P. 1997. 'Fictionalizing Family History.' *Toronto Star,* 5 July: L16.

Melo, F.F. de. 1994. *Os visitantes da América e reminiscências.* Toronto: Olive Press.

– 1996. *Nadine: A Sereia dos corais e reminiscências.* Toronto: Olive Press.

Minni, C.D. 1993. 'Dollar Fever: The Diary of a Portuguese Pioneer.' In Fanning and Goh 1993, 48–62.

Miska, J. 1990. *Ethnic and Native Canadian Literature: A Bibliography.* Toronto: University of Toronto Press.

Rodrigues, L. 1976. *Os bastardos das pátrias.* Lisbon: Distribuidora 'O Século.'

Simone, R. 1995. *The Immigrant Experience in American Fiction: An Annotated Bibliography.* Lanham, Md: The Scarecrow Press.

Teixeira, C., and Lavigne, G. 1992. *The Portuguese in Cânada: A Bibliography.* Toronto: Institute for Social Research, York University.

– 1998. *Os portugueses no Canadá: Uma bibliografia (1953–1996).* Lisbon: Direcção-Geral dos Assuntos Consulares e Comunidades Portuguesas.

Vasconcelos, E. de. 1997. *My Darling Dead Ones.* Toronto: Knopf.

Vincente, A.S. 1995. *Vida e tradições nas Aldeias Serranas da Beira.* Montijo: Sograsol.

16

A Sense of History

DAVID HIGGS

Historians deal with the past, and some of them raise questions about ethnicity in earlier times. There is a growing body of ethnic history in Canada (Iacovetta 1997). In the case of Portuguese – Canadians, social historians of the group are concerned mostly with the build-up of large-scale immigration, which began in the early 1950s. In the 1990s I would like to reflect further on what role the sense of history plays in Portuguese-Canadian identities among the first and succeeding generations and also to explore varying angles of historical perception among Portuguese Canadians. After this introduction, I ask, first, about how strong their sense of history is, and, second, how they conceptualize history. Third, I describe some exciting new methods of exploring Portuguese-Canadian history.

Perennial questions present themselves in the discussion of ethnic histories in Canada and elsewhere. Is ethnic identity some residual, ancestral bundle of characteristics never laid down, never lightened, and always weighing on the souls of its bearers? Is it the permanent legacy of the ancestors: in the case of the Portuguese, passed on from Viriato, the hero who resisted the Roman invaders, through Luís de Camões, the epic poet of the sixteenth century, to Rosa Mota, the young woman who won international marathon races in the 1980s?

Or, as seems likely, is ethnicity a state of mind that changes according to situation and setting? Are the Luso-(Portuguese) French, Luso-Brazilians, and Luso-Americans more French, Brazilian, and American than they are Portuguese in the second, or third, or fourth generations? Do regional origins within the Portuguese cultural space affect group behaviour?

In the 1930s, Gilberto Freyre (1946) stressed that the Portuguese colonizers in tropical Brazil showed a great ability to adapt to a climate, landscape, and social forms that differed from those of the homeland. He compared this to northern Europeans, who, in North America, had simply imported the agrarian techniques of their homelands. Freyre, in an essentialist statement about what this adaptability did to Portuguese emigrants to Brazil, argued that it brought about 'that perversion of the economic instinct which quickly distracts the Portuguese from the activity of producing values to that of exploiting, transporting, and acquiring them' (24).

Needless to say, other scholars would take issue with such a simplistic picture of the homogeneous impact of North Americans on agricultural production. One study of the farming success over fifty years of French Canadians, Mennonite, and Swedish under identical conditions on the Kansas prairies showed significant differences. Were these outcomes the results of a cultural, or some other, variable that made an imprint on the populations (McQuillan 1990)?

History is a vital part of the construction of Portuguese nationalism and identity, and it must enter into the encounter with Canadian history of adult Portuguese Canadians who have a knowledge of the Portuguese past. There have been no historical conflicts between Portugal and Canada. The ancient alliance between England and Portugal that began in 1373 extended over the colonial centuries until enactment of the Statute of Westminister in 1931. Leaving aside some unpleasantness surrounding overfishing of cod off the Grand Banks during the 1990s, there is no mythic history of conflict between Portugal and Canada.

Sense of History

How strong is the sense of history among the Portuguese in Canada (Ribeiro 1990)? Portuguese culture and education are deeply marked by a public discourse on the achievements of the nation, especially the age of discoveries. Under the authoritarian government of 1926–74, this invocation of the past was almost a civic cult, complete with monuments in prominent locations, celebratory radio and television programs, and numerous publications. The celebration of the Portuguese maritime discoveries is one clear continuity from the era of authoritarian rule to that which ensued from the Revolution of the Carnations (April 1974). A study – beautifully produced with the support of various official entities – commemorating the voyage of Vasco da Gama is an example of the culturally rich five hundred years of maritime contact between Portugal and India. In 1998 a wax museum was to be opened at Warehouse 2 of the Alcântara Dock in Lisbon with twenty-five settings and 180 figurines beginning with Viriato and concluding with 25 April 1974.[1] History has had a place of honour in the Portuguese primary school curriculum since the nineteenth century. Few Portuguese immigrants to Canada in the 1950s and 1960s had attended high school (*liceu*) in Portugal, and fewer still had a university degree, so they were untouched by the more complex formulations of historical and nationalist discourses encountered there (G.M. Anderson 1974; Matos 1990). Only a handful had a Portuguese university degree in history.

After 1974, the study of history within Portuguese schools underwent a change. The *Boletim* of Portugal's Associação de Professores de História (APH), discussing the 'social condititionalisms of Memory,' noted in 1986 how the presidential candidates were reaching out for historical references in their electoral campaigns: General Eanes considered Nuno Alvares Pereira an exemplary hero; Professor Freitas do Amaral said that his first act if elected would be to lay a wreath on the monument to the first Portuguese king in Guimarães; while Dr Mário Soares, a lawyer who was elected president, paid homage not only to the minister of the interior of the First Republic, António José de Almeida, but also to Camões, the epic poet. The writers of the *Boletim* wondered how they should respond to the emergence of the past in contemporary politics. How would their pupils deal with such historicized political discourse?

In his book *The Hero*, Raglan (1949) reminded us that only the smallest fraction of the human race ever acquired, or aspired for that matter, to take an 'objective' view of the past. Previous events are often remembered not as they were experienced, but from the perspective of the present. Professional historians are dependent on books and documents in the broadest sense (artefacts, photographs, interview tapes, and so forth), which subsist often fortuitously and without the intention of telling a coherent story. Establishing even simple chronology is often acutely difficult without written records. Whatever is not transcribed vanishes; if remembered in an oral tradition, it is often simplified into legend. Only relatively recently have ethnic groups been convinced of the necessity of establishing a documentary basis from which their own historical experience can be re-created.

Most first-generation Portuguese Canadians were adults with rarely more than primary education in the homeland. The place of books in cultural life was slight. Only gradually did the need for a coherent historical explanation of Portuguese life in Canada emerge. This narrative relied heavily on individual recollections retold orally. The drawback of reliance on oral witnesses has been obvious since the time of the father of history, Herodotus, who 'places the greatest emphasis on trying to understand events through personal ambitions and motives. He does not find it necessary to try to take account of the broader forces that may have a controlling influence on history, such as population growth, economic developments, social movements, and the value systems of different peoples' (Reinhold 1972: 175).

Historians in many countries are becoming more conscious of the manipulation of collective memory by monuments and ceremonies (Hobsbawm and Ranger 1983; Nora 1984; Boer and Frihoff 1993; Boer 1998). Collections appeared in Canada in the 1990s such as that dealing with the sites of memory in Quebec from 1930 to 1960 and a wider-reaching symposium on the place of history in Canada's past. As Raglan pointed out, it is unlikely that what is popularly remembered as tradition accurately represents the past. However, even if the chronology or factual details of an individual life story, to say nothing of the development of a group in Canada, are often garbled and inaccurate when recounted years later, there may be a symbolic significance in recurrent themes. Among migrants the emphasis on homesickness, for instance, and even the contrasting outlooks of those who migrate and those who stay in the homeland have interested psychiatrists (Grinberg and Grinberg 1989). It is no surprise that the Portuguese, one of the most migratory of all European peoples, have a whole esthetics of nostalgia, *saudade*. In 1420 the word was described as being peculiarly Portuguese: 'Love and absence are the parents of *saudade*, and as our nature among the other nations is known as being loving, and our prolonged voyages cause great absences it results that where there is much love and absence the *saudades* are more pronounced, and this was why these *saudades* are to be found among us as in its most natural centre' (D. Francisco Manuel de Melo, quoted in Serrão 1976: 58–60).

This nostalgia was often put in feminine terminology, as when men evoked a distant mother, wife, fiancée, daughter. It was not just in Portugal that migration led in the past to marital breakdown (O. Anderson 1997). Many migrants to Brazil were bigamists, marrying new wives in the New World (Higgs 1993). Nostalgia reflected a psychic need for a land of happiness, often an island, a desire of returning to a time in the womb before birth. Gardens, islands, and valleys are of course the context of the saudade of rural emigrants from the Atlantic archipelagos.

This transposition of a Kleinian 'good breast' landscape into nostalgia often accompanies an equally strong reference to the place of origin, the *terra*. One writer observed that *terra* does not translate well into English 'home,' with its indoors connotation. Instead 'Terra connotes earth. The idea has soil clinging to it. And it names our final resting place' (Conrad 1990: 123). To have abandoned the body of the homeland is to have been expelled from the larger family, just as the individual, or even the emigrant family, has been cut off from those close and dear. The first Portuguese-Canadian novel describing the experience of life in Canada has a title that can be translated *The Bastards of the Motherlands* (Rodrigues 1976). The emigrant could feel in some way illegitimate, at least for that author, and exiled from the lawful family rooted in the natal *terra*.

Conceptualizing History

Generational Shifts

Another question concerns how Portuguese Canadians conceptualize history itself. The first generation, educated in Portuguese primary schools before 1974, read primers similar to those used by small children in any other European country. To quote from one in wide use during the 1940s and 1950s: 'If history is the great master of life, and if ours [history] is the most beautiful in the world it therefore becomes necessary to ensure that the little scholars know it as well as possible, so that they may be strengthened by the healthy examples of so many of its remarkable men, so that they can receive and afterwards bequeath to generations of the future, the sublime inheritance of eternal Portugal' (Barros n.d.: 4). The title page bore an epigraph from Michelet 'It is needful that the Motherland be felt in the school.' Most men emphasized in such history books had dedicated themselves to purposes that glorified the motherland and defended the overseas territories. One could say of them pretty much what Friedelle Bruser Maynard (1972) wrote about the *Canadian Reader*s of her western Canadian childhood: 'Naive, jingoistic, unscholarly, sentimental, moralistic – they were all these. And yet the fact remains that they were also memorable and moving ... The world of the readers was a world of heroes. And in the end it didn't much matter, I think, that these heroes were dedicated to purposes which a modern finds questionable – the invincibility of the British Fleet or the glories of the empire. What mattered greatly to all of us who succumbed to its spell was the vision of men committed to a principle beyond self' (113).

'Exemplary figures of the national history' included even in a 1973 text such figures as D. Aleixo Corte Real, a native ruler in Timor, and Aniceto do Rosário, a police sub-inspector from Diu in India (Carvalho 1973: 87). The 1973 history book exhibited views similar to those current in the 1930s (Pinto 1938). Social process over time makes for a less stirring subject.

The second and third generations of Canadians of Portuguese descent may encounter among their relatives a historical sensibility different from that in school books intended for multicultural school environments in Canada. Those children in junior grades may also have encountered some pedagogical materials that are in Portuguese and address the life experiences of themselves and their elders. They may have learned words in a reader that show street scenes in Toronto or summer in 'Canadá e outros países' (Morais 1979). The School of the First Portuguese Canadian Cultural Centre in Toronto published the history of its first twenty-five years of activities illustrated with many photographs of teachers and pupils (Ferreira 1988). Maria de São Pedro Lopes, when working as a language instructor in Portuguese in the Metropolitan Separate School Board of Toronto, encouraged the pupils of a Catholic school in Toronto, St Luke, to interview elderly Portuguese. This led to the publication, from 1994 to 1996, of three instalments of a collection with the title *No tempo dos nossos avós: Duas gerações em contacto* (for more details, see Lopes and Lopes 1996). In collaboration with her husband, then a research officer at the Modern Language Centre of the Ontario Institute for Studies in Education in Toronto, Lopes organized a collection of essays to make the history of Portuguese emigration to Canada accessible to young children (Lopes and Lopes 1996). These initiatives were intended to heighten pupil's historical awareness of the Portuguese dimension of Canadian history and will help them relate to the symbols of historical allusions drawn from the Portuguese past.

Gestures of community benevolence in Canada often evoke history. Someone donates a bust of Camões, rather than a set of chairs, to a club, or an antique Portuguese musical instrument, rather than a scholarship fund of equivalent value, to a museum. In a Toronto park, a copy of a monument set up during the Renaissance to mark Portu-

guese landfalls on unclaimed islands and territories marks the pioneers who arrived in Ontario's capital by train, carrying cardboard
suitcases. The habit of translating North American experience into the
vocabulary of a national epic is not peculiar to the Portuguese. Glaser
found the same trait among Italo-Americans. Doubtless it has much to
do with the linkage of the sacral to the public, and of ritual to familial-
ism, in the popular Catholicism of southern Europe. The tradition of
historical experience in the homeland shapes what is celebrated in the
Canadian present.

Autobiography

Individuals telling their life stories unconsciously suppress whatever
does not fit their version of what the experience meant. They often forget simple details. Manuel Vieira of the parish of Agua de Pau, who
hails from the Azorean island of São Miguel, was the first man to leave
the Halifax immigration offices on 14 May 1953. In a 1978 newspaper
interview he mused: 'If I had known that I was going to take part in all
the commemorations of our twenty-five years here in Canada I would
have written everything down.'[2] Emigrants later ascribe forethought
where, in fact, there was simply an opportunity offered. To take a concrete example, the reasons cited to explain emigration often include the
desire to provide a better life for the family. The social historian looking at the overall structure of the Portuguese economy and at different
regional 'networks of contact' – to use Grace Anderson's phrase (G.M.
Anderson 1974) – emphasizes such factors as the inability of the local
economy to provide full employment, emigrants' contacts with sources
of credit that permit them to purchase expensive travel tickets, and
bureaucratic regulation. These tedious elements get left out of the individual's declamation of the pain of self-sacrifice for the betterment of
his loved ones.

   People in less affluent regions of Portugal presumably share high
hopes for their families, but they are less able to realize them by international migration. Research has shown that people in one mountain-
ous area of eighteenth-century Europe had a demonstrable 'link of
prosperity' to migrants who maintained their kinship networks and
returned periodically to their place of origin. By contrast, the 'hardship
migration' that saw whole social clusters moving away did not have
the same effect (Siddle 1997).

   The 'editing' of oral autobiography was noted in a book on Alberta
Ukrainians. Interviewing elderly members of the second generation,

the author found a wealth of information about early trials, hardships endured, language barriers, crass and insensitive officials and employers, and shortages of adequate clothing, food, and agricultural supplies. However, when she asked the same informants about the misery of the Great Depression, or about the 1940s, she found a striking reluctance to admit to any difficulties. Did this mean that there were none? Or, as she surmises, was it unacceptable to tell the stranger that after a lifetime in Canada not all Ukrainians had prospered wonderfully (Kostash 1977)? Grace Anderson and I became very conscious that personal interviewing led to a 'Horatio Alger' motif that omitted failures (Anderson and Higgs 1976). The Portuguese popular saying 'Se és infeliz, não o digas a ninguém (If you are unhappy, don't tell anybody)' is apposite here.

Regional Differences

It is fairly obvious to the casual observer, as well as to the sociological investigator, that there are differences among Portuguese-speaking people. In continental Portugal and the Atlantic islands, popular culture is localized, underlined by accent, agricultural economies, special religious devotions, and shrines, folklore, and cookery. There are also those who want to insert insular identities between the familial setting of the small town, or even city suburb, and that of Portugal. An editorial in an Azorean newspaper published in Toronto, on the twenty-fifth anniversary of the first arrival of the Portuguese in Canada, had an article headed: 'Azoreans Awake!' It proclaimed: 'We all speak Portuguese but we are all different.' The writer deplored the fact that celebrations had lacked an Azorean emphasis, even though immigrants from the archipelago of Atlantic islands constituted a clear majority of Portuguese Canadians. The editorial did not mention that Azoreans were, like all other members of the Portuguese-speaking public, invited to the initial organizational meeting, which had been publicized in the ethnic press, radio, and television. Instead, the following appeared: 'All together, let us name a co-ordinating commission exclusively Azorean, but worthy of this name, that uses the remaining months of 1978 to organize a commemorative programme about our, but only of our, pioneers to Canada, and that spreads to all the places where Azoreans live.'[3]

While the subsequent years have shown little meaningful support for such exclusionism, the editorial attested to the strength of regional identities in Canada at that time. At a more urbane level, the numerous Portuguese regional clubs that have been founded in Canada manifested a clear desire by Portuguese Canadians to socialize with those who share the same experiences on the basis of place of origin.

It is a commonplace of ethnic histories in the Americas that the emigration experience itself produces greater social malleability and a hybrid identity in the second and subsequent generations. Sometimes the hostility of the receiving country was enough to strengthen solidarity, like that felt among the Portuguese in Rio de Janeiro during the 1890s, attacked by the nativist *Jacobino* press and on occasion even chased through the streets to the insulting cry of 'Mata Galego!' (Kill the Galician) (Hahner 1976). In large Canadian centres, Azoreans, Madeirans, settlers from Minho (in continental Portugal), and others feel that they inhabit different social solitudes, each with a circuit of restaurants, clubs, shops, and houses that are 'known.' An individual from any part of Portugal, isolated in a remote location in Canada and unable to speak English well, would be drawn to others from any part of Portugal who spoke the same language.

The legends of Portuguese-Canadian history derived from exaltation of individual achievements. By inviting people to talk about themselves, one gains much information – but also an idealized version of motives, family, homeland, and self (Crépeau 1978). That kind of 'aural' history obscures as much as it illuminates. Of course there is an ongoing need to collect micro-histories of emigration in order to test the 'fit' of generalizations (Baines 1994). What is needed is historical analysis that draws on a larger framework as well as autobiography and simple collective biography. The legends are part of, but separate from, the broader social analysis of an ethnic group within Canadian society. However, in future we must explore the permanence of the characteristics of 'Portuguese' behaviour, of Portuguesismo.

New Historical Methods

Above all, future historians will need written and other records that can be collected now. They reflect the diversity of the experiences of Portuguese people in Canada. An interesting technique is to elicit responses to family photographs and to ask respondents to comment on those images of other places and individuals. That approach was used to considerable effect in a volume published in 1993 dealing with life thirty years earlier (Marques and Marujo 1993). In a history course at the University of Toronto during the 1990s, students born in the 1970s used family photographs to illustrate brief essays on their family histories, as researched through interviews with relatives in Toronto. In one case, an Azorean family had a double migration experience – first, to Massachusetts before the First World War and later, back to the archipelago, and then a second generation to Canada in the 1960s, to keep a son from impending military service. The oral lore of the family contained recollections of the United States prior to 1914, of international travel, and of the effects of the colonial wars, illustrated with pictures from the father's military service in Guiné Bissau at the end of the 1960s. The students became conscious of the different levels of historical sophistication found in family informants who had not studied history at the university level and in academic works.

Historians have noted the reluctance of the Portuguese to compile autobiographies and personal memoirs. That reticence may be a product of the exaltation of modesty and humility in the folk culture, a lingering memory of fears of denunciation to the Inquisition (1536–1821) for sinful conduct, or the need to be cautious in Salazar's Portugal with many informers operating for the secret police of the Estado Novo. We can hope that in the near future many Portuguese Canadians will write down the stories of their lives. Recent examples of Italian and Dutch immigrant accounts of Canada show what insights can be gleaned on the adaptation strategies adopted by individuals in different ethnic groups after 1945 (Colantonio 1997; Horne 1997). Complementary to these are studies of individual immigrant lives such as that of Martin Nordegg, born Moritz Cohn, who erased all traces of his life before his arrival in Canada in 1906.[4]

In 1986, the APH association of history teachers in Portugal considered the 'Memory of the Twentieth Century' and how this might be conveyed to a child. It mentioned several dates – 5 October 1910, establishment of the First Portuguese Republic; 1914–18, for the First World War; 1926, for the start of the military dictatorship; 1939–45 for the Second World War (in which Portugal did not take up arms); 1956, for the launch of Portuguese television broadcasting; 1961, for the beginning of the African wars for independence; and 1974, for the change of regime on 25 April. (The apparition of the Blessed Virgin of May 1917 at Fátima did not get listed, nor did the papal visit to Portugal fifty years later to commemorate that sighting.) The school teachers proposed that each child ask parents and grandparents about these 'particularly significant' events and then add to the table his or her own birth date and the birth, marriage, and death dates, as appropriate, of relatives.[5]

In a Canadian setting such 'time lines' for Portuguese-Canadian children might well take into account some memorable local events, such as the 1994 celebration, in Toronto's Portuguese districts, of Brazil's victory in the World Cup of Soccer over the Italians, who also had many supporters in the city. For adults, markers might be political changes in Canada or Portugal and stages in life such as house purchases and births, marriages, divorces, and deaths. However, older faces – those of the heroes of the Portuguese past – may also look out from picture frames in homes in Canada.

Conclusion

Consciousness of the Portuguese heritage among individuals varies widely, depending on education, personal experiences, linguistic environment in childhood, and degree of motivation to study Portuguese and Canadian cultures. It would be informative to know Canadian sales of historical works published in Portugal in the 1990s. It would be equally helpful to learn how many Portuguese Canadians have read historical studies of Canada and the place of Portuguese in that past, particularly since 1953 – although the oldest known document dealing with a Portuguese in Canada dates from 1671 (Higgs 1990). Controversy and questioning of the records of the past can only enliven an inert descriptive sociology of the Portuguese-Canadian communities. Many of the earliest works in the 1960s and 1970s on Portuguese Canadians implicitly posited a single, often academic, and atemporal authority in interpreting the cultural achievements of Portuguese Canadians and their children (Teixeira and Lavigne 1998). Happily, this is no longer the case.

NOTES

1 'Um Museu de Cera,' *Jornal de Letras* 17, no. 715 (11–24 March 1998), 7.
2 *Jornal Açoreano*, 30 June 1978.
3 João de Lima, 'Acordai, Açoreanos,' ibid.
4 See review by Antana Sileika, 'The Stories Immigrants Tell,' *Globe and Mail* (Toronto), 20 Dec. 1997, D14.
5 *O estudo da história: Boletim dos sócios, associação de professores de história* no. 1 (2nd series) (1986), 53–5.

A Sense of History 247

Anderson, G.M. 1974. *Networks of Contact: The Portuguese and Toronto*. Waterloo, Ont.: Wilfrid Laurier University Press.
Anderson, G.M., and Higgs, D. 1976. *A Future to Inherit: The Portuguese Communities of Canada*. Toronto: McClelland and Stewart.
Anderson, O. 1997. 'Emigration and Marriage Break-up in Mid-Victorian England.' *Economic History Review* 50 no. 1: 1–20.
Baines, D. 1994. 'European Emigration, 1815–1930: Looking at the Emigration Decision Again.' *Economic History Review* 47: 525–44.
Barros, T. de. N.d. (c. 1956) *Sumário de história de Portugal ... para a 4a classe do ensino primário*. Oporto: Editora Educação Nacional de Adolfo Machado.
Boer, P. 1998. *The European Challenge: Essays on Culture, Values and Policy in a Changing Continent*. s'Gravenhage: VUGA.
Boer, P., and Frihoff, W. 1993. *Les lieux de mémoire et identités nationales*. Amsterdam: Amsterdam University Press.
Carvalho, P. de. 1973. *História de Portugal para a 4a classe*. Oporto: Porto Editora.
Colantonio, F. 1997. *From the Ground Up: An Italian Immigrant's Story*. Toronto: Between the Lines.
Conrad, P. 1990. *Where I Fell to Earth: A Life in Four Places*. London: Chatto and Windus.
Crépeau, P. 1978. *Voyage au pays des merveilles: Quatre autobiographies d'immigrants*. Ottawa: National Museums of Canada.
Ferreira, H.B. 1988. *Escola do 'First Portuguese': 25 anos de história*. Toronto: First Portuguese Canadian Cultural Centre.
Freyre, G. 1946. *The Masters and the Slaves: A Study in the Development of Brazilian Civilization ... Translated from the Portuguese of the Fourth and Definitive Brazilian Edition by Samuel Putnam*. New York: Knopf.
Grinberg, L., and Grinberg, R. 1989. *Psychoanalytic Perspectives on Migration and Exile Translated from the Spanish by Nancy Festinger*. New Haven, Conn.: Yale University Press.
Hahner, J.E. 1976. 'Jacobinos versus Galegos: Urban Radicals versus Portuguese Immigrants in Rio de Janeiro in the 1890s.' *Journal of InterAmerican Studies and World Affairs* 18 no. 2: 125–54.
Higgs, D. 1993. 'Bigamia.' *Silva* 143–56.
Higgs, D., ed., 1990. *Portuguese Migration in Global Perspective*. Toronto: Multicultural History Society of Ontario.
Hobsbawm, E., and Ranger, T. 1983. *The Invention of Tradition*. New York: Cambridge University Press.
Horn, M. 1997. *Becoming Canadian*. Toronto: University of Toronto Press.
Iacovetta, F. 1997. *The Writing of English Canadian Immigrant History*. Canada's

Ethnic Group Series, Booklet No. 22. Ottawa: Canadian Historical Association.

Kostash, M. 1977. *All of Baba's Children*. Edmonton: Hurtig.

Lopes, J.M., and Lopes, M. de S.P. 1996. *Uma longa viagem: História da emigração portuguesa para o Canadá*. Toronto: Ontario Institute for Studies in Education.

McQuillan, D.A. 1990. *Prevailing over Time: Ethnic Adjustment on the Kansas Prairies, 1875–1925*. Lincoln: University of Nebraska Press.

Marques, D., and Marujo, M. 1993. *With Hardened Hands: A Pictorial History of Portuguese Immigration to Canada in the 1950s*. Toronto: New Leaf Publications.

Matos, S.C. 1990. *História, mitologia, imaginário nacional: A história no curso dos liceus (1895–1939)*. Lisbon: Livros Horizonte.

Maynard, F.B. 1972. *Raisins and Almonds*. Don Mills, Ont.: General Publishing.

Morais, D.M.C.M.R.N. de 1979. *Português à volta do mundo*. Oporto: Tipografia Bloco Gráfico.

Nora, P., ed. 1984. *Les lieux de mémoire*. Paris: Gallimard.

Pinto, A.C. 1938. *O valor da vontade na história nacional: Palavras Dirigidas aos rapazes da mocidade portuguesa da Ala de Mousinho de Albuquerque*. Leiria: Comissão Municipal de Turismo de Leiria.

Raglan, F.R.S. 1949. *The Hero: A Study in Tradition, Myth, and Drama*. London: Watts.

Reinhold, M. 1972. 'Historians and Biographers.' In R.D. Mead, ed., *Hellas and Rome: The Story of Greco-Roman Civilization*, 168–205. New York: New American Libary.

Ribeiro, M.A. 1990. *O Canadá e a presença portuguesa. Ante-projecto*. Toronto: Correio Português.

Rodrigues, L. 1976. *Os bastardos das pátrias*. Lisboa: Distribuidora 'O Seculo'.

Serrão, J. 1976. *Testemunhos sobre a emigração portuguesa: Antologia*. Lisbon: Livros Horizonte.

Siddle, D.J. 1997. 'Migration as a Strategy of Accumulation: Social and Economic Change in Eighteenth-Century Savoy.' *Economic History Review* 50 no. 1: 1–20.

Silva, Maria Beatriz Nizza da. 1993. *Vida privada e quotidiano no Brasil na época de D. Maria I e D. João VI*, 143–56. Lisbon: Editorial Estampa.

Teixeira, C., and Lavigne, G. 1998. *Os portugueses no Canadá: Uma bibliografia (1953–1996)*. Lisbon: Direcçao-Geral dos Assuntos Consulares e Comunidades Portuguesas.